10-11-17

Dear Erin,

As you journey through mother-hood, trust Him with all of your heart – even when it seems im-possible. He loves us with an everlasting love that never fails when we turn to it. I've loved watching your family grow.

In Him,

Nora Alexander (LSA)

He heals the brokenhearted and binds up their wounds.

Psalm 147:3

Bitter, Broken, Blessed

NORA ALEXANDER

WESTBOW PRESS®
A DIVISION OF THOMAS NELSON & ZONDERVAN

WestBow Press books may be ordered through booksellers or by contacting:

WestBow Press
A Division of Thomas Nelson & Zondervan
1663 Liberty Drive
Bloomington, IN 47403
www.westbowpress.com
1 (866) 928-1240

ISBN: 978-1-5127-7206-7 (sc)
ISBN: 978-1-5127-7207-4 (hc)
ISBN: 978-1-5127-7205-0 (e)

Library of Congress Control Number: 2017900612

Print information available on the last page.

WestBow Press rev. date: 08/08/2017

Contents

What If

What if God grows our trust through trials?
What if He teaches us His truths in our struggles?
What if darkness renders the Light brighter?
What if we gain strength because of tribulation?
What if desperation drives us to seek Him more?
What if tears are an integral part of cleansing and healing?
What if these are the very ways God uses to reveal Himself?
What if?

Dedication

To those who find themselves bitter, broken, or blessed may you find hope and restoration, and may you discover rest in God's mercy and peace.

To the generations that will live in decades to come, until Our Lord's return, may the good promises of our Father ring true for you. He keeps every one of them; not one of them fails—ever. (Joshua 21:45)

My prayer is that you will set your hope in God and not forget His works; you are one of them. (Psalm 78:7)

May God grant His transforming restoration and empower you to conquer influences of evil.

Acknowledgements

Thank you, God, for having a plan, giving me a purpose, and allowing me to tell my story.

Thank you to the Todd, Paul, Glenn, Richey, Jeffers, Gray, Benton, and Hack families who have chosen to see me through the eyes of Jesus. Your acceptance, love, and encouragement mean the world to me. Thank you for adopting me into the family. I love all of you very much.

I give my sincerest thanks to those in the Kingdom who have chosen to befriend me.

Everyone who helped in the editing process of this manuscript deserves my wholehearted appreciation; I offer it to you in abundance. Without your help, this piece would not have become what it is intended to be. Thank you from the bottom of my heart.

An endless "Thank You" goes to my brother in Christ, Hank Gray. The contributions of your time and publishing knowledge are priceless; I value you and them, deeply. I appreciate the investment you have made in my life on both a personal and professional level.

Special thanks to my new acquaintances Dr. Bea Haler and Shelia Moss. Their insights, influence, skill, and professional expertise helped polish this work.

Resounding thanks goes out to Kay Mack who introduced me to *Westbow Press.*

With a grateful heart, I offer abundant appreciation to Kayla B. Ray who has spent countless hours helping me rediscover my place in this world. God has endowed her with a special gift, and I am privileged to be the recipient of her willingness to be what He has called her to be. "Love ya', girl."

I am forever indebted to Kathryn and Clarence Todd. They live life intentionally as disciples of Jesus. They reached out to me, a stranger, and they chose to invite me into their world. My life is blessed beyond measure because of them, and I am eternally appreciative of everything they have done and continue to do for me. Thank you for choosing to love me; you have done it well. I cherish the treasure of our friendship.

Forward

Be prepared to fall in love all over again—with Jesus. This memoir of "the lullaby singer" will have you singing praises when you trace God's hand in her story from deep brokenness to healing and restoration. With gripping intensity and not easy to put down once you start to read, you can smell the fragrance of Christ as you see her life of ashes turn to uttermost beauty. It is my prayer that the words and poetry she has penned will give hope to many who seek a life of new beginnings. —*Renee; Franklin, TN*

Nora has poured out her heart and soul as she relates her tragic, yet triumphant, story. She gives the reader a poignant peek into her heart-wrenching life challenges while encouraging her readers with her tenacity, optimism, hope, and uncompromised devotion in serving her Lord. —*Sherilyn; Northborough, MA*

Nora, thank you for letting me read how God brought you "through the fire" and set your feet on solid ground. I got hooked just reading the Dedication and Preface. It took me a long time to insert my own name in God's Promises. I simply LOVE, LOVE, LOVE the Introduction! —*Mary Jane; Franklin, TN*

Thank you for writing your story and speaking up for those of us who just can't. I have been on a roller-coaster of emotions while reading this book; I have laughed, cried, and found myself relating to your words. Bravo! —*Teryn; Deridder, LA*

Nora and I joke about meeting each other when she sat in my chair in Sunday school. Although partially true, our long-term friendship began at that moment. Hearing her stories and seeing God working drew my heart to her countless times, especially when

I heard her say, "God did that for me." Reading her book three or four times, plus our friendship, are constant reminders that God really did *that* for me. Our prayer is that readers will be drawn to our Savior through her story of deliverance from bitterness to being blessed. —*Kathryn; Franklin, TN*

Bitter, Broken, Blessed is the remarkable, heartfelt story of how Nora Alexander overcame a lifetime filled with hardships, tragedies, disappointments, betrayals, and failures. This painstakingly written, authentic story vividly describes how God's grace enabled her to arrive at a place in life where she is forgiven, restored, blessed, loved, and victorious. —*Patrick; Longview, TX*

Preface

The content of these pages is the accounting of my journey: the pains, joys, loves, and sorrows of life in the process of being lived. These are coupled with lessons learned and truths discovered along the way. Some of these lessons were much harder to learn than others. Many of the experiences became too painful to bear. Other issues were so confusing I lost direction and parts of who I am in the process of trying to survive. These trials could have utterly destroyed me; they almost did. Instead, God used the sum-total of these events to teach me and mold me into the person I am today.

Does this mean my life is now perfect, and I have no problems with which to cope? Far from it! It solely means I have been delivered and am extremely blessed by a loving Savior. He has revealed to me the fact that He is real. His promises hold peace, comfort, and security for those who trust Him; these assurances are waiting for each of us to claim.

To some people, my writing might sound like irrational ramblings from a mind in need of psychiatric treatment. At one time my mind and emotions were broken, filled with damaging thoughts. I confess that at one point I was anxious and frenzied, in desperate need of professional help; however, I contend and proclaim to you there is much more than insane ramblings written in these pages.

You will observe a broken life in critical need of a renewed relationship with Jesus Christ. You will witness actual events designed by our loving God to bring an error-ridden child back into His fellowship, and you will discover proof that His sheep hear His voice. He knows them, and they follow Him. There will be evidence that those who belong to God are safe and protected. God who has given them to Jesus is greater and more powerful than all, and no one will ever be able to snatch them from His hand. (John 10:27–29)

You will behold a child of God caught in despair, seeking in complete desperation the waiting Father who "inclined to me and heard my cry. He brought me up out of the pit of destruction, out of the miry clay, and He set my feet upon a rock making my footsteps firm. He put a new song in my mouth, a song of praise to our God" (Psalm 40:1–3, selected sections).

My earnest prayer is that "many will see and fear and will trust in the LORD" (verse 3). My desire is that the words penned here will bring encouragement to those who find themselves in similar circumstances. There may be others who are in completely different situations who can relate to and draw strength from my story. This writing is for those who think they cannot make it through what is happening in their lives. It is also for those who feel they cannot escape the pain and scars of what has happened in their past. My prayer is that all people will find hope, strength, and healing in the life-changing power of the cross.

I have learned that my life is unique. It cannot and should not be compared to anyone else's. To some people, my experiences might seem filled with many terrible things; while to others, my trials might seem trivial or uncomplicated. I have found that some individuals have had a more tragic, traumatic, or painful existence than mine. At the same time, other people have been blessed with a more fairytale-like lifestyle. Whichever the case, I know this is true for everyone: if we live long enough, every single one of us will experience disappointments, trials, and traumas.

Am I jealous or envious of those who appear to have had things easier? No. Everyone has a life with issues to face and burdens to bear. What we do with our lives, how we confront the challenges, how we conduct ourselves, and to whom or what we turn to in our desperation are what matter most.

The recording of events in these pages is by no means meant to be a blaming tool for the direction my life has taken. It is not an itemized list of excuses created to justify the place in which I find myself at this stage in life. This project is not written with the intent of embarrassing or degrading anyone I love, nor is it designed to hurt those I have cherished in the past. I could offer insight and background on individuals represented in this manuscript, but their stories are not mine to tell, and I do not have their permission to do so. I can only share how these issues impacted my story.

My hope is that people will discover it is never too late for a life to be healed. Unfortunately, restoration will not be attained by everyone, but it is definitely a possibility for all. Eternal renewal does not come outside of Jesus Christ. We must recognize the fact that the past is the past. It forms parts of who we are, but it does not have to consume or destroy us; nor does it automatically dictate a bleak future. I believe there is nothing that has happened during one's existence that cannot be overcome by the power of Christ. As long as we draw breath, we are never too old to learn, and it is never too late to seek deliverance. A broken vessel can be made beautiful, useful, and productive no matter how damaged it appears. The mercy and grace of God have caused anyone found in Christ to be a new creation, "old things have passed away; behold, all things have become new" (2 Corinthians 5:17, NKJV).

Hopefully, readers will gain the understanding that even though God hates all sin, He does love the sinner. According to Romans 3:23, every individual is guilty of sin. God desires to grant full pardon and forgiveness because He wants to fellowship with us. He is the Great Physician who is always on duty and the superb Counselor who offers twenty-four-seven accessibility. He's always there, ready to listen when we call.

I do not know what your deliverance will look like, for each story is unique. I can tell you this: complete, irreversible healing took place when I came to the end of myself. I realized I had to stop looking for all of my answers in this world's solutions. I had to stop trying to fix and protect everything by myself, no matter the costs. I had to stop struggling and fighting in my own strength. I just had to be still and rest in Jesus; there is a point of full surrender.

I had to look to Him first and discover how everything else fits into His word and ways, instead of the other way around. I was broken and poured out before the Holy God of heaven, seeking Him with every fiber of my being. This much I know: there is bright hope for every tomorrow when Christ is involved.

Finally, my aspiration is to share my story so others may find restoration and transformation through God's love; He is a treasure worth finding. He will grant victory over sin and deliver us from whatever holds us captive. He empowers us to become conquerors of our past. Most of all, I yearn to see God reveal Himself through these pages. I pray He will receive honor and glory for the magnificent things He does.

"That in all things He may have the preeminence."
(Colossians 1:18, NKJV, italics are mine)

Introduction

I sat and listened to my pastor speak during a presentation made to first graders. As I reflected on his remarks, I was struck by the simplicity and truth of his comments. One statement was a profound theological thought, yet simple enough for a child to grasp. He said, "Not only is God's story in the Bible, but each child's personal narrative and our very own story is there waiting to be discovered."

I pondered this statement and wondered what my journey would look like if it came straight from the pages of God's Book. I think it would look something like this:

> Nora, do not fear, for "I have redeemed you; I have called you by name; you are Mine. When you pass through the waters, I will be with you; and through the rivers, they will not overflow you. When you walk through the fire, you will not be scorched nor will the flame burn you. For I am the LORD your God, The Holy One of Israel, your Savior." (Isaiah 43:1–3)
>
> Nora, do not forget, "I know the plans that I have for you, plans for welfare and not for calamity to give you a future and a hope." (Jeremiah 29:11)
>
> You are redeemed, Nora; you will have everlasting joy on your head. You will obtain joy and gladness; your sorrow and sighing will flee away. (Isaiah 35:9–10)

In my brokenness, I, Nora, have called out to Him saying, "But you, O GOD, the Lord, deal *kindly* with me for Your name's sake; because Your lovingkindness is good, deliver me; for I am afflicted and needy, and my heart is wounded within me. I am passing like a shadow when it lengthens; I am shaken off like the locust. My knees are weak, and my flesh has grown lean, without fatness." (Psalm 109:21–24, selected sections)

Remember Nora, the person who "has no rule over his own spirit is *like* a city broken down without walls" to protect it. (Proverbs 25:28, NKJV)

My desire is to be found in Him so that I will know Him and the power of His resurrection. (Philippians 3:9–10)

Nora, remember with those of generations past: "The joy of the LORD is your strength." (Nehemiah 8:10)

This small sample shows just how delightful and astounding God's Word is. I could go on and on through the Bible from beginning to end and find my story throughout its pages. My pastor was right: God is found between the covers of His Book, and our narrative is established there.

We all have a story. I pray as you read the account of my journey, you will discover yours along the way. As you travel through this writing, may God's words and all He teaches enlighten you and shed hope on your life's chronical.

Enjoy the journey.

PART 1

Bitter

CHAPTER 1

Where Am I

Fact or Fiction

I do not know my name, nor my age. Sparkly bright lights flash against a dark backdrop similar to the static found on a television station that is off the air. I think I am alone. I feel deserted with nothing around me; no one else is present. Eerie sounds echo all around me, pelting me with their presence. A few moments pass, and I find myself waking up in a dim, dull, white room. I am wearing blue paper pajamas, and my hair has been cut extremely short. My arms are bandaged from wrist to elbow; the painful wounds throb and ache.

Pain is coursing through my skull. Lights from the hallway hurt my eyes as I battle an all too familiar migraine, and I ache all over. I am excruciatingly tired and downright exhausted; I am cold. I will learn at a later time that I weigh 103 pounds. This number is unbelievable to me. I have been overweight my entire life, at one time I tipped the scales at 287. Now, they are telling me I am anorexic, and I need to relearn how to eat. Each bite makes me nauseous, and I fight to keep every morsel down.

I do not understand the "why" of all of this. Two days pass before I come to the realization I am in a hospital somewhere in a southern state. Several days pass, and I discover I am in the psychiatric lockdown unit of a prominent medical center. My concerned, loving brother—desperate and at his wit's end—has brought me here to be evaluated; hoping I can be helped. This move to the hospital followed an almost successful attempt to end my life, which culminated in a complete emotional breakdown; I am totally separated from reality.

Hallucinations and factual memories take turns randomly racing through the chambers of my mind. Sometimes, I cannot tell the difference between fact and fiction because both appear to be real. I'll learn to differentiate between the two in time, but at this moment they are entangled in battle. Each one is trying to dominate my thoughts, each trying to rule over the other. The facts are authentic recollections from my past; the hallucinations are manifestations of my memories and details from my life that are painful, distressing, and troublesome. These things are too excruciating to deal with in a direct, straightforward manner. They have been buried or suppressed for a long time.

Who Cares

My first recollections of events are intense. My version of traveling dictates I slept all the way to the hospital. The actual account reveals I talked speedily and nonstop the entire trip. I spoke so rapidly no one could make sense of my babbling. Upon arrival at the emergency room, I was placed in a holding area where patients are evaluated, observed, and monitored for a nonspecific amount of time; allowing the staff the opportunity to determine the level of intervention and care I needed.

My report of events indicates I was lying on a bed in a room with bright lights, burrowed under a blanket with my eyes tightly closed and covered. I was waiting for someone to come and check on me. The truth exposes the fact that I was extremely vocal and rather abhorrent during the intake process. I understand my southern accent and impersonation of a famous television cook are not very accurate.

One of the first steps in the treatment plan was to discontinue my prescription medications, all twenty-one of them. Once settled at the hospital I desperately wanted to sleep, but I couldn't. I laid in my bed curled in a fetal position so tight my head bent forward reaching my knees; they touched my nose as my heels contacted my fanny. I constantly wriggled, trying to curl into a tighter and tighter ball. I rocked, hummed, and moaned.

A faucet dripped relentlessly. It seemed as if the sound had been magnified ten thousand times as it resonated off the walls of my room; it was maddening. I screamed for the noise to stop. I did not know what being in a dungeon was like, but I envisioned a dark, damp cell; and I was in its grasp. I became very ill. I didn't realize it at the time, but the ravages of drug withdrawal were beginning to wreak havoc on my body.

My surroundings terrified me. I kept wondering why no one would come and help me. In reality, the people working the unit could do nothing at this point. I was safe and under observation. They were doing their jobs; they were watching and monitoring me closely. I turned a wheelchair on its side and placed it in the doorway of my room to prop the door open; this created a barrier or trap for anyone who might try to cross the threshold. I wanted to make sure anyone entering my room would make a lot of noise. I spent the majority of my time crying and moaning; I felt abandoned and alone. I desperately wanted someone to care. I was afraid of everyone, and I trusted no one.

I kept asking if I could make a phone call to my immediate family. I hoped it would reveal some small piece of evidence that someone once close to me might be concerned about what was happening in my life. After what seemed to be eons, I was granted permission to place the call. My youngest daughter answered the phone. It had been a long time since I had seen or spoken to her. She took the phone to her dad as I requested. The message I received was loud and clear. The man on the other end of the phone had distanced himself from me, and he didn't care. I was no longer "his problem."

I had not come to grips with the fact that I no longer had a personal family to contact; all of those relationships had been severed two years earlier. I was searching for my identity. I was no longer Nora: pastor's wife, mother, neighbor, friend, teacher, children's Bible leader, or any other title I had worn. When the call ended, I felt a worse emptiness and a greater sense of loss and loneliness. The realization I did not have an immediate family hit me hard.

Not Who I Thought

Dejected, I hung the phone on its hook and wandered through the halls. After a few rounds through the maze of corridors, I found myself standing outside the door of another patient's room. I peeked inside and stood in the doorway for a while; my eyes had trouble focusing. The male patient had the same general build, hair color, and facial expressions of a man from my past, but there was something a little off.

He was seated on a bed, and a blanket was draped over his shoulders. I thought he was wearing a policeman's uniform with a badge on his dark blue shirt. None of this made any sense to me. I finally sat down on the end of a gurney which was located just inside the door of his room. We began a conversation; eventually, I got around to asking him his name. He instantly replied, "Christian."

I was startled by his response. My ex-husband's favorite novel is *Pilgrim's Progress*; the main character's name is Christian. I jumped to the immediate conclusion that this was my husband, and he was finally here to talk about us. When I called out my former spouse's given name, the man on the stretcher scowled, got up, and moved toward me. The blanket fell away to reveal a hospital gown, not a uniform. As he advanced across the room, I saw his wounded neck and face.

His injuries encompassed his entire frame. At first glance, it looked as if thousands of staples tracked across his body. I later learned that he was a real young man who had been severely wounded by his own hand. He had received over 150 staples to close his wounds.

Christian was not my husband, but everything in me wanted him to be. I intensely desired to be cared for and loved—not abandoned and alone. The next thing I remember is being back in my observation room.

Special Messages

Before being transferred to the main lockdown unit of the hospital, two more significant episodes took place. The first event concerned three of my cousins, the children of my dad's brother; the second involved a coffin. I watched the scenes described below unfold before me. They were very real, as real as anything I have ever witnessed. I would discover later that these happenings were figments of my mind and never actually took place, but I experienced them just the same.

Episode 1: Cousins

I was standing at a door looking out of a small window into what appeared to be a parking garage or bus terminal of some type. The steel gates to all of the street's exits and entrances were down and locked. The female cousin had long blond hair. She was dressed in a seventies-looking outfit, complete with numerous beads around her neck and a brown leather headband that was wrapped around her forehead. She was in her late teens.

Her tall, slender, older brother lovingly walked over to her and took her suitcase. She was crying. He hugged her, turned her around, and placed his arm around her shoulders. He gently led her away, guiding her steps as they maneuvered their way toward a bus. I knew they were headed home.

Tears streamed down my face as I watched this scene unfold on the other side of the door. In a whisper, I called out their names as I softly patted the small window. I begged silently for them not to go, but neither looked my way; soon they were out of my visual field. I stretched and strained to keep them in my sight as long as possible.

I cried awhile and then wheeled my chair away from the door and rolled myself into a small sitting area. When I finished positioning myself at a table that was located next to a far wall, I looked toward the far end of the room. I saw the same girl cousin being rolled into the area by her other brother, the younger of the two. She was now dressed in a hospital gown and sitting in a wheelchair.

The girl was lethargic and despondent. Her head hung forward; she looked dejected, almost lifeless. The young man lovingly laid a blanket across her lap, wrapped it around her legs, and tucked in the edges. He took her lethargic hands in his and bowed his head in prayer. I watched as his mouth moved in intercession for his sister. He rose softly, took her chin in his hand, raised her head, smiled at her, told her he loved her, and placed a gentle kiss on her forehead.

It was excessively cold in the room; my teeth chattered. Even though I was wrapped in a blanket, my entire body shook. My cousin took a few steps over to a chair and sat down. He was now on the same side of the room as I. Suddenly, he raised his head and stared straight at me. He held my teary gaze in his. He lifted his right hand and revealed an opened, palm-sized Bible which he held out for me to see. The words I read that were now printed across a poster-sized page said this: "For He Himself has said, 'I will never leave you nor forsake you. The LORD is my helper; I will not fear'" (Hebrews13:5–6, NKJV, selected sections).

Audible words were never spoken, but my cousin mouthed: "You are loved." I withdrew my gaze, hung my head, and closed my eyes for a few seconds as tears fell into my lap. When I looked up, no one was in the room. I was completely alone.

I know these cousins are individuals of much faith and prayer. I found it comforting in future days to think: *there is the possibility that these family members were praying for me at the very moment I saw this vision.* I also wondered if someone dear to me had suffered a similar event, and God was revealing to me she had survived.

Whatever the reason behind giving me this message, I know God was telling me there was still hope and I was not utterly alone.

Episode 2: The Coroner

The second event before my transfer upstairs to the lockdown unit involved a visit from the county coroner. She came to issue a mandatory commitment to the psychiatric ward; it had been determined I was an immediate threat to my own safety and well-being. I don't know if the next portion of this event happened or if it was imagined; I do know it felt very real. The coroner took out her measuring tape and calculated my height; I thought she had measured me for my coffin.

Haunted

I do not remember my actual transfer to the tenth floor where another of my earliest recollections takes place. This event involved the terrifying illusion of being chased by savage, black, wolf-like dogs with red eyes. Their sharp fangs looked ready to devour whatever was in their path, which at that moment happened to be me. They were chasing me through a thick dark forest. After a relentless pursuit, these animals managed to trap me in a heavily wooded area.

I tried to escape them by attempting to climb a gnarly tree that was covered with black bark. Eventually, I took refuge in a small cave. These ferocious creatures managed to hunt me down and wear me out. They were ravenously scowling as they snapped at me with their teeth. I was screaming and crying, hitting at them with all my strength.

As my nightmare turned into consciousness, I became aware of the fact that I was in the shower. The hallucination was there with me, and the scene was very real. Nurses tried to pry me out of the corner of the shower, where I was cowering. I was crying, screaming, and hitting the staff. I was battling the fierce wolf images I thought I saw. The attendants gave me a massive injection; it hurt.

I was unconscious for quite some time. With each passing day, the menacing creature's eyes grew weaker and less piercing. As time dragged on, they finally stopped stalking me. Eventually, they disappeared. I have not seen these villainous animals since the early portion of my hospitalization.

How did this forty-eight-year-old daughter, sister, mother of four, teacher, children's group leader, Sunday school teacher, women's ministry director, honored sales consultant, preacher's wife with a seemingly healthy, long-term marriage end up in such a precarious place?

CHAPTER 2

Lost in the Balance

The Sound of Laughter

Approximately one week after I first discovered I was in a hospital, professionals informed me that I was emotionally unstable and very ill. Experts were telling me I was suffering from the effects of a mental illness caused by severe emotional trauma. Soon after I came to comprehend this information, I broke down in complete remorse for having had an unloving attitude toward a member of my extended family who lived with the ravages of a mental disease.

As a Christian, I should have shown love, kindness, compassion, and gentleness toward him. I should have made every effort to gain some understanding of his illness and its disabling effects. I should have offered friendship and acceptance. Instead, I dished out disdain, disbelief, and personal judgment in ample portions.

I remember being physically ill, lying face down on the bathroom floor and beating the tile with my fists. I pled vehemently, begging that person to forgive me. I was screaming out my profuse apology for the way I had judged him. I had come to the point where I comprehended, and now understood, the devastation mental disease inflicts on someone. This event ended like many others, with a painful injection.

Things from my past continued to surface. At times, it seemed as if I was living in the exact moments of those events. I experienced some memories repeatedly. For example: though in my hospital room listening to the laughter of other patients travel down the corridor, I thought I was at my grandmother's house in the country near Cross Bayou. I was twelve and on vacation—I had been transported back in time.

My family was gathered in my paternal grandmother's tiny apartment. They had just finished a day filled with enjoyment. They had been fishing, and an impressive catch was the prize. It was late evening, and we had all consumed a great country-cooked meal. My dad told a funny "fish story," and everyone was laughing. While the adults and older kids were having a pleasant time, I was in the bedroom supposedly going to sleep; but I was hanging on every word that traveled from the adjoining room.

As I stood in the doorway of my hospital room, I leaned longingly into the hallway and stretched my ear toward the pleasant sounds of laughter I heard coming from the other room. I strained trying to cling to every sound that drifted toward me. I became painfully aware that I was not where I imagined myself. I shrunk back from the entry and pressed myself against the wall of my room; I was crying. Sometime later I crumpled, slid to the floor, and crawled across the cold tiles. I curled up in the corner, lamenting and longing for the comfort my joyful memory possessed. I do not know how long I remained there. Later that evening, I awoke to find myself face down on the chilled tiles; I realized it was late.

More episodes of laughter would drift through the hallway and make their way toward me. One event, in particular, involved my oldest brother who had a distinctive laugh. I would describe it as somewhere between a boisterous chuckle and an advanced round of jolliness. His infectious snicker was always present when he watched episodes of *The Roadrunner, The Little Rascals*, or *The Three Stooges*. It was contagious when he became lost in a full-blown incident of laughter. I couldn't help but smile with this memory, and at times I joined in the fun and giggled right along with him.

During one of my flashbacks, I heard two of my brothers laughing and cutting up as they told stories about their fishing partners of the day. Everyone was enjoying homemade ice cream—I was not allowed in the room; I was supposed to be slumbering. I was quiet, but I was not sleeping. I was listening, clinging to all that was happening in the next room. Somewhere in the midst of this memory, I fell asleep. Once again, I awoke to find myself curled up in the corner of my white hospital room, on the floor near my bed.

Encounters with these particular memories gave way to bouts of tears and weeping. It is strange how grief manifests and reveals itself. I think these events flooded my existence because they are some of my most cherished memories from childhood. My soul was in desperate need of comfort, and my mind was finding it in the only place it existed—in my fond memories. Even as a child, I had a strong sense of family; I enjoyed summers and the visits we made to see relatives.

I discovered the reason I thought of my oldest brother so often during my stay at the hospital; I had not dealt with his death. I learned that the impact of his untimely and unexpected demise three years earlier had taken a much greater toll on me than anyone realized. I was the only one of the remaining siblings that did not get to attend his funeral and that saddened me greatly. I desired to go, but my husband didn't want me to drive by myself, and I had no other way to get there. I wanted to console and comfort my brother's wife and their boys; I wanted to be there for them. I also wanted to say goodbye. I wanted and needed to go to his funeral, not attending left a gigantic void in my heart.

Now, I realize I had not found closure in this loss. I've learned that paying last respects to someone we love is an important part of letting go, no matter how difficult. Part of the grieving process and getting through the death of a loved one is coming to grips with the loss. I could not visualize this event because I had no first-hand knowledge or memory from which to draw. My mind kept searching for a connection, but it came up blank every time.

I went into the bathroom and shut the door. A teary venture to the chilly corner of this room is where I finally bid my brother farewell. I told him I loved and missed him; I also let him know how sorry I was for not being there the day he was remembered and mourned. I asked him to forgive me for that omission. I felt a sense of release that night as I revered his memory. I am glad I was finally able to process the passing of my eldest sibling. I had finally found peace in the loss of my brother, and with that came closure.

Intense Meltdowns

I recall a time when I became totally distraught, crying uncontrollably. I was sitting in a room filled with people I didn't know and could not visualize; it was as if I was blind. I was eating but had no clue what I was consuming. The food was devoid of flavor, and I could not see it. Strange sounds vibrated all around me; some of them resonated like gunshots.

I sobbed. I jerked, flinched, and recoiled each time the loud racket reached my ears. Confused and overcome with fright, I became increasingly shaken with each shot. After one of these blasts, I ended up on the floor under my chair in a tornado drill position. Orderlies had to pull me out of my safe place; another injection was given.

The gunshot sounds were made by other patients stabbing their silverware through the Styrofoam containers that held our food. It astounds me to think of the intensity to which my senses were magnified for the duration of my initial recovery, especially my hearing. Hearing these sounds is significant because I am hearing impaired; I have a severe loss in both ears, and I was not allowed to wear my hearing aids during my confinement.

I didn't want to be around people, noise, or things. Part of the program at this center helps patients who have disconnected emotionally acclimate back into their surroundings. I learned that many of the noises and actions going on around me were intentional. Other patients were enlisted to help; they assisted in the process of reconnecting me to the real world. It worked. Each day I found myself slightly more present in reality and less involved in an altered world. Eventually, my clouded and impaired sight returned to normal.

The view from the tenth floor was astounding; many times, both day and night, I stood and leaned against the window sill of my room. The coolness that radiated from the glass pane felt delightful against my hot, achy head. I spent hours staring out across the eminent metropolis that spanned below. I gazed at the lights of the city, observed traffic moving through the streets, and watched pedestrian movement unfold along the avenues of the town. The peace I found in the activity of looking out across the city was addictive. The comfort that flooded my being when I participated in this quiet pastime was soothing to my spirit.

Over time I started recognizing cars, traffic patterns, the habits of people walking, and the shadows that reflected on the walls of my room; even the birds regularly roosting on the stoop outside of my window in the afternoon were always the same. Eventually, my peace and comfort turned into a season of paranoia. In my mind, I had become thoroughly persuaded that I was on the third floor of the hospital, not the tenth. After several days of watching these scenes unfold, I determined a film loop was being played over and over again. I came to the illogical conclusion that there was a projector installed in the vent casing which ran across the top of the wall; it was parallel to the window from which I viewed the outside world.

I was convinced that staff members had the capability to flash images onto my window. I determined that these pictures made it seem like I was on a higher level of the hospital. I was sure an elaborate scheme was in place to make me think I was locked in with no way out. I was convinced that this deterrent was set into play so I wouldn't make another break for freedom. I tried to flee the unit once, but I was chased and tackled by two attendants. They inoculated me and placed me in solitary confinement.

During my season of paranoia, I spied a wheelchair parked in the hallway. I had been transported to and from therapy in it every day. The words TELEMETRY UNIT were stenciled on the back of it. Because I didn't know the meaning of this medical term, I assumed I was receiving a secret psychiatric treatment of some kind. I was also persuaded that the orangey haze I saw on occasion was a direct result of my therapy, and related in some way.

Later, I discovered the word telemetry is a term used to describe an intermediate, cardiac care unit. Special machines are used to monitor patient's stats, like changes in blood pressure and heart rhythm. I don't think the chair had anything to do with my care plan; it was just located in the wrong area of the hospital. I have no idea what the orange haze was, or from whence it came.

It didn't dawn on me until much later that the patterns I watched develop across those days were easily explained by simple, natural occurrences. The sun's position, the normal progression of a given day, and the labor patterns of hospital employees during shift change were the most elementary of reasons for the same things happening at the same time every day. Once I entered into the mindset that they—the hospital staff—were out to get me, everyday events and activities became suspect.

Why did I develop this frame of mind? A tormented mind in limbo seeking its way back to normalcy can cause one to believe numerous fallacies to be frightening truths. My inner strength was frail, and I trembled in weakness. A wise man named Solomon put it this way, "The spirit of a man will sustain him in sickness, but who can bear a broken spirit" (Proverbs 18:14).

One of the earliest issues I struggled with was dealing with the fact that I no longer had a spouse. Where was my husband? There seemed to be no particular person who cared about what was happening to me; this translated into the belief that nobody cared. My brain accepted this fallacy as truth. It totally crushed me to think that the person I had loved most in this world deemed me unsatisfactory and unworthy. It acutely hurt knowing that I had disappointed him. He, in turn, found me worthless and undesirable; he erased me from his life. As I faltered and tried to deal with this situation, my mind continued to escape to the place where it felt safest—non-reality.

One day while waiting in the lunch line, I was standing in front of a door with a small window; I was turned facing that door. People behind me were getting angry because I wouldn't move. I stood there leaning on the door, patting the small window with my hand as tears coursed down my face. I kept repeating, "You promised me, but you promised me!"

In those moments, I desperately wanted to talk to the person with whom I had spent over twenty-five years of my life discussing everything; I wanted to run into the arms that used to afford me great comfort. In my mind that was my friend and partner, my husband. I couldn't communicate with him; he would not see me, and he did not want to talk about anything that had happened. I was speaking to him the only way available to me—in my altered world. Orderlies came and removed me from the line; I received another injection.

Echoes of My Own Screams

Anguishing cries flew through the halls making their way to my ears, infiltrating my mind. They seemed to be coming from the farthest, darkest end of the corridor. Vivian was screaming for her daddy; occasionally, she called for her mom. Her terror sounded exactly like my gut-wrenching cries; only many of mine were still buried and hidden inside. I whimpered, "Mom; Mom," repeatedly. I was forty-eight-years-old, and I desperately wanted my momma.

I heard the fear in Vivian's screams as she cried out for help. I recognized the loneliness, and I knew what this poor woman was feeling. Of all the patients in the ward, my heart went out to Vivian; I identified with her. I detected the torment and sorrow in her cries; she genuinely needed someone to care. As I witnessed Vivian's struggle, I realized I had spent the majority of my life searching for acceptance and love. I spent a substantial portion of it believing

I wasn't good enough or worthy of such. I recognized my spirit's anguish in Vivian's cries.

During the years leading up to this moment, I had experienced one emotional hurt after another; they piled higher and higher, one on top of the other. I had been the victim in a multitude of events; many times, I was treated like the perpetrator. I had spent a lifetime on this earth seeking acceptance precisely as I am but never finding it. I tried desperately to be perfect and do everything right; I wanted my parents to be proud of me. Later in life, I transferred this desire and looked for it in other relationships. I tried to be everything I thought others wanted. If I could fulfill expectations, then maybe I would hear what I was seeking. As a child, I never heard the words I desired to hear. This kind of fulfilling acceptance does not come from this world. I was looking in the wrong places.

Shortly before I left the lockdown unit for minimum security, Vivian ventured out of her room for the first time. I remember looking up and feeling strange when I saw her. She was making her way down the hallway toward me; it felt as if I was watching myself. My journey in this ward was ending, and her steps into realism were just beginning. I do not know if Vivian was an actual person or not. Because I remember her from the times I was present in reality, I think she was real. If she was an illusion, I believe God allowed her to appear to be real for a reason; maybe because I was leaving her behind and stepping into my future.

Root Causes

I sat with the lead doctor and my team of professionals in a room of the counseling center. I was coming into consciousness, and I was weeping. I was told that I had been in the hospital for several days. Unknown to me, I had attended psychotherapy sessions daily. My medical team was telling me things about myself they couldn't possibly know, and I don't recall telling them anything; I do not remember talking to anyone. Apparently, I poured out a litany of events from my life that had been chewing me up inside for a long time. I told my doctor things I had shared with only a few people in my entire life; some things I had never verbalized. There was an abundance of issues with which I thought I had dealt, but they had come back with a vengeance to torment me.

During a later session with my care team, I was told I had been in a depressive cycle for a long time. Before this moment, I had never heard the name of the disorder the professionals were giving me in association with my illness, but medical records indicated the findings had surfaced at an earlier date as a possible diagnosis. I don't know why my mind did not absorb this information; I knew I had suffered bouts of depression, but I did not know this disorder can be so severe it leads to problems in multiple areas of life. I had come to the point where it was impossible for me to function emotionally or physically. I had crossed the threshold of stability and entered the world of severe mental illness; when left untreated, life is lived in a nightmare.

Bouts of severe depression followed periods of super energy and euphoric well-being. Over time, the melancholy intensified in length and depth. As the pendulum swung in opposite directions, it got to the point where there were no in-betweens. Each episode of gloom and despondency lasted longer than the one preceding it. Eventually, the high times ceased to exist, and I could no longer function physically; this included the simple task of getting out of bed each day. I felt like I was on an extended roller-coaster ride. Only this time, my car left the track and spiraled out of control. I was trapped in the depressive portion of the rotation, headed for a fatal crash.

My doctor explained that I had suffered a psychotic break, meaning I had experienced total separation from reality; some people call this a nervous breakdown. She told me I was very sick and emotionally fragile. Lack of restful sleep and too many of life's stressors had caused grave problems to develop in my life.

The professionals told me if I pulled out of this episode, the proper medications would help me live a less chaotic life; they would help keep the chemicals in my brain at stable concentrations. Therefore, my thought processes would remain level, helping me stay mentally and emotionally healthy. I do not believe medication is the primary solution to mental and emotional health issues, but it is a vital component in treatment.

The Edge of Darkness

The powerful effects of trauma had gravely wounded me. Physical and emotional affliction had moved in, causing massive destruction at every turn. Cruel, relentless amounts of damage had been inflicted upon me. My mind was ravaged with illness, and my body was riddled with pain. Ordinary ceased to exist; being physically well and psychiatrically sound were things found in my past and doubtful for my future.

As I continued on course toward reality, I found myself facing spiritual issues. One evening, things came to a crisis point. I was laying on the cold floor of the hospital, crying out to God. I had come to realize I was emotionally frozen, physically crippled, socially isolated, cognitively confused, and spiritually comatose. Personally, I had given up, and I was overwhelmed with paralyzing fear.

This fright brought with it a torrent of self-doubt, loathing, isolation, guilt, shame, feelings of worthlessness, and loss of purpose. I had landed in a sea of total hopelessness and despair. I had slipped off the slippery slope of my earthly existence and had begun my journey toward death. The captive arms of severe depression and mental illness had engulfed me. I had embarked on an adventure unlike any I had ever experienced. It cost me dearly, and I barely escaped with my life.

I was in the psychiatric unit of this hospital for approximately one week before I begged God for the strength to fight my way back into reality. The first ten days of confinement were mandatory. By the next round of five, I agreed I would benefit more by staying than leaving. I decided to remain there on a voluntary commitment basis. By day thirteen, I graduated from the lockdown ward and moved to the minimum-security wing. On day fourteen, I was promoted to the coveted exit hall. I remained there for three more days. On the first day of October, I was released into the care of my brother and sister-in-law. Though I had been in this hospital only seventeen days, I learned that this particular cycle of my illness had connective threads as far back as three years, possibly even further.

I didn't realize until the undertaking of this writing project that I was hospitalized for a total of seven months; a hospital or similar facility had been my place of residency from March through October first of that same year. Life events had landed me in a horrific pit. Endless darkness, extreme pain, and profound loneliness had beaten me down. Bitterness had entangled every aspect of my life, and it was choking me to death. Because I am a Christian and was at the time of my breakdown, it is of utmost importance to understand how and why I reached this breaking point. I will use a phrase from a famous radio personality from my generation to help. In the words of Paul Harvey, you need to hear: "The rest of the story."

PART 2

Broken

CHAPTER 3

Way Back When

In the Beginning

Martin and Lillie traveled from the chilly climate of the northern United States to the hill country of the Deep South to visit family; this trip was a yearly, sometimes biannual event. It was a windy spring day, and the extended family was enjoying a meal together. Lillie was pregnant with her third child; two sons had already been given to the couple. Walt would turn seven shortly after the new baby's birth, and Kevin would be three in the fall. Lillie was secretly hoping this wee one would be a girl.

The meal everyone had enjoyed was completed, and a few of the ladies rose from their seats to begin clearing the table; Lillie was one of them. She leaned over the array before her to pick up a dish, straightened, and turned to move into the kitchen. As she did, she looked down and realized she was standing in a small puddle of water. The backache she had been experiencing all morning now made complete sense. Immediately, Lil knew she had gone into labor, but it was too soon. The baby wasn't due for another two months.

Martin was a thirty-three-year-old, World War II decorated Army veteran; he was the oldest of his siblings. He was of medium height, slender, and ruggedly handsome. He was employed as a tool specialist who worked with notable skill and strict precision. He was capable and mathematically inclined. He grew up in the rural

South. He had been to war and was involved in both the European and Pacific campaigns. Martin had undeniably experienced the world outside of the small southern homestead on Morton Road.

Lillie was a thirty-year-old mother of two, and waitressing was her chosen profession. She had stopped working in diners to take care of her home and family. The busyness of motherhood filled her days. Based on the socially acceptable guidelines of the era, Lillie was an at-home-mom. In the vernacular of the times, she was a "housewife."

She grew up on a small southern farm. Feeding chickens, slopping hogs, haying cattle, planting and reaping gardens, hauling water from the creek, milking cows, churning butter, and gathering eggs were all on her daily schedule. Each of these activities produced more chores associated with country survival. Every day held plenty of work to fill the hours from dawn to dusk. Sunday, even though called "the day of rest," held chores that needed to be completed for simple existence to be maintained.

How did these two people find each other and become a family? Lillie Reeves was a twenty-year-old country girl who left the farm to become a waitress. She went to work at Willa's Café, a small diner located in a nearby town. She was five foot three, had wavy dark brown hair, creamy beige skin, and hazel eyes; she was absolutely stunning. She was the oldest girl of six children. She graduated from high school and found a job in town serving tables. She was the friendly, smiling, pretty face people met as they entered the diner.

The Great War had ended a few years earlier, and a new era was dawning. Martin was safely home from battle and had found work at a small munitions plant near the town where Lillie was employed. One Saturday, he went to town and stopped at Willa's for a sandwich and a cup of coffee; the petite waitress caught his eye. After that first visit, Martin seemed to make his way back to the café every Friday or Saturday. One day out of the blue, he altered his pattern and started showing up a few times every week, then numerous times during the week. Each time, he made sure he sat in Lillie's station; eventually, he mustered up the courage to ask her out on a date; she accepted. After work one evening, they went to a "moving-picture show." They got to know each other pretty well over the next year.

Martin arrived at the restaurant early one evening and sat at the counter where he ordered a cup of coffee. He asked Lil if she could take a break; he had something he needed to tell her. Her supervisor granted her permission to speak with the handsome customer. They found a corner table and sat down. Martin began telling this young woman—of whom he had grown quite fond—that the pay where he was working was not great, and satisfactory jobs for a man with his particular skill set were hard to find. Gainful employment was difficult to procure because there were few factories and industrial plants in this region of the country.

He confessed to her that he had been corresponding with companies in the North, and one of them had offered him a decent paying position with terrific benefits; he was giving serious consideration to their offer. He continued, finally getting to the actual reason he had come to see her that evening. He tried to tell her how he felt about her and proceeded to ask for her hand in marriage. He wanted her to become his wife and accompany him to his new destination.

She said, "Yes."

They made plans; and on a spring day, just after the turn of a new decade, dressed in a petal-pink linen suit with matching netted hat, white gloves, pearls, white patent pumps and purse, Lillie and Martin stood before a Justice of the Peace and said, "I do." They left the officiator's premises and ventured forth into their new life. Lil had led a protected, simple life in the red clay hills of farm country. Leaving for parts unknown and an alternative way of life had to be nothing short of daunting for this country girl. Nevertheless, she embarked upon her new adventure.

Third Addition

It was early March and eight years after saying "I do." Lillie was twenty-nine and pregnant with her third child. Realizing she was in labor, she became frightened; her due date was at least eight weeks away. The couple grabbed a suitcase and headed to the nearest community with a hospital. In a small northwestern town of the state they were visiting, Nora Jean Alexander made her way into this world. She arrived two months early, weighing in at four and one-half pounds. In that era, this was a life-threatening, scary event.

"It's a girl!" announced the doc.

Things began to happen quickly. Nurses scurried around collecting an incubator and breathing tubes. The doctor began examining the infant thoroughly; she was tiny and frail but holding her own. She went home after a two-week stay in the hospital, but she contracted whooping cough (pertussis) in her third week of life. This teeny-tiny girl whose momma carried her around on a pillow would battle serious health issues for the next three months.

Martin returned to the North after a week because he had to go back to work. Lillie, her two sons, and baby Nora remained in the South. This allowed time for Nora to gain enough strength to travel and her oldest brother would complete first grade.

Nora would battle various respiratory issues throughout her childhood. Later in life, she would discover being premature and sickly, or prone to "catching everything that came her way" was a minute problem when measured against the bona fide evils that exist in this world. The parallels in this mother-daughter existence were similar; so much so, they would define "history repeating itself." No one knew it then, but Nora would be a lot like her mom; she was a survivor from the very beginning. One day she would become a conqueror, just like Lillie.

A Few of My Favorite Things

My earliest memories go back to approximately four or five years of age. We lived in a northern state in a metropolitan area, on Macon Street. I used to play with dolls in the foyer of our living room. Playing house was a much-loved pastime, and nothing pleased me more than to sit at my miniature table and chairs with a new box of crayons and my Yogi Bear coloring book. Barbie dolls were also favorites.

My mother made all of my clothes. To this day, I have vivid memories of some distinctive outfits. The navy blue, puffy-sleeved, smocked dress was a treasured garment. The red calico with tiny yellow flowers got torn in a game of *Tag* which involved climbing neighborhood fences. The gorgeous peachy-orange, organza-covered, chiffon dress was worn on my first day of kindergarten. The light blue, cotton dress and the country-blue overcoat were for Easter. The forest green, gingham dress was my favorite third-grade outfit. The cute lavender and white pantsuit with dark purple flowers and yellow centers made me feel mature. They all have a place archived in my brain.

I look back on my memories of clothes and realize these are the things from which my love of color and matching outfits comes. Add this to my favorite childhood pastimes of playing in my mom's shoes and purses, and digging through my grandmother's jewelry boxes, one finds a big girl who loves to shop. To this day, there is nothing I love better than spending a Saturday shopping and matching outfits. Finding the perfect accessories to accompany the clothes and finishing the ensemble is bonus fun.

Sometime around the age of ten, I started sewing. My mom allowed me to work on some projects with her, and she taught me how to do handwork first. When I was in fifth grade, I made my first garment; it was a nightgown. In seventh grade, I took Home Economics where my skills in sewing and cooking were pushed to higher levels. I loved both of these activities and would excel in each of them.

Seasons

In the northern region of our country seasons are specific and stunningly beautiful. I remember all four of them; they were diverse, vivid, and markedly distinctive from each other. Northern climate differs from the South where there are generally two major times of the year, hot and sizzling or wet and cold. Humidity in the southern portions of our country is extreme and significantly affects how temperatures feel, making climate a huge factor in coping with the weather.

Spring is exquisite in the northern United States. The crabapple and cherry trees are incredibly gorgeous and in full bloom. The apple trees are budding, getting ready to bear fruit in summer and early fall. Ice and snow may hang around in some places until late March or early April, leaving large patches that had not completely melted away and perfect weather to play *Lost in Space, Cowboys and Indians*, and *Army*. Spring brings the return of other favorite outdoor activities like *Kickball* or working on gymnastic moves. It's the time of year we pull out my candy apple green bike, complete with banana seat and monkey handlebars. I spent hours practicing, learning to ride with no hands, and I exhausted countless hours skipping rope and bouncing on a pogo stick.

June arrives, bringing the close of a school year and the long-anticipated break which moves us to the next grade. Summer holds fun of its own: swimming, kickball, baseball, bike riding, barbecues, picnics, camping, and fishing. Whizzing down the street on a bicycle pretending to be the *Flying Nun* was enjoyable. More games came with the advent of summer. Neighborhood kids would gather together to play *Freeze Tag, Mother May I, Red Rover,* and my absolute favorite—*Three Feet in the Mud Gutter.*

Fishing, camping, fishing, picnics, fishing, vacation, fishing, baseball, and fishing were all treasured summer events. Did I mention fishing? Everyone in my family loves to fish—except me. The worms are slimy; the fish are ugly; their fins hurt when they stick; and, they stink. Some fish even bite. One gets scorched and sweaty while sitting in a boat, on the water, in the sweltering sun, trying to catch a stupid fish. Being quiet and sitting still in a boat all day long is troublesome. Because of my contempt for fishing, there was serious family debate as to whether or not I was truthfully an Alexander. My family concluded that I undoubtedly missed receiving the "fish gene" when being formed in my mother's womb.

Every year during summer vacation, we traveled from the northern to the southern regions of the States to see family and celebrate Independence Day. Spending a few weeks with Uncle Claude and Aunt Martha was always the highlight of summer break. To this day, nothing brings my siblings and me greater joy than spending time with these incredible people and their extended family.

Fall ushers in the new school year, bringing with it new supplies, clothes, and the hope that I would get the best teachers. The decision to take a sandwich or buy a hot lunch for thirty-five cents was of utmost importance. There would be field trips to museums, the cereal plant, and the soda pop bottling company; these were always highly anticipated. The weather would grow cooler, and the vivid colors of nature would show themselves in glorious splendor. Hot cider; warm raised, cinnamon-sugar doughnuts; and pumpkin pie were in ample supply. At this time of year raking leaves, Halloween, mom's famous cornbread dressing, turkey, and homemade pies were in my near future.

Winters are breathtaking in the North. Sledding, building a snowman, snowball fights, constructing forts, and making angels in the snow were marvelous fun. Going to a country lodge to sing with the school choir and riding in the horse drawn, jingle-bell clad sleigh was a junior high highlight. Every winter my brothers built an ice rink in our backyard. How many hours did I pretend I was an Olympic figure skater going for the gold? There were too many to count. Ice fishing and staying out in the cold all day were common occurrences. I will never forget the year my younger brother was walking across a frozen lake. The ice cracked, and he fell into a hole.

He will never know how much that scared me; I had nightmares for a long time.

Christmas has always been my favorite holiday, even when I was young. Each year, I couldn't wait to erect the tree. I wasted no time helping decorate it so I could lie in front of it to watch the lights and sing carols. Homemade cookies and hot cocoa were always on the menu.

I have two treasured memories and one lesson that was learned the hard way associated with this holiday. The first recollection concerns the time my little brother and I got up in the middle of the night to raid the cookie jars that had been filled with freshly made goodies. We had spent the day helping Mom in the kitchen and decided we had not tasted enough samples. We almost got caught! We hid behind the rocking chair in the living room until Mom and Dad went back to bed. The second memory is the taste of homemade ice cream made from freshly fallen snow—yum.

One Christmas, I learned a valuable lesson about peeking at and snooping for presents. I was in fourth grade which made me about nine. Somehow, I managed to sneak around and find out what every single one of my gifts was that year; Christmas morning was ruined. I never peaked after that; and, I have never had the desire to discover what my gifts are beforehand, ever again.

Golden Rule Days

We all have recollections of school days. I liked the learning part of attending school, but I faced a few times when some subjects would cause me problems severe enough to almost result in failure. Acquisition of knowledge did not come easily for me in my elementary days; I remember working hard in school. There were two occasions when math would almost hold me back: fifth grade (*multiplication and division*) and ninth grade (*Algebra 1*). My mom made sure I mastered these areas by providing extra tutoring opportunities for me. My freshman year of high school arrived, bringing a challenge in the form of ninth grade science: simple machines, inclined planes, gravity and— — —. Need I say more?

I loved stories. I loved to listen to them, read them, and write them. Exposure to stories may be why I fell in love with history; it is a series of grand stories. Though I am fond of reading now, it did not come without much effort. I recall sequencing, inference, main idea, cause and effect, and other comprehension skills that took a lot of effort and hard work to master.

Once again, Mom came to my rescue. She placed a small rocker, a table, and a lamp in my room. During my primary days, she would make me sit in my rocking spot to read a book silently. When I finished, I had to find her and read the story aloud. She would then ask me to read the book orally to my dolls and stuffed animals. It should not surprise anyone that I still love to sit in a rocking chair to read a book.

My elementary teachers always read books to us. I loved that part of the day after recess when we would come inside, put our heads down on our desks, and listen to our teacher read a story out loud. I couldn't wait to go to the library every week to check out new books and take them home. *Sam and the Firefly, Little House on the Prairie* (the series), *Nancy Drew Mysteries* (every one of them), *Harriet the Spy, The Family Nobody Wanted, From the Mixed-up Files of Mrs. Basel E. Frankweiler,* and every Grace Livingston Hill novel ever written made their way into my possession. These superb pieces of literary art laid the groundwork for my current adoration of reading.

I liked school most of the time, but I was not proficient at the socializing part until my junior and senior year of high school. In elementary years, I was shy and painfully timid. I became consciously aware of this when I was in the second grade. We had recently moved from a large metropolitan area to the suburbs.

We all know how cruel children can be at times. There was a group of students at my new school who traveled home the same way I did every day. Instead of befriending me and helping the new kid on the block, they taunted and teased me unmercifully. Some days, they would get more physical than others. They would run by and knock my red plaid satchel from my hand, and they would throw small stones and rocks toward me. I don't know if their intention was to scare me or if they were trying to hurt me.

One particular day, these kids were exceptionally mean. The boys ran by and knocked my book bag from my hands. When I bent down to collect my things, the girls in the group proceeded to bump me as they passed by; the whole time, they were jeering and calling me names. Whoever said, "Sticks and stones may break my bones, but names shall never hurt me," lied!

I was so angry I hit one of the boys in the head with my lunch box. It was me against five of them. Needless to say, I didn't win that fight. I had yet to learn the valuable lesson of "choosing your battles wisely." Apparently, my math skills were challenged even then; five to one odds are not good.

Of course, there was the "mean girls" scenario that happened in seventh grade. This event occurs when one person from a group is singled out and intentionally ostracized by all others within that group. More times than not, one individual pits the other friends against one particular person within the group. Girls are particularly bad about entertaining this behavior. I was "the one" outside of the cluster.

These events and some others would affect my socialization skills for a long time. I remained timid and introverted. I walked the halls at school clutching my books tightly to my chest, and my eyes were always diverted downward. I walked home from school, generally choosing to walk alone. When riding the bus, I tried to sit alone whenever possible.

To this day, I remember all of my teachers and the influences they had on me, both expert and substandard. There were a few who needed to find a new career; but for the most part, almost all were good; many were great, and a few were exceptional. When I reached third grade, I knew I wanted to be a teacher, and

I never changed my mind. Throughout my career as an educator, I used many "tricks of the trade" that I learned from my mom and instructors. The "rock and read to stuffed animal friends" works fabulously with primary school kids. I must give credit to Mr. Beckham for *Mini Math*; it works wonderfully at every grade level.

The Impact of Memories

Childhood memories have an effect on all of us, and some of my own stand out quite vividly; it is as if they occurred yesterday. I have fond memories of the times I took an apple to my teacher, and she said something nice to me; it made me smile inside and out. I remember one second-grade recess when my new best friend and I were running on the playground; she fell and broke her arm. I will never forget the day I got busted by my fifth-grade teacher for being the classroom candy thief. I was totally embarrassed, and I felt horrible about what I had done. However, the day I finally regained the trust of my teachers and was allowed to participate in the service squad program was awesome. I clearly remember the time in eighth grade when one of my favorite teachers told me how "nice" I looked; I was wearing a green and white dress with white sandals. One day an eight-grade instructor asked, "Are you sure everything is okay; are you alright?" I wanted to scream, "No!" but I didn't.

Good or bad, great or small, the influences of these and other events helped form the person I would become. My childhood and young life were filled with many marvelous, happy, and joyful occurrences. However, there was the presence of some very dark, sinister things that infiltrated my existence, and they severely scarred me. The happy, momentous events helped form outstanding parts of my personality. The menacing, troublesome, annoying ones became problematic for me; they would become integral parts of my development as well. They would assist in molding some of the "not so appealing" portions of my character.

CHAPTER 4

Life's Influences

Discipline Styles

The emotional expansion of a child's mental health plays a key role in how he learns to handle the situations life sends his way as an adult. The number of siblings we have and our position in birth order—otherwise known as our ranking in the chickadee line—play a vital role in our development and emotional makeup. The effects of acceptable rules of social interaction must also be taken into consideration when evaluating a person's emotional and social coping skills. To get a full picture of what I am talking about, one must understand the philosophy of discipline during the era in which my siblings and I were reared.

I am a late Baby Boomer. A late nineteen fifties birth date makes me one of the last of this group able to claim that label. The sixties would soon dawn and usher in a new generation who would no longer identify themselves as being from the post–World War II Era. It was a time when old fashion ideas about family, discipline, and religion were changing, and roles within the family were fluctuating. Social issues such as unwed mothers, drug abuse, adoption, and abortion were battling their way from being whispered about in private to being openly discussed at the dinner table.

These words: family, home, mom, dad, and the entities themselves should foster feelings of love, comfort, happiness, peace, joy, acceptance, and safety. My personal definitions for these would render these exact emotions. However, in my childhood home experience, these words and the reality of their meanings leaned more toward fear, anger, disappointment, hurt, and pain. My definitions did not match.

Child rearing was different in the fifties, sixties, and early seventies. There was no such thing as time-out, grounding, or talking with a child and giving them an opportunity to choose an acceptable option concerning behavior; these did not exist in my world. Spanking with a belt, a paddle, a switch, or an object of some kind was always the punishment of choice; reasoning with a child was not considered an option. "Don't. No. Why did you? And, I told you," were the most commonly spoken words on any given day in my household. Statements like these, coupled with commands and demands, were in abundant supply around our house. A thorough tongue lashing was never far away.

I have learned that the decades in which I grew up, held differing parental styles and choices. Physically correcting a child was not the only form of discipline available to parents then, even though I thought this to be true. Spanking was a traditional and widely accepted method of punishment during my childhood. There is an immense difference between a spanking for corrective purposes and a punishing beating. Being hit over and over again, until the disciplinarian is tired of striking, is undeniably abusive behavior.

I will not say I never deserved a spanking. I can look back and see there were times I deserved this form of correction. For instance, the time I bit a chunk out of my brother's arm after Mom told us to stop fussing and fighting is a notable example. My brother and I agreed not to tell on each other because we knew we would "get it good" if either of us told. We were fine until Bryan showed Mom the massive-sized bite in the crook of his arm. I must say, the way he chose to inform her of this misdeed was priceless. His announcement was: "Hey, Mom! Look, a big mosquito bit me!" I knew I was in trouble when I heard: "Nora Jean Alexander, go to the basement, NOW!"

There was also the time I cut my baby sister's hair—completely off. Her beautiful brown locks were Shirley Temple curly. My stringy, blonde mane was board-straight. No one ever noticed my cute pigtails, but they sure seemed to love her gorgeous bouncy curls; I was so jealous of her. I got especially tired of people oohing and ahhing over her precious ringlets. Oh, I forgot to mention I used my mom's pinking shears to cut it, and I was old enough to know better. The punishment I received fit the crime. (On a side note: I would have tried to find out why the child had done this.)

I cannot forget to include the time in seventh grade when I decided I was old enough to go to a friend's house after school without asking permission. No one knew where I was going. I should have arrived home by three-thirty in the afternoon, three forty-five at the latest. By five thirty, my two older siblings and my frantic mom were combing the darkening neighborhood streets looking for me. I scared my mother horribly. Needless to say, I got what was merited; and as long as I lived at home, I never again went anywhere without asking permission.

Spanking a child daily, or multiple times per day, for everything is beyond destructive. Not only was corporal punishment used liberally in the household within which I grew up, verbal and emotional abuse were prevalent as well. In my home, if a child was not receiving stinging comments about herself she could hear them being spewed toward a sibling or spouse. Being told I was stupid, ignorant, lazy, or dumb, and being constantly reminded that I would "never amount to anything" was beyond damaging. Eventually, these negative messages worked their way into my mind and stuck there.

As a child, I began to process and believe what was being repeated to me over and over again. We, my siblings and I, always seemed to be in a constant state of being corrected. Do not mistake this as being in a continuous learning environment; they are nothing alike. "No" is a necessary concept that needs to be learned, but there are many positive ways to teach the meaning.

Analyzing and discussing issues with a child were not practiced in our home. We were told what to do, how to do it, and what would happen if we did not comply. We were never given choices. Things didn't just happen in my world. When they did happen, someone had to be at fault; there was always a responsible party. There was no such thing as a glass of accidentally spilled milk. Once the perpetrator was identified, they would be dealt with accordingly.

A child who deliberately picks up a bottle and smashes it should be disciplined in some way. At the very least, she should be spoken to about the dangers and inappropriateness of such behavior. (I think it is a good idea to uncover the reason behind the destructiveness.) This event differs from the little girl who trips over three milk bottles, causing her to fall down the stairs and taking them with her as she went. She should be consoled and asked if she is alright. She should be treated gently and loved. She should not receive a spanking for being careless or blamed for breaking the containers which would cost the family deposit money for the replacements. All of these insults naturally caused more emotional pain.

The preteen girl who becomes ill while enjoying the evening meal with her family should be helped out of the room and made comfortable. She should be removed from the table and gently tucked into bed. She should not be spanked with a belt while being led down the hall to her room. Accusing her of being the culprit who has been eating all of the snacks in the house doesn't help matters. It was cruel to toss her to the bed while proclaiming that eating too much was the reason she vomited. Declaring that excessive eating is the reason why she is so fat only made things worse. None of these actions are acceptable. The stinging comments heaped more forms of pain on this child who was already suffering physically. Over the course of the next two days, she proved to be very sick. Somehow, a peeled orange offered by the disciplining parent didn't quite say "I'm sorry," even though she loved fruit.

A teen who is trying to accomplish the chores she has been asked to complete should be encouraged and thanked. The adults in her life should try to find something about the job that can be praised. If needful directions become necessary, give them in a way that is instructive, not destructive. Do not tell her she is lazy and that she will never be worth anything. Do not badger her about how "sorry" she is, and do not ask her why she never does anything right.

The thirteen-year-old washing dishes for her aunt who is busy tending to a sick child should be commended for helping out in a frustrating situation. She should not be verbally berated in front of family members—her favorite aunt and uncle—for being too slow in bringing the requested washcloth. The girl became so taunted, she hid in the back hallway of the house and sobbed in a corner until she could gather herself together. She stayed hidden for quite a while.

The fourteen-year-old young lady who is missing her mom—who had flown a thousand miles away to check on her parents because they had been in a fatal car wreck that crippled the grandmother—should be dealt with kindly. She should be spoken to with understanding when she asks, "Do you think Mom has made it yet; can we call her?"

"I don't know; let's call and find out," would be an excellent response. The teen should never be shoved into a corner, slapped, and told how stupid she is for not figuring out there is no possible way her mom could be there yet. Adding a verbal shower of insults depicting her presumed ignorance makes the situation even sadder.

These are only a few examples of how discipline and teaching proper, acceptable behaviors were carried out when I was young. Negativity abounded in my home, and verbal berating was in ample supply. Physical punishment and correction were administered on an almost daily basis. By today's standards, an investigation into my childhood home would find it to be a mentally, emotionally, verbally, and physically abusive environment. I believe this would be the case if measured by the standard of the era in which it occurred as well.

The Inequity of Things

Gender bias was in abundant supply during my childhood. Chores were divided into masculine and feminine categories. Guys raked leaves and gals mopped floors; but, the girls could help pick up grass and leaves if their inside chores were completed. Boys created laundry, while girls did the laundry. It was clear that garbage collecting was for men and maid service for women.

My brothers cut the lawn and did yard work. They worked on cars and all things mechanical, technical, or electrical. The guys took the trash to the curb for pick up. They managed the tool shop and kept the garage tidy and in order. The lifting of heavy, bulky items and the moving of heavy things was man's work. Almost every outside job went to the fellas; this included: painting, building things, repairing broken items, and taking care of vehicles like boats and bikes. All of these areas were categorically a boy's domain.

Girl territory consisted of things deemed domestic, meaning all things that need to be cleaned inside of the house. These jobs consisted of dusting, mopping, sweeping, waxing, and vacuuming floors. Laundry was a girl's job. It included: gathering, sorting, washing, drying, ironing, hanging, folding, and putting items away. Females collected household trash and placed it in outdoor receptacles. Making beds fell to the girls, and cleaning toilets and bathrooms were a girl's lot in life as well; the guys messed them up, and the gals scrubbed them.

Cooking was the funny twist. The boys could cook if necessary, but the majority of kitchen responsibilities fell to the girls, especially clearing away dirty dishes and baking goodies. Make no mistake, my brothers and my dad did some KP duty (*kitchen patrol*), particularly when Mom returned to work full-time.

Desired careers were categorized by gender, and remarks concerning professions were heavily laced with male or female identifiers. I could be a clerk in a store, a cashier, a waitress, or a secretary; being the manager, boss, or owner was out of the question. My alternative was to train to be one of the employees, not the employer; becoming a doctor, dentist, or lawyer was not considered possible; those jobs were for men. Though suitable for women, the option of going to college to be a nurse or teacher was never presented as a choice in my early years. The reason: one had to be genuinely smart to pursue those careers; I was not smart enough.

Grades were an area of non-equity as well. Guys could make C's, even D's, and get away with it; the girls needed to generate B's or higher. I never understood this thinking; especially if the boys were going to be the owners, the bosses, and the highly skilled professionals; and the girls were destined to be lower level employees or housewives. Why was grade acquisition not the opposite or at least the same all the way around?

I was always trying to find ways to please my parents; I tried very hard to make them proud. In tenth grade, I made a concerted effort to work diligently and achieve the highest grades possible. My efforts paid off in personal success and accomplishment. I attained Honor Roll that year and proceeded to gain straight A's the remainder of my high school career. Unfortunately, if I received an A-minus my father always wanted to know why the minus was there. There were never rewards for a job well done; it was expected. I would strive to do an efficient job to avoid the consequences that lurked in the offing if my efforts were considered sloppy, inadequate, or incomplete. There were no words of encouragement, and there was always room for improvement.

It's strange what a difference five years make in the way things are viewed. I was born in the late fifties and very domestic in my roles, the doer of all things considered girly. I sew, cook, crochet, keep a neat house, and I love to decorate. I tend to be on the pink and prissy side of being feminine. I love to have dinner parties with a menu which is served on china, and tea is poured into crystal glasses. A prize-winning meal must be presented on a beautifully-set table. I love dresses, skirts, nightgowns, and most things lacy, frilly, and cute. The right hairstyle, make-up, and manicure are all equally important. Of course, shoes and the right jewelry make an outfit, and adding an impressive handbag is always a nice touch. I love all of these things about me.

My sister learned many of the same domestic skills as I; but being born in the mid–sixties, she approached them in a different manner. She broke the gender mold in our family. She enjoyed baseball, fishing, hunting, and building things; she still does. She cuts grass, works outside, and she is an excellent woodcrafter. She works shiftwork in a manufacturing plant, something I don't think I could ever do. She is a good housekeeper and a superb cook, but the frilly details do not matter to her. When serving company, nothing beats paper plates and plastic cups.

She is a blue jean wearing and boot-shod woman who loves the outdoors. Hair is something she must keep, and make-up is not a necessity. She is the best "Git 'Err Dun" person I have ever met. We are as variable as night and day, salt and pepper, hot and cold, and black and white. I have no desire to see her change. She is my sis, and I love her. I do not know how she managed to break the girly mold, particularly in our strict home environment; but she did.

As I look back on the years of my childhood, I see many things that were not satisfactory and should have been different. However, there is one thing I know for sure: though wrong about some things, misplaced and misguided about others, I think my parents did the best they could with the knowledge they possessed at the time. Their hearts were in the right place. They desired nothing more than for their children to become responsible, respectable people. My parents did many things right; all of us have grown to be productive, decent, successful adults.

I cannot speak for anyone else brought up in the same environment as I; I can only voice how I viewed things from childhood, and how they affected and influenced my mental and emotional growth. Somewhere in the maturing process, we must personally identify the things that have shaped us, both positively and negatively. If we find a need to change those that are not right, unattractive, unpleasant, or downright wrong in our lives, then we must access resources available that help us do that. We make choices on a daily basis that create the final production of the person we become. We are responsible for the choices we make as we mature.

Unspeakable Things

The generation in which I grew up was spoken to more openly about issues that were considered unsuitable topics of conversation in the past. The inappropriate use of drugs and alcohol was talked about more freely. Plenty of discussions on acceptable dating behaviors were offered; they included the subjects of living together before marriage, unwed mothers, and teen pregnancy. However, there were still a few topics that remained taboo. They were never spoken of frankly, at least in our home they were not; if discussed at all, they were whispered of in secret.

A ten-year-old girl who has entered the hormonal stage of growth and needs to find the courage to tell her parents that one of these taboo topics has infiltrated her life, and has been present for several years, should feel loved and safe enough to do so. Her dark secret that someone has been touching her inappropriately for as far back as she can remember should not cause her to be so petrified of the adults in her life that it prevents her from taking proper action. She should never be more afraid of her parents than of the wrong being inflicted upon her by another person; this is not a respectful, healthy kind of fear. It is mental anguish and emotional torment.

This child should know it is always right to tell, tell quickly, and keep telling until someone listens. She should not have to worry that her dilemma is a forbidden subject, forcing her to choose silence. She should never be caught in the bondage of fright, concerned that she might get into serious trouble if she divulges the truth. The fear and worry produce unnecessary anxiety and stress. She should never be spanked and told that she is being punished for "letting him" do this. She should be held, guarded, and protected while being reassured that absolutely none of this was her fault.

How could this situation possibly get any worse? This young lady happens to overhear part of the lecture her perpetrator received. He was verbally scolded and told, "Make sure you never do it again." She had finally mustered up the nerve to tell; he got "talked" to, and she was punished. What kind of twisted message was that?

Approximately one year later, she certainly wasn't going to tell it was happening again. She was terrified that her punishment would be even worse. The offender finally got caught. He was dealt with more harshly by his parents, but her mother dealt with her as well. This time, she was spanked with a switch. Many whelps developed, but they disappeared over time. The visible wounds eventually scabbed over and vanished, but the emotional injuries left scars for decades. It was the worst beating of her young life.

The inappropriate touching never happened again. After eight years, at the age of twelve, the unacceptable behavior finally stopped. This child would be sixteen before anyone told her that she was the victim in this ordeal, and none of what happened was her fault. That event left its mark; she would never tell an immense, dark secret again. Many years later this do-not-tell fear would almost cost her, her life.

CHAPTER 5

Life Changing Experiences

The Gospel Message

The following portion of my life is the most significant of all. If omitted, I believe everything in my story would be altered, and the ending completely changed. Without God's truth becoming a reality in my life, I would have had no hope of restoration, joy, or deliverance concerning the nightmare I was living as an adult. Outside of this chapter, life would mean nothing. The same events may have taken place but minus this one situation, this book may have never been written. If it did get penned, I believe the contents and outcomes would be different.

This portion of my story is about the time someone who did not know me reached out and shared truths from the Bible with me. This episode was the turning point that completely changed how I view and react to things in this world, and in life. I know the Gospel Message (The Good News of Jesus Christ) is the essential element that has been the most impactful and influential throughout my life, especially when I faced times of trial, grief, heartache, difficult decisions, healing, or spiritual renewal. This message is for all humankind to hear and contemplate.

I am writing and including this section because many do not know the truth about Jesus, God's Son. Oh, how I pray that you do. If not, know this: God does not lie, His words are truth for "no lie is of the truth" (1 John 2:21).

Here are some nuggets contained in the Gospel Message of Jesus:

God loves us. His Son, Jesus, died for us; and, we can spend eternity with Him. This gift is available to everyone, but not everyone will accept it. (John 3:16; John 3:36; Romans 5:8; 1 John 4:10; *propitiation means an appeasement for; to satisfy; a substitution for; payment for.*)

Jesus died on the cross because we—every single one of us—are sinners. (Ecclesiastes 7:20; Romans 3:10)

We were all born in sin. (Psalm 51:5; Psalm 58:3; 1 John 3:4)

Because we are sinners (1 John 1:8, 10), we fall short of God's glory. (Romans 3:23)

Sin is in this world; we cannot escape it or its end result. (John 3:17–18; Romans 5:12; 1 Peter 2:24)

The consequence of sin is death. (Romans 6:23, first portion of the verse)

If we do not settle the issue of sin in our lives before we die, we will be separated from God's presence forever. We must accept who Jesus is, recognize He is our only hope, and follow His ways. (John 10:9; John 14:6; Romans 10:9; 1 Corinthians 15:55–57; 2 Thessalonians 1:7–9; 1 John 2:23)

Because Jesus is this hope, we must face the issues of salvation and eternal life. "There is salvation in no other; for there is no other name under heaven that has been given among men by which we must be saved" (Acts 4:12). (1 John 5:11–13)

The Bible tells us the truth of how all of this can happen. God has given us a gift, salvation in

Jesus Christ; and, it costs us nothing. (Romans 6:23, second portion of the verse)

To receive this free gift (Ephesians 2:8), each one of us must personally answer Jesus' question: "Who do **YOU** say that I am?" (Matthew 16:15; Mark 8:29, bold caps are mine)

Once we recognize the fact that we are sinners in a sinful world (1 Timothy 1:15), we must decide our answer to Jesus' question, one way or the other. Either, "No, I do not believe this," or "Yes, Jesus is Lord."

If we confess our sins, God will forgive us (1 John 1:9).

If we declare: "Jesus is God's Son," believing that He died for us, and God raised Him from the dead, then we begin our journey of obedience to His ways. In this, we are saved; we will abide (be with) with God, and He will abide with us. (Romans 10:9; Romans 10:13; 1 John 4:14–15)

Once confronted with the question of Jesus, we will make one of two decisions: We either accept and follow Him, or we reject Him. (Matthew 10:32–33; John 3:36)

The latter option means we have turned away from God. Choosing not to believe His words indicates we are stepping into our own strength and following the ways of the world. (Psalms 81:12; Romans 12:2; 1 John 2:15–17)

The decision to reject Christ carries a hefty penalty, and it will cost us everything. (Matthew 10:33; Luke 12:9; John 3:36)

Remember, God has provided the way for us to solve our sin issue: through His Son, Jesus Christ. (John 14:6; 1 John 5:11)

Had this pivotal moment not occurred, I believe my life would have ended with the traumatic hospital event written about in Part One of this book. This particular chapter is fundamental to understanding my story.

The Most Important Questions in Life

I recall the moment I met my Savior with profound clarity, thankfulness, and awe. The following account is my personal testimony of salvation in Jesus Christ.

Growing up, my youngest brother Bryan and I were very close. Barely two years separated us, and we were great buds; we did a lot together. We even managed to get into trouble; we were partners in crime. Sunday was a play day for us. If we finished all of our chores for the weekend, completed homework, and the necessary items needed for school were prepared, we were pretty much allowed to enjoy the day.

We never attended church. Our family unit had no religious factor in its content. My dad was a self-proclaimed atheist. My brother and I almost always spent the day together doing something.

One Sunday morning, I got up planning to make pancakes for breakfast. I thought for sure Bryan would be in the den viewing *Davey and Goliath*, an animated clay cartoon that he loved, but the television was not on. After further inspection, I discovered he was nowhere to be found; he was not in the house or outside. I was not a happy camper.

I made breakfast, ate, did the dishes, and got a book to read. I parked myself in a chair and waited in the living room for Bryan to return home. I was waiting like a cat anticipating the arrival of the resident mouse.

It was after one o'clock in the afternoon when he arrived. I was thoroughly agitated by the time Bryan got home. I grew angrier when I saw him get off of a church bus. He went to church, but he didn't invite me. How rude! (One must understand my displeasure had nothing to do with me wanting to go to church. It had everything to do with my brother getting to go somewhere I didn't get to go.)

When Bryan arrived, I grilled him unmercifully. I hurled a string of questions and a statement at him, all at once. "Where were you? Why didn't you invite me? Who is Keith? Why were you gone so long? What was it like? Why did you ride a bus? Are you going next week? I want to go." They all came out of my mouth in rapid fire procession.

When I asked my brother if he was going back and said I wanted to go too, all he said was, "I don't know." I was determined I was going, whether he invited me or not. He was not about to get to do something I couldn't.

The next Sunday, I got up early, got ready, and I waited—maybe for nothing. The bus showed up about eight-thirty; Bryan and I went to church. For a few weeks after that, my brother continued to go with me; but eventually, he stopped. I never knew why.

Mr. and Mrs. Hanson were on the church bus; he was the driver. They reached out and intentionally invited me into their midst. They picked me up every Sunday morning. Eventually, they went out of their way to provide transportation to Sunday night service, Monday evening meal and visitation, and Wednesday choir and prayer meeting. (This was significant because my father refused to take me to church for anything. He told me if I wanted to go, I'd better find my own way; neither he nor anyone else in the household was taking me.)

When I was old enough to participate in youth activities, Mr. and Mrs. Hanson made sure I had a way to get there. They drove several miles in the opposite direction of the church to come and get me. Because of their efforts to help me plug in, I found a church family, a place to belong, and a place to grow in the things of God. Two women at this church took me under their wings. They helped me discover God's word, taught me how to pray, and encouraged me to praise through music.

Six or eight weeks into this new experience, and about six weeks after my fourteenth birthday, I was sitting in the balcony seats of the church listening to a sermon about salvation. The preacher said our relationship with God begins when we have a personal encounter with Jesus. It is a matter of what happens in our heart, the innermost part of us. It affects what we think in our minds, and alters how we view everything in this world; it also determines our behaviors and changes many things about us.

I sat there asking myself the tough questions I had been hearing from the pulpit throughout my weeks of attendance at church. Did I have a relationship with Jesus? Did I think I needed this Savior? Did I know I am a sinner? Did my life look any different because of what I believed? Did I believe Jesus is God's Son? Did I believe Christ died for me? Did I believe He rose from the dead and conquered death? Did I believe Jesus is the only way to heaven? Had I confessed Jesus as Lord (Master/Ruler)? Did I want to be a follower of Jesus Christ?

As I stood there during the invitation, I began to cry. I knew my answers to every one of these questions except the last one was, "NO." The answer to the final one was, "I don't know, but I think yes." In those quiet moments, everything in me desired ALL of the answers to be, "YES." I realized I am a sinner in desperate need of the Savior, and if I died at that moment, I would face death and eternity without Him.

I wanted to go to the altar at the front of the church to meet with a counselor who would show me how to be saved, but I was terrified to go down to the front of the sanctuary by myself. As I stood there facing the questions of eternal life and salvation, I came to the realization that someone was standing beside me. It was a sweet, five-foot tall little lady with a beehive hairdo. She slipped her arm around my waist and asked me if I was okay. It was Mrs. Hanson.

I told her I knew God was dealing with me, and I wanted to follow Jesus; I wanted Him to be Lord (Ruler) of my life. I confided in her I was too afraid to go down to the front of the church. She told me God could save me right where I was; I didn't have to go anywhere. She said, "Honey, He knows where you are; you just have to talk to Him. You know, Nora, when a gift is placed in front of you, you simply believe it is for you; and trust that it is honestly yours. Hopefully, you accept its validity and know it is for your good. A gift is of no use if it is being held out to you, but you do not take it; it remains unopened and useless. You must reach out and accept it and unwrap it to experience the joy it brings. You must utilize the gift if it is to be of any use to you; it does no good to open it, then hide it away somewhere never to be seen again. Nora, God's gift is right here waiting for you."

I do not know what happened in those moments, but all of a sudden it was okay. I felt an instant calm, and I was no longer afraid; I wanted to go. In fact, it felt like I couldn't get down to the front of the sanctuary fast enough.

Mrs. Hanson walked with me to the altar, and we got on our knees. She opened her Bible and laid it on top of the prayer bench then proceeded to show me scriptures that talked about many of the questions I mentioned above, and she included those that stated I am a sinner in need of forgiveness and repentance. I had to turn to God. After explaining everything to me, she asked me if I was ready to proclaim Jesus as Lord and become a follower of Christ. I shook my head yes as a teary, nervous smile shot across my face.

Mrs. Hanson gave me a warm hug; then, she took both of my hands in hers. She said we were going to talk to God and tell Him why we were there, stating that this was a prayer she could not pray for me; it was personal between God and me, so I had to talk to Him myself. Mrs. Hanson explained that she would start and then signal me by squeezing my hand when it was my turn. She advised me to just talk to God as if He and I were sitting here having a conversation. She said there was no rush; and when it was my turn, I could start when I was ready.

A few minutes later there I was, bowing before Almighty God, voicing the first prayer of my entire life. I opened my mouth and verbally proclaimed:

> God, I believe Jesus is Your Son, and He is Lord of everything. Thank you for loving me and sending Jesus.
>
> I believe He died on the cross for me; and because of that, I can have eternal life. I believe Jesus rose from the grave and is in heaven with You.
>
> Lord, I understand I am a sinner, and I need to walk in Your ways. I don't understand very much of the rest; help me learn. I want to be saved from my sin; please forgive me. I want to follow Jesus; please guide me, and help me live for You.
>
> Thank you for dying for me, for saving me, and for giving me eternal life.
>
> In Jesus name, Amen.

My life was transformed forever in those precious moments on that spring day, and my journey continues to this day.

The following Sunday, Mrs. Hanson waited for me in the wings of the baptistry. (My parents were invited to come, but they did not attend.) She watched as I publicly shared my decision to follow Jesus. I was proclaiming to everyone present that I had accepted Jesus as my Lord and Savior, and I belonged to Him; now, I was part of God's Family. I made this profession by being baptized; it was my first step of obedience to the Ruler of my new life. (Mark 16:16; Acts 2:38; Romans 6:4)

Have I been perfect? No way! Have I behaved flawlessly since that day? I wish I could say yes, but the answer is no. Do I have a problem-free life? No, again.

There is one thing I do know, and I cannot be swayed from it: *As I peered inward and saw my sin and then gazed upward seeking the Savior, God looked down from heaven and saved me.* Just as He knew my exact location and circumstances then, He knows where each of us is right now. God is aware of what is happening in our lives, and He is ready to meet us where we are. We don't have to be prepared or cleaned up before we go to Him; He took care of all of that on the cross. He accepts us just the way we are; all we have to do is agree with Him about sin and who He is. If we seek Him with our whole heart, we will find Him (Jeremiah 29:12–13).

Illumination

In far-future days, I would be cloaked in a veil of darkness while dwelling in the midst of the valley of the shadow of death, trapped in a horrible pit controlled by evil. The only speck of light present was the small fragment that remained, abiding deep inside of me. It had almost been extinguished by the weapons of the enemy, but it was still there because once given it can never be taken away. It is an everlasting ember. It is the light Jesus placed there when I proclaimed Him as Lord and Savior of my life. When I returned to the Source of this boundless light, God fanned the speck and ignited a flame that illumined everything around me so I could clearly see what was there. (Job 33:28; John 6:12; John 8:12; Ephesians 5:8)

I cannot imagine what cowering in the depths of darkest black, engaged in battle with evil would be like without my Heavenly Father; it is a frightening place of encounter. He is the only way we can find our way back into the full beauty and radiance of the light for He is the Light (Luke 11:34–36; 1 John 1:5), and it is how we break free from our fear (2Timothy 1:7, NKJV).

My sincere prayer is that you will seriously consider these truths and examine them in your life.

> If you have already accepted the free gift of salvation, and your relationship is fully brightened because of the closeness of your Source, then you are in a wholesome place. I would count it an immense

privilege and joy to celebrate with you because you are my brother or sister-in-Christ.

If you are His, but your life is cloaked and burden down like mine was, for whatever reasons, please stop and run to Him now. Call out to Him; talk it all out and settle it. Take as long as you need to sort through things, and then leave them with Him; release and surrender all of it to Him. Talking with God will not take away all of the issues you face in life, but it will reenergize your relationship with the Light; it will embolden and empower you by shedding fresh light into the darkened arena that keeps you captive. A conversation of confession with God is key to freedom from bondage.

My prayer for you is that He will send His light to expose the hidden and troubling things in the dark spaces of your life so you can be refreshed and renewed; you do not have to stay where you are. I know the Light will infiltrate your darkness; and you will see much more clearly, becoming strengthened and encouraged to move forward.

Oh, precious person, if you do not know my Jesus, nothing would bring me greater joy than to know you have discovered Him and have asked Him to be your Savior and Lord. You can go straight to God and talk to Him at any time. Salvation will not instantly fix everything in your life, but you will discover the support you need to deal with everything you are facing, especially the nightmares that haunt you. This kind of help comes only in God's gift to us, Jesus; He is waiting for you.

Culture Shock

My mother once told me, I didn't have a clue what her life had been like throughout the years. She was right; as a fourteen-year-old, I was not aware of the emotional and psychological battlefields she had encountered in her lifetime. I doubt that at the time she said this, I could have fathomed the emotional stress created by the extreme cultural differences between growing up learning the ways of the rural South and living in a big northern city. She was correct; I had absolutely no clue, but I would find out.

A few short years after she made this comment to me, I would discover the war zone of emotional stress created by culture shock. I would come to comprehend the mental battles my mother must have endured, for I experienced the same jolt when this scenario played out in reverse during the sixteenth year of my life. It was the second most influential event that happened to me up to this point.

It was time for my parents to move back south and take only part of their family with them; my older brothers would be remaining in the North. The company my dad worked for was sold, and he no longer had gainful employment. My parents had to provide for their family and take care of them. They did just that, with the only resources they had available to them. They did what they had to do, and it was the right thing. This part of their journey would begin twenty-four years after Martin and Lillie had first ventured into marriage and new territory up north.

The summer of my sixteenth year came to an end, and the shock of a total lifestyle change was about to floor me. When I was growing up, the penny store was located at the end of the street. It was the perfect place to get ice cream, candy, and soda pop. We walked to and from school every day. Four-lane traffic that ran all directions was three blocks away from our house. There was a Farmer John's Grocery Store, Wonder Hills Shopping Center, and a Reed Drug Store; they were all within walking distance of my home. This house was strategically placed; it was the perfect location for a sixteen-year-old girl gainfully employed as a babysitter.

In September of that year, my life changed, literally overnight. I would find myself in the middle of nowhere. My new home was so far out in the country, I would be headed toward a town no matter which direction I chose to travel when turning out of the driveway. The area in which I came to reside was located just outside of a small southern town, approximately twenty-three miles from the nearest city big enough to have a major grocery store, a franchised burger joint, a discount center, and a movie theater with two screens.

There was no such thing as ordering a pizza for delivery or driving to the nearest chain hamburger establishment for a quick burger. Soda, or pop, no longer existed; everything was now called Coke. The roads near my new home were narrow. The one leading away from my house was steep, surfaced with red clay, and topped with gravel. The next series of roads were paved but had no lines of division. If I drove long enough, I would eventually find myself on a highway that would lead toward town—no guarantee it has double lanes.

My city high school had close to one thousand students registered in grades ten through twelve, with over three hundred in my commencement class. My new school housed grades seven through twelve with approximately two hundred students total. My new graduating class consisted of thirty-six students.

Our first two years in the South, we grew eighty-five to ninety percent of what we ate; meat was hunted, fished for, or raised for slaughter. Most of our food did not come from the store anymore. Eggs came from the small coupe out back and had to be gathered twice every day. Milk didn't come in a carton anymore; it came directly from the cow—twice daily, morning and evening. It was squeezed into a bucket, strained through a cheesecloth, and stored in glass jugs. Vegetables no longer came from a can or bag purchased at the local grocery store. We grew all of these items, and I learned how to can and freeze things for future use. Ketchup is no longer found in a bottle labeled Heinz; now, it is in a jar that says Ball, and it has been processed in our kitchen.

Heat did not originate from the touch of a button on a wall. Trees were cut down, branches sawed off, and the entire tree chopped into manageable sized pieces. The resulting logs are burned in a hole in the wall called a fireplace. Winter mornings are freezing in a house being warmed solely in this manner.

The move south created vast loneliness and isolation in my life. Knowing absolutely no one, starting my junior year of high school with no friends, being moved from the suburbs of a big northern city to the country just outside of a small southern town, and being separated from my older brothers caused tremendous emotional pain to develop in my life. I was also forced to leave my first boyfriend behind; that hurt as well. Besides all of that, the nearest mall was over an hour away, and I lived too far away from town to be employed as a babysitter.

Though I would eventually count this move one of the better things that happened in my life, I would face extreme apprehension, trepidation, uncertainty, and insecurity for a long season. It was a difficult time of adjustment. Today, I know my mom faced many difficult days like I did because adjusting to an entirely different way of existence is challenging. Now, I recognize that my mother was a strong, determined woman; she was a survivor and a conqueror.

Many prized treasures came into my life because of this move. Better friends than I ever possessed became mine, and I found acceptance by peers, something I had not experienced prior. I had been a Christian for only two years when we moved, and God continued to grow me in my relationship with Jesus and guide my spiritual walk. I had the privilege to learn from great people of faith and expand my knowledge of His Word, absorbing sound theology and biblical precepts along the way.

I learned many things about being self-sufficient and resilient. I learned the value of discernment and discretion. I continued to learn about music and singing. These would become highlights and be empowering strongholds in my life. Many of the marvelous traits that belong to me, God bestowed when He formed me; but many of them grew and matured when He allowed me to transfer to the southern portion of our country. Most importantly, He would teach me the importance of "learning to bloom where I am planted."

CHAPTER 6

Young People These Days

Off to College

By the time graduation from high school rolled around, I experienced friendships and acceptance like I had never known. God instilled in me a desire to do and be my best. The two years I attended school in the South, I made straight A's and graduated with honors; I was tenth in my class.

The relationships formed at this institution are the ones I remember when I recount my high school experiences. Much later in my life two dear friends from this era would reach out and help me during a most difficult time in my existence, even though they had not seen me in many years. The only fond memories I have of high school in the North are centered on my involvement in the choir and the ensemble group in which I was privileged to participate.

Early in my new walk with Christ, I developed the desire to go to a Christian university or college. I also felt a distinct calling on my life at the age of sixteen, shortly before we moved; I knew I was being called to be a preacher's wife. I did not know how God would combine and use my dream of being a teacher with this call, but I trusted He would reveal that to me in time. I surrendered my life to a distinct service for the Lord, asking Him to use my skills as a teacher to influence my students and to show me how to be a godly woman, and how to do it well.

I didn't realize I would have to fight and stand my ground to go to college. I knew I wanted to be a teacher, but I also felt college was out of my reach. The move south and being placed in a smaller educational setting did great things for my confidence level. The majority of my teachers were wonderful. I studied harder than ever, and my grades made me feel smarter. When friendship and acceptance by peers were added, I discovered a new-found belief in myself and a liking of who I am; I wasn't so bad. Most of my new girlfriends were all talking about going to college. I started thinking maybe I could go too. Eventually, these thoughts turned into believing I was college bound.

As time went on, my desire to be a teacher grew stronger. My dad had clear-cut ideas about what jobs were appropriate for women. By his standard, the best I could hope to be was a skilled secretary, and I didn't need college for that. According to him, a year or two of training and practice of my typing skills would set me for life. I once asked him why I couldn't be a nurse or a teacher. His reply, "You have to be intelligent to do those things."

There was also the issue of money. My father told me outright that he had no money to send a girl to school. If I wanted to go to college, I would have to figure out a way on my own; the challenge had begun. I decided I needed to get an after school and weekend job so I could start a college fund, but my parents would not allow this. My next plan was to talk with the guidance counselor at school. I collected information about scholarships and grants. Most scholarships were not available to me because my freshman GPA (*Grade Point Average*) lowered my final overall average to just under the requirement. I did not have enough extracurricular activities to include in my biographical information because my parents did not allow me to participate in these. When the grant program was explained to me, I got super excited. I knew I would qualify because my dad had been unemployed for a long time.

I went home armed with information and dangerously excited. I was shot down from the first word; I encounter a major problem.

My parents, specifically my father, have always been private people, as were many from their generation. He did not want to fill out the financial section of the grant application. He said the government already knew more about him than he wanted them to know, and he was not going to tell them anymore.

My oldest brother came to my rescue; he talked to my parents. Dad would not listen, but Mom did. Without Dad's approval or permission my mother filled out the paperwork, and I submitted it. Secretly, I battled my hidden emotions and feelings of deceit. My actions could appear to be disrespectful to my father; disrespect was never my intention. My dad was opposed to the grant process, and I felt trapped between a rock and a hard place. I had my mother's blessing, and I knew I could not attend college if I didn't apply and qualify for a grant. I had sound teacher recommendations, and my grades were good; by government standards, I met the criteria for the funding, and my application was approved. The award money, coupled with a job on campus, made financing possible; I was going to college.

Battle number two: "You are not going away to school. You are not going off by yourself. There is a perfectly fine university right here in the city." These were the responses I heard every time I brought up the subject of going away to further my education. My dream of going to a Christian college was fading. My father wanted me to live at home and go to the local university, thirty minutes away. I began the process of searching for a Christian school relatively close to home. I discovered a college two and one-half hours from our home; this is where I decided to go. My goal was to learn all of the theology and Bible stories I could. I seemed to have no knowledge of these, but everyone in the South appeared to be infinitely familiar with them.

Once again, my oldest brother and mom intervened on my behalf, and Dad finally stopped arguing. I never knew how instrumental my mom and brother would be in winning the college war and other battles for my future, but I do know I can never thank them enough for stepping in and helping.

Disillusioned

My first two years of college life were challenging. Besides dealing with overwhelming homesickness—which totally surprised me—I discovered the unfortunate reality of some professors in schools who find intense joy in tormenting certain students. I had the opportunity to experience one such teacher. I would survive that particular class. I would retake it under a different professor and do rather well. Apparently, the first one just didn't like my writing style.

Old and New Testament classes were not at all what I expected, and I quickly became disillusioned; neither one met my expectations of discovering the stories in God's Word and the meanings behind them. I survived New Testament my first year but dropped Old Testament at the beginning of my second. On top of my discontent with the religion aspects of the school, college courses were a bit different from high school, and I had to tweak my study habits.

I also fell into a trap many college kids face; I attended church for a while and then slacked off toward the end of my first year. The first semester of my sophomore year, I grew increasingly unhappy with classes. Coupled with not taking care of myself spiritually, I became quite disgruntled. My grades began to slip, and I developed an upper respiratory infection. By the time semester break rolled around, I was not doing well physically, spiritually, or academically; disenchanted is an understatement.

Sometime shortly before Thanksgiving, I called my mom. Subconsciously, I knew something was seriously wrong at home. I stayed on campus during the holiday, and I prayed a lot. By the time students were coming back for the last few weeks of classes, I knew I would not be returning to campus in January. Calls home had left me wondering if I had done the right thing in leaving. I remember being struck with the thought: *I had escaped the tyranny of my dad;*

but I had left my mom behind, alone to deal with him. When I went away to school, my parents were sleeping in separate bedrooms and barely speaking to each other; they just existed in the same household. My mom decided to make me her confidant when we moved south; she had no one else. Even though I was guilty of nothing, I experienced guilt and blame; I felt I had abandoned her.

Changing Course

There was only one reason I regretted leaving the small college I had chosen. I had met a young man, and a friendship was developing. I will never forget the first time I saw him. I was sitting in West Parlor playing my guitar and singing a song I had written. I looked up when he walked into the entry. He smiled at me, but that is not the only thing I witnessed. I saw a young man with a glow about him. I will never forget the immediate thought I had: *I am looking at my future husband.*

My new-found friend and I talked about everything. We shared our salvation experiences and how God had worked in our lives, particularly in bringing us to this school. We disclosed childhood memories and shared family backgrounds; the similarities in our lives attracted me to him even more. We didn't date much because we couldn't afford it, but we did spend considerable amounts of time together talking and getting to know each other.

I was amazed by the way God had redirected his life. He was a high school dropout with a GED (*Graduation Equivalency Degree*) and a vocational training certificate; yet here he was, in college. I was intrigued by his salvation testimony. This good-looking young man was saved through the witness of a young lady he did not know; a stranger shared the Gospel with him. He was also influenced by two family members whom he greatly admired. He was in school, studying hard, and he loved the Lord. I was very impressed; smitten would be a better description. Beyond all of that, he was quite handsome.

If I was so intrigued by this young man, why was I contemplating leaving school? It was because I had finally taken care of the spiritual issues in my life; I was attending church and spending time in prayer. In the innermost part of myself, I knew I was being led to go home. Semester break arrived, and I had to tell my new friend I was not returning after Christmas. However, just as I felt the conviction about him when I looked up and saw him in the parlor, I knew my mom needed me at home.

I also had to think about the call on my life to be the wife of a preacher. After careful consideration of all these things and prayer, I knew I was leaving. As far as I knew that was the end of our friendly relationship, I would never see him again. Besides, he was studying finance; he wasn't studying to be in the ministry. God would help me get over it.

I had not fully recovered from the respiratory infection I contracted, and by the time I reached home I was very sick; I would get even sicker. The new term at the local university—the school my father wanted me to attend in the first place—would not start until March. This campus operated on an alternative reporting system; I would miss one session, and all of my class credits from the other school would not transfer. Both of these situations caused me to fall two enrollment units behind in my studies. It would add time to my school career, but I could handle it.

Double Take

The first thing on my agenda was to get well; this took Christmas break and all of January. Second, I would no longer have library and dorm monitor duties from which to draw income; I had to find work. When I got well, I looked for a job. During this portion of my journey, I would meet an exceptional friend whom God would use to come to my assistance on more than one occasion in my future. Talk about a servant's heart; she has one.

I walked into Safe Haven Daycare and met the owner. She was willing to work around my school schedule, knowing it would change occasionally; and one dollar and ninety-five cents per hour sounded suitable to me. Our relationship began as boss and employee, but it grew into dear friendship. I started work in February, and college courses began in March.

Because I had missed part of a full year, and all of my credits did not transfer, I decided not to take a break during the summer session. I continued to work for Melissa Jane as a daycare provider. I registered for summer school, and in June classes began. There were two sessions, and I attended both. The first portion was June through mid–July; I took Political Science and Music Appreciation. The second session was from mid–July through August; it held Tennis and State History.

Summer rounds began. Session one was at eight o'clock in the morning, Political Science, located way up in Connor Tower. There were five rows of desks in the classroom. I picked a seat in the first row, about the fourth seat back. The door opened and in walked a guy who looked really familiar; I knew him from somewhere.

No way! It can't be him. He walked by me and didn't say a word. I thought: *I must be mistaken.* I kept watching him on and off during class, saying to myself: "It is him. No, it's not. Yes, it is. No— — —"; I caught myself staring.

The bell rang, and the first class of summer school ended. The young man walked by me and still said nothing. That settled it; surely, I was just confused. Don't we all have a twin somewhere in the world? My eyes were playing tricks on me. I decided to follow him to the elevator. I tried to reach through the crowd to tap him on the shoulder to get his attention, but there were too many people. The elevator arrived, he got on, and I had to wait for the next one. I was determined another day would not pass without me knowing if this was the person I thought him to be. It wouldn't take long to discover because class met every day, Monday through Friday. In a few short hours, I would finally know.

I arrived to class early the next morning and sat in the same seat as the day before. He walked through the door and plopped down in the seat right in front of me. "It is you!" I exclaimed as I smiled.

"Why didn't you speak to me yesterday?" I quipped.

"You didn't speak to me, either." he replied.

"You are right; I did not. Is it really you?" I asked, smiling.

"Why did you leave school?" I questioned.

I do not remember his reply, but I did know he was my good-looking friend from the Christian college. We started talking that day and continued to do so every day afterward, and he walked me to my car when it was time for me to leave for work. We did this for the entire six weeks of classes. Once again, we talked and spent a lot of time getting to know each other. This time of continued companionship and learning about him was the first time in my life a young man ever showed extreme interest in me. He seemed to want to spend huge amounts of time with me, and we never ran out of things to talk about; I felt special.

The second session of summer school began after Fourth of July break. My first class of the day was Tennis; my second was State History. I no longer saw my handsome fellow every morning, but I was thinking about him. In fact, several days went by before I realized the likelihood of randomly meeting on a large campus was not very high.

I found a parking spot relatively close to the building where my last class would take place and parked there every morning. About the fourth day of classes, I headed across the parking lot and noticed someone sitting on the hood of my vehicle. As I drew closer to the vicinity, a guy jumped off and came walking toward me saying, "I knew if I found your car and waited, sooner or later you would show up."

I think I smiled bigger than I ever had before that day. We saw each other every day for the next two weeks, and then he finally asked me out on a real date; I was so excited. The big day finally came; it was a Saturday. I was babysitting some kids at the daycare where I worked for extra cash. I would be finished by two o'clock and have the rest of the day free; he was going to pick me up at five.

A Practical Joke

Around eleven o'clock, I noticed someone was parking a dark green K-Car at the curb; it was him. He came in and helped me with the kids; we fed them lunch and put them down for naps. He talked about how he couldn't wait to have kids of his own. While the children were napping, he told me the real reason for his visit.

"I hate to do this, and I don't want to; but, I have to break our date tonight."

"Why?" I know I sounded disappointed; I was.

"I got a new job. I was supposed to start Monday evening, but they called this morning and asked if I could come in tonight at five. The other cashier is sick."

"Oh. Well, you can't jeopardize your new position, so we'll have to reschedule." I said.

"You're okay with it?" he asked.

"Sure. It's not your fault that the cashier is sick. You could have called me; you didn't have to come by here to tell me."

"I was supposed to get to see you today, and I was making sure I did."

"Thank you. Where is your new job?"

"I am the new night cashier at Henry's; it's over on the service road."

"You have got to be kidding me!" I squealed. "My mom is the supervisor on the night shift; you'll be working with her tonight."

We spent the next hour scheming, planning a practical joke to play on my mom. During a lull in the evening, he was going to talk about how glad he was to have a job and everything, but he would complain that it was messing up his date life. Then, he was going to tell the story of running into a girl here in town whom he had met at college in another city. We were hoping my mom would pick up on the names of school and town, and then make a statement something like: "Oh, my daughter went to school there for a while." She came through; that's what she said, verbatim.

Next, he would talk about running into the girl at the local university. He would describe her and draw things out. Then he was going to look straight at my mom and say, "Maybe your daughter has mentioned this girl to you; her name is Nora Alexander." My mom was so surprised she almost dropped the tray she was carrying. We got her, and we got her good. Contriving this hoax to play on my mom is a favorite memory.

The young man I had felt would one day be my husband was back in my life, spending time getting to know my mom and me. The only problem was dealing with the calling on my life to be the spouse of a preacher. He was going to be a finance officer, a Christian one, but not a pastor; well, maybe he would be involved in a ministry of some type. I would figure that out later; anyways, we were just friends.

I Do

We both worked and went to school full-time. Spending a few hours together each evening was the extent of our dating. We went to the movies once, to get a bite to eat a few times, and we visited his Aunt Sally who lived twenty miles away; he was living with her during this time. Mostly we went to my apartment to talk, study, or to eat a meal I had cooked. I would describe our experience more like courting than dating. In September, he asked me to marry him. I said, "Yes."

We originally planned a May wedding. It was scheduled to take place after the spring grading session ended. We would have the summer to adjust to being married before school would start again in August. After spending fall session trying to juggle work, school, and trying to seeing each other, we decided to move the date up to November during the session break.

The wedding was not going to be big or fancy, just family and friends gathered at our small country church. My mom and I made the food, and a friend made my cake. My fiancé and I bought a few single stem flowers for the wedding party. My dress, veil, and accessories totaled 150 dollars. The guys wore tan suits that they already owned. My mom bought my sister's dress, and my matron of honor had a dress in the same color scheme. My friend's daughter would be the flower girl, and her peach dress went perfectly with the rust and tan. My boss's six-year-old son said he would be the ring bearer. My brother agreed to take photos, and we mailed simple invitations. We were in outstanding shape for a ceremony.

My dad had granted his approval for the wedding and agreed to walk me down the aisle. Even though things were strained between us at this time in our relationship, it was still important to me to have his approval. I wanted to respect him by seeking his permission to marry. When the photos of the wedding came back, there was one that I treasured greatly. I was holding my dad's arm as he escorted me down the aisle. I was broadly smiling, as I looked toward my groom. On a beautiful autumn day, I became a married woman. I genuinely loved my new husband.

CHAPTER 7

Making Choices

Wisdom Verses Judgment

There were two things I had to grapple with before our wedding, and I knew I had to settle them before I ever journeyed down the aisle to link my life with this man. During our engagement, my future husband and I discussed pretty much everything imaginable about marriage. We seemed to be on the same page and in agreement on all the major issues, and on the majority of the minor ones as well.

The first matter in our relationship that I had to ponder was my experience as a sixteen-year-old, distinctly knowing I was being called to be the wife of someone in ministry; I felt God was leading me to devote myself to becoming a preacher's wife. I prayed about this a lot. I had read in my Bible: if God has called us to do something, He will be faithful to equip us and supply everything we need concerning the situation, (Philippians 4:19; Hebrews 13:20–21). Just as God always provided what He promised to those who obeyed him in the scripture, I knew He would do the same for me because His word does not change and neither does He.

I also had to consider my experience from the dorm, when I had the fleeting thought I was going marry this man; now it was happening. My dilemma: "He's a finance guy, Lord." God's answers came to me from His word, and I heard in my heart: "Well, Matthew was a tax collector, and I used him to write the Gospel. Luke was a doctor, and I used him for My glory. Paul was an enemy of My loved ones, and I still used him. As long as a man knows Me and serves Me, I can use him in My kingdom; it does not matter what title he bears. Nora, you can be a godly wife to anyone I send, and I can use any of My children who are willing to be used." I had such a perfect peace; I didn't think about it anymore.

The second issue with which I had to deal was evaluating an event that happened about a week before our wedding. We had never quarreled or argued, and we enjoyed being with each other. We had both witnessed unrelenting parental arguing while growing up, and we decided we did not want to carry that into our union. We had known each other slightly over a year, but we had only spent significant amounts of time together for the last five months. I had never seen my fiancé angry.

I do not remember why he got mad. We were in my car; he was driving. I do not recall where we were going, possibly to or from Aunt Sally's home. Joe, his brother and best man, was in the car with us. I made a remark about something and watched as my fiancé went from zero to boiling point with anger in less than thirty seconds. He became enraged and began spewing words, driving erratically all over the road.

I became frightened and cried out for him to pull over and stop. He swerved off the road and slammed on the brakes. We skidded to a halt, barely missing a tree. He got out of the car to walk, rant, and rave. I was watching a frenzied, grown man pace before me; he was throwing an absolute fit. My future brother-in-law tried to console me; then he went to speak to his brother. I did not get out of the car. We traveled home in silence. I did not say good night, and he did not walk me to my apartment.

I spent the night crying. I seriously considered returning the ring and calling off the wedding. I could not figure out what I had done. (Why did I assume it was my fault?) As I calmed down, I got out a piece of paper and made two columns; what I loved and liked about my fiancé and what I didn't. There were a few items in the "do not like" column, most I could handle. The worst was a seemingly violent, raging temper. The like-list was great, and I smiled as I read over it.

Next, I looked at what God says about faithfully loving someone. Acceptance, forgiveness, compassion, understanding, and trust all came to my mind. I looked up scriptures for a few hours. At the end of my vigil, I came to the conclusions that I was not trying to change him. He was not perfect, but neither was I. I had plenty of weak areas in my life that needed work; I just happened to witness one of his. I had been a Christian for six years at this point, and I knew my journey of growth was still in the early stages of development. My fiancé had only been a follower for two, almost three years. So, where did that place him on the spiritual maturity scale? Was I acting judgmental, or did I need to seek wisdom in this?

I remember getting on my knees and thanking God for this man who claimed to love me; who by all appearances was sent for me to love. That night, in the wee hours of the morning, with 1 Corinthians thirteen opened on my lap, I chose to love my future husband, even in an unlovable moment. I was going to accept him as he was and journey in growth and faith with him. I fell into a peaceful sleep with a smile on my face, as I anticipated the next day and the forgiveness it would bring. We exchanged vows and wed the following week.

The Unspoken Truth

Our first year together was tremendous; I loved being married. It was "give and take." We were learning to compromise and discovering likes and dislikes along the way, all while enjoying each other. We only had a few minor disagreements, and I thought we were great together. We did not fuss, and life was good. The following year was my senior year of college and it was shortly after our first anniversary; we experienced our first intense marital altercation. It was only a slap; I reasoned with myself. I had survived much worse in my life. *Anger and Rage* had reappeared for the first time since the incident in my car, hinting they were lurking in the shadows waiting for an opportunity to pounce.

By our second anniversary, I had graduated and gotten a teaching position in a neighboring county. During that time span, a dented car hood from being pounded with a wrench, some books being hurled across the room, a slapped, and a broken piece of furniture were the spoils of matrimonial discord. I thought we were adjusting, and I was learning to deal with the presence of anger. When things were going well for us, they were pleasant. When they were bad, they could be incredibly taxing; particularly when his temper reached an explosive level. I thought this was the norm and accepted it.

We got through those episodes and moved forward. We started our third year of marriage and rented a house in a neighboring town. During our tenure in this home, we had our first knock-down, drag-out fight. He decided I was out of line, and he was going to get me under control. His statement was something like: "If the only way to get you to cooperate is the way your dad treated you, then I'll treat you the way he did." He was going to use the method my father had always incorporated to get my attention, physical force.

For the first time in our relationship, I found myself in a wrestling hold from which I struggled to escape. When I finally got away from my husband's grasp, I implemented a tactic I would carry into future years of our marriage. I jumped into the car and drove away. I stayed away until I cried out my fear and anger. I screamed and yelled until I was exhausted. No one could see me or hear anything I said. I thought things through, stayed away long enough to calm down, and then I returned home to apologize. Though I didn't know it at the time, our cycle of abuse was established.

I called my mom shortly after this wrestling incident and asked her if I could come home. She told me returning home was not an option. I had a husband and a home of my own to manage. I had to learn how to settle problems when they came up in my marriage, and I couldn't run home to momma every time we had a spat. She told me I had made my bed, and now I had to lie in it. I wondered if she had heard these words in her younger days.

Later that year, we decided to move to an apartment in a town located several miles north of us; this would put us halfway between his school and work, and my job. Things were decent again, and we started over. The next year and a half went great. We even talked about having a baby. He was about to graduate from college, and we were more settled. We loved our church, and life was good.

Close to the time of his graduation, my spouse began to pull away from me. He became quiet and withdrawn. He seemed distracted and distant; I was worried. True to habit, I started trying to figure out what I had done wrong. We had been through a few major marital adjustments, but I thought things were looking hopeful. I had decided after the wrestling incident that physical confrontation was something that plagued all marriages, and every couple had to figure out how to get through it and deal with it.

Based on my background with my dad and his temper, it should be no surprise that my thoughts told me: *I had it much better than most because the physical stuff didn't happen every day.* My folks quarreled, and married couples spat; therefore, we argued. My father had disciplined me severely to keep me in line or get me back to a place of obedience; I bought into the lie that it made sense for my husband to do the same. After all, he was the head of the household.

Furthermore, there was all that teaching about being submissive to one's husband, and he was ruler or master of the home. I was learning the art of compromise—so I thought. In reality, I was being influenced by false teaching laced with some truth, causing me constant confusion. I was actually withdrawing, justifying an abusive environment; something I had watched my mother do for a long season in her life. Hers was mental and emotional abuse; I never saw my dad strike my mom.

My conclusion on all of this: *he may not show it at times, but at least my husband "said" he loved me.* I determined abuse was a fact of life, and it reared its ugly head in every relationship. Some couples would defeat it, while most tried to manage or hide it. I decided this was the unspoken element of marriage; it was one of those taboo topics of which no one ever whispers. Deep inside, I knew better; but I set out to find a way to deal with this daunting flaw in my marriage, so I rationalized and became proficient at it. I was praying that my experience with abuse would end here, and we would conquer it. I clung to the hope that we could do all things through Christ who strengthens us (Philippians 4:13).

Not a Mistake

I did not understand why my husband's new reclusive behavior had set in or why he was no longer speaking to me; he completely shut me out. One night, I couldn't stand it any longer. I marched back to the bedroom, slammed the door, and locked it. I stood in front of it and said I was not leaving, and neither was he, until he told me what was going on with him. I was so afraid he was going to say he wanted a divorce, which made zero sense because we were doing extremely well as far as our relationship was concerned. We had never discussed separation or divorce, but that is where my thoughts went. Maybe he only acted like he had gotten over the wrestling thing a year or so earlier; maybe, he was still harboring some angry.

He looked at me from the bed and began to cry; I was not expecting that. He had his red Bible in his hand—the item with which he had been spending all of his time lately. Tears made their way down his face, and I became unsteady. "Please, tell me." I cried.

He started to speak through his tears. He was broken, and I could barely make out what he was saying. "I don't want to do this, but I have too. I don't know how, and I don't know why; of all people, it should not be me."

"What are you trying to tell me?" By now, I was crying. I slid down the door to the floor and buried my head in my arms. There we sat, on opposite sides of the room, weeping; me thinking my marriage was over, and he not knowing how to tell his wife what had been happening in his life.

I heard his voice travel through the now dark room, "I'm not going to be a finance officer when I graduate."

"Yes, you are. You finish in a few months. It's been a long time coming, but it is finally here."

"You don't get it. I'm not going to be in business. I can't."

"Why?" I asked.

Next, I heard the most startling statement, "God is telling me to preach the Gospel, and I can't say no."

I jumped to my feet, and in an excited voice I said, "Is that what this is all about?" I ran to the bed and wrapped him in my arms. My eyes overflowed with tears of joy as I confessed, "I thought you were going to tell me you were leaving."

"No silly," he said through his tears, as he hugged me closely. We cried ourselves to sleep that night, shedding tears of joy and relief.

The next day my sweetheart came in from school to find me crying. He asked me what was wrong. I brokenly shared with my husband my experience as a sixteen-year-old, and what I thought God had revealed to me. I told him the calling God had put on my life at that time was coming to fruition because of the call being placed on his life now. "I'm going to be a preacher's wife," I sobbed. That weekend, we spoke with our pastor.

We entered an even sweeter season in our marriage, one that would last many years. We had plenty of trials ahead of us, but we were united and headed in the same direction, growing together and supporting each other in many ways. The rage thing seemed to have disappeared. The next several years were great, in that there was no physical abuse. However, there was a life altering tragedy waiting for us. It would take almost three years for us to resurface and find a way to live life joyously again, instead of merely enduring it.

CHAPTER 8

Then Comes Baby: Cameron's Story

I Quit

It was spring, late March or early April, and school was going great. My seventh and eighth graders and I were winding down another successful year. There is also a stomach virus going around, and it's a rough one. I started the week off not feeling well, and Thursday I called in sick. I had to make the call from the bathroom floor; I was vomiting so much, I could not leave the commode. I couldn't even hold down chicken broth, Jell-O, or toast.

I felt horrible, but my throat was not sore, and I did not have a fever. I concluded I had contracted that pesky virus, and I would be out of commission for the rest of the week, possibly even the weekend. Monday came, and I was still vomiting and very sick. I wanted to stay as still as I could, curled up, with my eyes closed. By Tuesday, I had lost a few pounds and was dehydrated. I called my mom to give her an update, and she quietly asked, "Honey, do you think you might be pregnant?"

I reminded her I was going to see a fertility specialist on Thursday. Over the past two years, I had been disappointed many times by negative pregnancy tests, both at the doctor's office and at home. I didn't want to waste the money or be discouraged again. She gently encouraged me to do an at-home test, anyway. I went to the drug store and bought one.

In that decade, the stick tests didn't exist. First thing in the morning, I got up and collected the appropriate sample for the test. Using the enclosed dropper, I placed a specific number of drops in the tiny test tube. I added a few drops of the solution which is included in the kit, inserted the cork, shook the tube, and mixed it all together. I placed the tube back in the stand and put it in a safe place where it would not get jostled or bumped; then, I waited several hours. If brown sediment appeared in the bottom of the tube the test was negative, no pregnancy. If the reflector mirror beneath the tube revealed a dark brown ring with a lighter center the test was positive, and there was a baby on board. In that day, it was not as effortless as turning pink or blue, or the quick appearance of a positive or negative symbol.

After spending the day alternating between vomiting and sleeping, I went to check the results in the test tube; that was the most marvelous brown ring I ever saw. I called my obstetrician and made an appointment. I called the other doctor and canceled an appointment. I called my mom who said, "I thought so!" I could hear her smiling on the other end of the phone.

I did not call my husband; there were no cell phones or frequent communication way back then. He was in class at the local university, taking a test. He got the news that evening when he came home from work. We were both excited; and all the while, I threw up.

One evening I called my mom. I was in tears, sniveling. I whined into the phone, "I don't want to do this anymore. This part is supposed to be over. It's called morning sickness, not all day sickness. I expected things to get better in the second trimester. I don't even like coffee, but it's the only thing that does not make me vomit. I quit!" At the end of my tirade, I heard my mom's soft chuckle at the other end of the phone. She said, "Honey, I don't think you have a choice. You can't quit now; it's a bit late for that." It is never fun when your mother is so totally right.

Things got a smidgeon better toward the end of my second trimester. I had lost thirteen pounds, but I found all of them and more in the last three months of my pregnancy. I still had to be careful around certain foods and smells during early morning and late evening hours, but it did get better.

Fall came, and school was scheduled to begin. We decided since the baby was due during the holidays, I would not teach that particular year. I didn't think it would be fair to my students to get a new teacher halfway through the year, especially if I decided not to return. I wanted to be home with my newborn; my spouse and I were in agreement on this. Besides, my husband had surrendered to the ministry about a year earlier. He would be graduating from college at the end of the summer, and we would head off to seminary in the spring.

I enjoyed my time away from school. My pregnancy was during the last days of not knowing the sex of the baby; I didn't have an ultrasound during this pregnancy. My grandmother came to stay with me for a while, and we made everything for the baby's nursery. We chose yellow gingham. My favorite thing that Grandmother and I made was a nine-patch quilt. I embroidered the baby animals on white cloth squares; she hand-pieced and quilted the blanket. It was beautiful.

Shortly after Grandmother and I finished the baby items, my husband and I decided to move in with my parents to save money and prepare for seminary which would begin early in the coming year. The second week of December (ten days beyond my due date) I was pretty uncomfortable, miserable to be exact. I remember being told about the nesting syndrome which happens right before the baby comes—it does exist. I cleaned house all day, cooked, and got all the Christmas decorations out so we could decorate the tree. My husband had worked all day, and he was not interested in a tree. He was pretty tired when he got home, but he put up the tree for me anyway—twice.

He had gone to bed, and I started to decorate—one of my absolute favorite things to do. I decided the top of the tree was too close to the ceiling, so I removed the lights and ornaments. Then I went to my exhausted, resting husband and asked him if he would take the tree outside and shorten the trunk six or eight inches so the topper would fit. He did! Let it be known, that this was a supreme act of love. He restrung the lights, gave me a kiss, and went back to bed; I stayed up to decorate. Did I mention I love Christmas? There is just something about this holiday that brings out the best in me.

I went to bed around midnight. An hour later, I was awakened by cramps. I walked through the house and started timing the pains. Sometime during my venture, my mom joined me. The contractions were coming regularly; they were fifteen minutes apart. My parent's house was an hour-and-twenty-minute drive from the hospital. After walking around for a bit, I realized my contractions were not going away. I went to the bedroom and sat by my exhausted husband. I leaned down, awakened him and said, "Honey, you're not going to believe this, but— — —."

Off we went. Nineteen and one-half hours later our son, Cameron, was born. My husband and I celebrated the birth of our son by ourselves. There were no family or friends in the waiting area. That fact did hurt but not enough to hamper the intense joy we felt. He was a beautiful, eight-pound nine-ounce baby. His daddy cried, and so did I. What a gift and blessing; what a miraculous work of God.

A Blue Malibu and a U-Haul

Remember the twice erected Christmas tree? One of my favorite photos is a picture of Cameron being held by his daddy on our first evening home from the hospital; that tree was the backdrop for this particular photo. The cherishing expression on this father's face for his first born, his son, was captured on film that day. At that moment, I knew my husband would be a good dad.

He would be different, not just a father who worked and disciplined which is what we both knew growing up. He would be a dad who did both of these things, yet he would mix them with quality and content. He would spend time with his children. He was one that would read to, play with, and talk to his kids. We had discussed the importance of being responsible parents and what we thought that meant. My children are blessed to have a father who greatly values his time with them.

We stepped into this new chapter of our lives with tremendous joy and anticipation. We were looking forward to being parents and experiencing all that goes with it, conquering the trials and treasuring the memories. We had no idea of the daunting trial that lay ahead of us. We could have never endured it had we known what was coming. Three months after Cameron was born we packed up our blue Malibu, hitched a small U-Haul trailer to the back, and headed to middle–continent America. We were bound for seminary.

Our first semester things did not turn out as we expected. We had confused some dates, or we had written them down incorrectly, and we arrived at the wrong time; classes had started the week before we got there. We regrouped and went to Georgia; we decided to visit my in-laws for a few days. While we were there, my husband's parents invited us to stay until fall term started. We spent the rest of spring and summer with my husband's parents.

Once again, we loaded our car, hitched the trailer to the back, and ventured toward our new home. It was mid–July, and we were relocating in preparation for the seminary year which would start after Labor Day. We found an apartment we thought we could afford and established ourselves with a local church. We made sure everything was in place for school, and my husband began looking for a job. I applied for a teaching position with the city school board. Numbers were not in yet, per student enrollment so it would be a few weeks before I would hear from them. The first few months in our new town, our diet was not nutritious. We ate a lot of fried cornbread, beans, and mac-n-cheese. It was food, inexpensive, and filling.

One of the biggest ordeals I remember from the first month of our move was the washing machine in our apartment being broken, and the dryer ran but did not dry; Cameron wore cloth diapers. The bathtub became my washing machine, and our living room looked like a laundry house. I had clothesline strung back and forth across the living room and in the dining end of the kitchen; diapers were hanging everywhere.

The local school board contacted me in late August. They said projections suggested they would need several teachers, but it would be after Labor Day before they would know exact locations and grade levels. I was so glad they called; now, maybe I could stop worrying; at least there was the possibility of a job. All we had to do was survive; those first few months were really tough financially.

An Unsettled Spirit

I was getting perturbed, which is the wrong thing for a child of God to do. I should have trusted my Father in Heaven. Though frustration and annoyance are common human reactions, I dishonored God by worrying, fretting, and stewing over matters of which He had knowledge; He was aware of our needs. Our money was gone, and we had to make it another month before any income would be available to us. Where would we go to get the rent? How would we buy baby food? We had an electric bill to pay, gas to put in the car, and insurance was due; on and on went my list. My mind would not shut off. It was like the Energizer Bunny; it just kept going and going and going. It was evident that I was not trusting Him.

The number of things we collect that we do not need is staggering. It is astonishing how much we accumulate that stays hidden in a closet, under the bed, or crammed into a drawer with the likely possibility of never being used again. It is strange to realize how many of our belongings are things we want to keep or have around, just in case we need them. They are not items required for daily living, otherwise known as necessities.

Tennis rackets, a chair, our bed, shoes, and all of the infant clothes Cameron had outgrown were grand possessions, but they were not needful. Some items were nice to have, but they were not necessary for survival. This bundle of stuff made a superb collection for a yard sale. We had stuff other people wanted, and we were able to amass a nice chunk of change by selling it. By October my husband would be drawing a consistent paycheck; and hopefully, I would be working somewhere with steady compensation by November. I had it all figured out.

Things had not gone smoothly in Georgia; in fact, they were quite stressful. (My husband always said he lived a thousand miles away from his family for a reason; through this experience, I understood why.) I must confess, I was struggling during this phase of my Christian walk; I was twenty-five and had been a child of God for eleven years. I knew I was a believer, but I was in a season of doubt and questioning.

My unrelenting inquiry for my Father was: "God, why is getting established in seminary so hard?" I had heard stories of how families, churches, and scholarships were helping others attend school, lessening the cash burden. Why were we not worthy of any outside help? We did the college thing with no help from parents; why did we have to do it again? It wasn't fair. All of these complaints flowed from my griping lips to God's listening ears. I was battling the emotions of being grouchy, angry, jealous, envious, disgruntled, and worried.

The area of town in which we found an apartment to rent was not safe. A prostitute propositioned my husband while the baby and I were in the car. There was a young boy on drugs who tried to break in the front door of the building where we were living. The police were called, and I watched five officers take this boy down. No, it was not extreme force. This boy was still fighting and trying to get away when officers tried to arrest him. I found myself saying in my spirit, "God, do you remember that we are here trying to prepare for a future working for You? I am trying to understand, but this is hard."

Eventually, I found myself whining instead of praying, complaining instead of seeking, and pouting instead of studying. For the first time in my Christian walk, I was uncertain. I had cut myself off from communication with God. I was not reading His Word or talking to Him in prayer; I was blaming Him for everything wrong in my life. Satan had ensnared me and had me right where he wanted, in a sea of doubt far away from my Source of perseverance. The Devil loves nothing more than to steal our joy, destroy our confidence in Christ, and kill our witness; he will do this if we fall prey to his antics.

My spirit was a fertile field, and I was perfect prey for the enemy. I was a child of God, but I was acting like a whiney brat. I couldn't sing or pray; the two things God always used to soothe and comfort my soul, no longer calmed me. Where was my assurance; where had it gone? Where was my steadfast peace; why did it flee? Where was my joy; why did it disappear? Skepticism had crept in, and I wondered if everything I believed for the last eleven years was a bunch of lies. I was spiritually ill, and Satan was celebrating.

Family Giggles

It was Saturday, and it was the day of our yard sale. On this particular morning, I awakened to Cameron's sweet sounds. We had slept on the living room floor because we were selling our bed; it was not a necessity. Sometime during the night, I had taken Cameron from his crib. As I followed the sound of his giggles, I looked into the kitchen and found him playing in a pile of laundry that I had left on the floor. I woke my husband and told him to look. Daddy smiled and called to his son. When Cameron recognized his dad's voice, he stood up, and we watched him take his first steps toward us; he was eight months old. We had a fabulous time that morning.

The Wednesday before our yard sale, I took Cameron to a local store for a photo shoot. I was thrilled that his cheerful nature and delight were captured in a portrait. How in the world could I afford baby pictures? My husband asked the same question; in fact, he and I had quite a discussion about it. Something inside prompted me to capture my baby's joyful spirit in print, even though I knew we couldn't afford the expense. That is one argument I am glad I chose to pursue; I had no idea how important this photograph would become.

The day of the sale, Cameron played outside all day in his playpen and rolling about in his walker. (We called his walker the tank.) He was a sweet-natured, happy baby, very energetic and expressive. We had a circular drive where we lived, one way in and one way out; the building was nestled in between the entrance and exit. Cameron went around the apartments in his tank three times, quite a hike and grand achievement for such a little guy. I smiled and laughed when I looked at his feet; they were black from the coating on the pavement, nothing a wholesome bath wouldn't fix.

It was a splendid day. The three of us were together the entire time, and we raised enough money to survive another month. We paid the rent and the power bill, and there was enough left over to purchase the pictures when they arrived. We put some cash back for gas, and bought a few groceries; we splurged and celebrated by eating hotdogs for dinner. We went to bed on the floor that night, but we had a roof over our heads, and the air conditioner was working. Outwardly, things were good; inwardly, I still struggled.

I tried to share some of what I was feeling with my spouse earlier that week, but he didn't want to hear it. In fact, he started quoting scripture to me from James and Philippians. Let's just say; it did not thrill me for my preacher husband to toss scripture my way when I was seeking sympathy and a comrade in "poor pitiful me" territory. I sulked and pouted inwardly; outwardly, it was evident I was troubled.

I needed my husband to be understanding and supportive; he wasn't. I needed him to listen and care because I was going through some tough stuff, too. He was dealing with finances, trying to find a job, and preparing for school to start; he had enough on his plate. He did not need a teary-eyed, insecure wife adding to his stress. He walked away when I needed to talk to him; in this case, I was complaining. There was an unpleasant silence between us, but I came to understand his side of the situation. From that point on, I chose to keep my feelings about all that was happening in my spirit to myself.

With our money needs for the month settled, full tummies, and happy memories floating through our heads we all drifted off to sleep. My husband and I had no clue that the unfinished weekend would bring a series of events that would alter our lives forever. We were about to experience a tragedy for which no one is ever prepared.

CHAPTER 9

Living a Nightmare

Longest Night of My Life

Sunday morning after the yard sale, Cameron awoke in a fussy mood; it was Labor Day weekend. I took his temp; it registered 100.6-degrees. His cries sounded hoarse, and I noticed his appetite was not good. He did not want to nurse, so I gave him some weak tea to drink. We decided not to take him to church services that morning; I stayed home with him. I gave him some infant Tylenol and rocked him. He got sicker as the day continued and by noon his fever was 102. I gave him more Tylenol and tried to keep water or tea in his body. Mid–afternoon brought chills and moaning from my child.

I rocked him all night. I gave him cold sponge baths and administered Tylenol as often as the label allowed. Every time I repositioned him, he winced as if in pain. Cameron's temperature was now 104, and nothing I attempted to use to help lower it worked. When he tried to open his eyes, it seemed to be difficult; they were glassy and dilated. Diarrhea hit; my baby was very sick.

In the wee hours of Monday morning, I called the doctor. He told me it was probably a virus because the symptoms had come on so quickly. He was not worried because he had seen Cameron earlier in the week for his well-baby check-up, and he was perfectly fine. My gut was telling me to go to the hospital; but we had no money, no insurance, and the pediatrician didn't seem to think it was necessary. He told me if the baby was not better by Tuesday morning, I could bring him into the office. I tried to tell the doctor I felt this was serious; it was different, and I was scared. I knew something wasn't right.

The doctor was patronizing, and I will never forget what he said, "Nora, this is your first baby, and it's his first major illness. I just saw him last week, and he was perfectly healthy. Babies always seem sicker than they really are, but they are very resilient. New moms tend to over react and get quite anxious. Try to calm down, by this time tomorrow he will probably be getting into everything."

I was tired, and I was angry because this doctor did not understand that I was frightened. My husband went to the store to purchase more Tylenol, Pedialyte, and disposable diapers; we continued to care for Cameron as best we could. All day long he grimaced and whimpered, but he didn't cry or open his eyes. My brain continually battled between the thoughts of taking the professional's advice and following what my gut was telling me—go to the hospital.

I laid him down at about twelve o'clock Monday afternoon so that I could take a shower. When I came back to pick Cameron up, his skin felt like it was on fire, and he was completely limp. I took him to the bedroom and measured his temperature. I watched with grave concern as the thermometer measured 105.4-degrees; I became even more worried and frightened. I didn't know what to think. I bathed him with cool water and tried to make him comfortable; I held him the rest of day. I was trying to pray, but my spirit was terrified, and I was scared. I couldn't focus on anything except my sick child. Inside, I was in spiritual turmoil, and I was petrified with fear. All I could say was, "Oh, God. Oh, God please."

I must have fallen asleep. I awoke about five o'clock that evening; my baby was lying limp in my lap, and there was no change for the better. He still could not open his eyes, and he wanted the coolness of something in his mouth, so I held a bottle for him, non-stop. He was not actually drinking; he was just chewing on the nipple now and then. He was excessively hot, so I took his temp and watched in disbelieve as mercury in the thermometer raced all the way to the end in a matter of seconds, passed the 106 mark.

I called the doctor immediately; I wanted him to meet us at the ER. He told me there was no need for that; it was a holiday, and the regular staff would not be in until tomorrow. "Nora, get Cameron through the night, and bring him to my office first thing in the morning, around seven-thirty. Place him in a tub of ice and water; repeat this every few hours and keep doing everything else. I'll see you early in the morning."

A battle raged within me the whole time I listened. I knew we had no insurance, and there was no way we could afford a trip to the hospital. It was only ten more hours until we would be in the doctor's office. I was trying not to be a drama queen. I was trying not to be the over anxious, nervous mother of an eight-month-old with a high fever. I was trying to keep calm and keep my wits about me. I wanted to trust my physician, and I was trying to trust my God, but I was failing miserably at both. I kept thinking I should go to the hospital. I was tired, confused, anxious, crying, worried, and very much afraid.

That was the longest night of my life. Cameron was listless at this point, and I couldn't support him in the tub or sink; I did not want to let go of him. I sat in the tub and cradled him in my arms while his dad poured ice water over both of us. We continued this all through the night, as we waited for Tuesday to dawn. His fever never dropped below 105. My husband and I did not sleep.

The next morning, we raced across town to the doctor's office. It was a twenty-five-minute drive that felt like twenty-five hours. We walked in just as a nurse was coming up the hall to the desk; she took one look at Cameron and knew something was terribly wrong. She asked me—in what seemed to be a scolding, accusatory voice—why I had not contacted a doctor. I started to cry, and I told her that I had. As the pediatrician rounded the corner, she asked, "Who?" I pointed his direction and blubbered, "Him!"

The nurse grabbed Cameron and put him on an exam table. Staff people were running every direction. They poured buckets of ice on top of my baby; in less than a minute, he was completely covered, literally buried. In those fleeting moments, I had a vision of my child lying in a coffin; I knew in my innermost self that he was not going to survive. I turned to my husband and choked on the words, "He's not going to make it."

Thoughts and images of Abraham flashed through my head; all I could mumble in my mind was, "Please God, don't take my son from me; please do not require my son. I can't do this; please God." (Genesis 22, Abraham offers Isaac as a Sacrifice)

A Parent's Worst Fear

My husband and I stood against the wall clinging to each other; I think we were holding each other up. I was confused and numb. The doctor told us to get in our car and drive thirty-five minutes back across the city to Children's Hospital. I do not know why we were not sent by ambulance. Did the doctor not know how long it would take us to cross this big city during morning rush hour traffic? Cameron had his first seizure in route to the hospital. We arrived shortly after nine that morning. We bolted out of the car and darted into the hospital.

The staff at the doctor's office told us to get to the hospital as soon as possible, and they were going to call ahead and arrange everything for our arrival. We were instructed to go to the emergency room, and we would be seen immediately; everything would be ready and waiting for us. When we got there, the receptionist was located behind protective glass. We told her who we were and gave the name of our pediatrician. We told her the doctor's office had called ahead to prepare everyone for our arrival. They should have been expecting us.

To my surprise, the receptionist told us to go and sit in the waiting room. I wanted to climb through the window and shake her. I stood there crying with my comatose, convulsing child in my arms. She was telling me to have a seat because we had to go through processing first. I yelled at her; I told her processing would be easy. I was irrational and irate, and I screamed out: "We have no money, no insurance, and my baby is dying; that's all the information there is to process." We were escorted to the waiting room.

We finally went through the admissions process, an hour later. We were sent back to the waiting room for another delay. It was approximately ten-thirty when we were finally called back to triage. The nurse took Cameron's blood pressure and temp; his fever was still over 106-degrees; he experienced more convulsions. Okay, now things will happen faster, I told myself. Wrong!

We were sent back to the waiting room and told we would be called when there was an exam room available. Sometime after eleven o'clock, we finally got summoned to the treatment area. We were put in an examination room and waited some more. I was livid by this time; I kept repeating, "My baby is dying. Where is everyone? Why won't they do something? Why aren't they here yet? They are going to let my sweet boy die."

Shortly before noon, a physician finally came into the room. Within seconds, things began to move and move rapidly. She barked orders faster than I could listen. Once the emergency room doctor took over, I had no complaints about Cameron's care or the services provided by the hospital; they were incredible.

We were advised to call family, and ushered out of the room so the medical team could work; we went to find a telephone. We were new to the city and had been going to church for only a few months; we did not know many people. I think we called the seminary. We did contact our Sunday school teacher, and he spread the word about our child. Prayers were spoken on our behalf across the city. We were alone at the hospital, trying to support each other. To say we were terror-stricken and horrified would be an understatement.

I called my mom. As soon as I heard her voice, I fell apart. I tried to tell her what was going on, but I didn't know any details myself.

My baby was extremely ill; that was all I knew. Mom told me to calm down and try to get a grip. I was aggravated because people kept telling me this. I asked her if she and Dad could make the six-hour trip to be with us. She said she did not think that was necessary; I was probably making a mountain out of a molehill as usual. I was offended, but I let it go. I asked her to tell my dad because I knew he would come.

Two years before Cameron's illness, my dad and I had burned our bridges behind us, and we were discovering a newly found, special relationship. Mom called me fifteen minutes later. She told me as soon as my dad heard baby and hospital in the same sentence, she was to pack and be ready to leave in twenty minutes; he was on his way home. It generally takes twenty-five to thirty minutes to get from town to the farmhouse; he made it in fifteen. They made the six-hour trip to the hospital in less than four hours.

We called my husband's aunt in Shelby and his parents in Georgia. The grandparents headed our way immediately. I have no idea what we told them about this darling boy and what was happening. Whatever it was I am sure it marshaled anxiety, panic, and fear for them that day. While we were speaking with one set of our parents on the phone, I do not remember which, we were being paged to the PICU (*Pediatric Intensive Care Unit*).

We hung up the phone and hurried to the unit. We were escorted into the area by a technician, and Cameron was no longer in the front section of the space. He had been moved; he was now in the middle of the area. I learned later that the patient's location within the unit indicates their level of illness; Cameron was in critical condition.

My child was hooked up to oxygen and IV's. The doctor told us the test results were back; Cameron had spinal meningitis. "There are several strains or types," he said. The medical professionals are telling us that this particular bacterium is the worst of the bunch; this one is known as the killer meningitis. The germ multiplies so quickly, the antibiotics have trouble destroying it fast enough.

I am trying to comprehend what they are telling us. "If your baby survives, there is a grave probability he will be severely handicapped, mentally and physically. Your little boy is critically ill." They informed us that most people come in contact with this microorganism at various times in their lives; usually, it settles in the mucous membranes of the body and causes a virus or cold. Sometimes an infection from another part of the body can travel and cause complications with this bacterium. The doctors explained that in this case, the microbes found their way into my baby's bloodstream; they attacked spinal fluid and the fluid around his brain. Every organ and nerve in his body were compromised. This illness started out as a simple ear infection, but it turned into a deadly disease in a matter of hours.

A surgeon explained that they needed to place a valve in Cameron's skull to release the pressure which had built up in his brain from the infection. I remember telling them they could probably do the surgery without anesthesia because he had been unconscious for so long; I didn't think he would feel anything. I was speaking from fatigue and worry. I was on my third day of little sleep, and I was listening to devastating news about my child. I think I rambled from sheer nervousness and exhaustion.

The doctor asked us to consider signing organ donation papers, in case Cameron coded on the table during the surgery. My immediate unchecked response was: "No! No! There is no way you are going to cut and chop my baby into pieces and send his body parts around the country." I was adamant and visibly shaken by this appeal. After the initial shock of the request had worn off, I realized if we signed the papers it could possibly save several other parents from the nightmare and agony we were experiencing, that of losing a child. We signed the forms.

I Need to Know You are Real

When they wheeled Cameron into surgery, I told my husband I needed to find the chapel. I did not tell anyone that I was in crisis.

I needed God. We walked into the chapel; my spouse went to one side of the altar, and I went to the other. I needed to be alone with my Father. I did not make any deals with Him. I was there for one reason—to take care of my spiritual heart.

I do not think for one second that this was happening because of anything I had or had not done. I do believe that God knew this was going to take place in my life. My challenge was finding the courage to trust Him, even in the toughest of situations.

I knew as I bowed at the altar, I was not right in my spiritual life. I needed God more than ever, and there were too many things I was doing that were against what God's word says; I talked to Him for a long time. I named all the ways I had wronged Him in the past few months, and I begged Him to forgive my whining attitude and lack of trust. I admitted I wanted my son back healthy and happy. I pleaded with Him to safely return my child to me; I laid prostrate on the altar in that chapel and poured out my heart as I cried out to God in prayer.

> O Holy God, Savior of my soul, I do not comprehend any of this, but I do not have to understand. Father, I confess my doubt, anger, worry, and confusion to You. I am laying these burdens and sins at the foot of the cross. Please forgive me.
>
> Jehovah, I thank You for forgiving me. Thank You for loving me when I am not lovable. I know You are the Great Physician and if it is Your will, my son will be healed and leave this hospital. You know this is the desire of my heart.
>
> In the midst of my doubt, I am giving my confusion to You. I am choosing to believe that You are who You say You are, and You can do all You say You can do. Whether You return Cameron to me or choose to take him to heaven is beyond me; it is in Your hands.

> *Father, I need to know two things. Please, God, I need to know Your promises are true, and I need to know You are real. Whatever happens, please show me I have not believed lies; I want to trust You; I am afraid. Please reveal Yourself to me so that I will know the truth and reality of Your existence. I don't want to doubt You; I just really need to know.*

I was broken and spilled out before the Holy God of Heaven in those moments. Almost instantaneously, peace I had not felt in a long time rolled over me; I was being girded up from within. I was still crying and very emotional, but I no longer shook uncontrollably; the trembling stopped. There are no words to describe what happened in those moments, nor any to tell of the peace I felt.

I know it was a Holy God intervention. Within seconds of ending my prayer, a voice came over the intercom system; it was paging my husband and me. The message: "Return to PICU, stat." By the time the announcement was being repeated, we were in the elevator headed that direction.

We walked into the Pediatric Intensive Care Unit, and the surgeon was there waiting for us. He took my hand and told me he thought I was right earlier. Cameron probably didn't need anesthesia; he would have felt nothing. However, the doctor assured me that everything possible was being done to guarantee my baby's comfort. He also told me that they would not be able to use any of our son's organs or tissue; they were already infested with bacteria. Once again, thoughts of Abraham raced through my mind. We had become willing to offer Cameron's organs to other families, but the sacrifice was not required of us.

When we came back to the unit, the staff had placed Cameron on the back wall of the PICU; this was not good. The pressure bolt was protruding from his skull. His head was bandaged, and he was hooked to every pump and fluid line imaginable. Tubes were coming from every opening in his body; others had been added via various avenues throughout his small frame. We were told it would only be a matter of time, but no one knew how much. My baby was not going to survive.

My husband and I walked toward the bed. He went to the left side, and I stood on the right; we were both crying. I looked down, and there was our precious boy fighting for his life. I could sense he was still present in his body. I took one of Cameron's tiny hands in mine, and his dad took the other. My husband and I joined hands across the bed so we could encircle our son. My head was bowed, and my eyes were closed. Tears coursed down my face as I prayed silently.

> I have only shared the next portion of my journey with a few people over the past years. It is told, precisely as it happened. Some have been vocal enough to say this was a figment of my imagination or a manifestation of an overloaded mind that could not handle the stress of the situation. I tell you *emphatically* that it is an account of just how marvelously and miraculously my God works in the lives of His children.

Suddenly, I sensed a presence in the room; I thought a doctor or nurse had entered. There was a calm stillness in the unit that was not normal. As I opened my eyes and looked around, they were drawn upward and to the right, to the area over my child's bed where the wall met the ceiling. I watched in wonder as a tiny speck of intensely bright light broke the line. It slowly grew larger and larger, and it became brighter as it extended its reach into the room. It traveled down toward the bed where my son was lying, and it slowly expanded until he and the bed were fully engulfed by its glow and warmth. The light became extremely bright and seemed to glow within itself. Cameron became entirely illuminated.

I tried to speak, but I couldn't. I wanted to know if my husband was watching or aware of what was happening. I cannot tell you if his eyes were open or not because I couldn't see him on the other side of the bed. The light was so intense, I couldn't see through it; I was in the midst of it, but I couldn't see out of it. I could only view what was within its borders. I watched in awe as the light slowly subsided, growing fainter as it went. It disappeared into the place at the ceiling from which it had come.

I looked down at my child and realized he was no longer present. His body was there, but his essence was not; he was gone. I tried to say something, but I still couldn't speak. I do not know if what I tried to voice was audible. I think my lips moved, but the words stuck in my throat; if they did emerge, they barely came out as a whisper. I was trying to ask my husband, "Did you see that? Do you know what I just saw? Jesus was here, and Cameron is gone. My baby went to heaven; he's not here. He left with Jesus."

I had been in the presence of the Holy One, and I had witnessed the transport of my child from earth to heaven. God had shown me His reality; He revealed Himself. He proved that He does not lie, and He does exist. I knew with everything in me, God heard my prayer that day. I believe with every fiber of my being that He showed me the trueness of Himself in those excruciatingly painful but precious moments. He allowed me to witness my little boy's journey to heaven. For me, the question of God's reality was settled; my cry to Him had been heard. I had been in His presence, and He was with me. No one will ever convince me otherwise.

I Need to Rock

Within seconds of the light's departure, nurses and techs came running to Cameron's bedside in answer to alarms that sounded on the machines; one of the assistants escorted us away so the rest of team could work. When we returned, our baby's body had been moved into the glass cubicle in the back-left corner of the PICU. He was in the death room, now on total life support. The nurses arranged things so I would have access to a chair. I wanted to hold my baby; but the tubes, cables, and machines hindered this.

Cameron spent the last day and a half of his existence on earth in that glass room.

The doctor had to perform a series of neurological tests before he could proclaim Cameron legally dead. Failure to respond to stimuli would prove he was brain dead; this meant his brain could not function in a manner that would cause his organs to work of their own accord. Machines were his sole source of existence; and over time, even they would not be able to sustain life.

The pediatric staff was incredible, and many of them cried with us; they catered to our needs and helped us with everything possible. They supplied items ranging from heated blankets to food, and they helped us fix a place on Cameron's bed so I could lie next to him. My heart hurt for the young doctor in training who was assisting with our case; I could tell it was all he could do to keep his composure. I asked him if he was okay. He pulled out his billfold and showed me a picture of his son who was only a few months older than Cameron.

The doctors let us stay for the third and final neurological test. A syringe was filled with ice water, and it was shot into Cameron's ear canal. His pupils were observed and watched for dilation while brainwave responses were monitored and measured by a machine. Nothing registered; there was zero activity. The respirator was disconnected, and we waited for chest movements or any other evidence that he was trying to gasp for breath; there had to be some indication he was trying to breathe on his own. There were none. The machines were not reconnected, and this time they were deactivated; life support was suspended. His heart and lungs no longer received assistance, and they made no attempt to function on their own. The doctor called out the time of death, and the nurse wrote the final numbers in the chart.

I wanted to hold my baby. I needed to rock him. I wanted him disconnected from everything. I had brought a pair of his jammies, a blanket, and his stuffed doggie from home. The doctors removed the pressure bolt from Cameron's skull and put a Band-Aid over the incision. All of the other tubes and machines were removed, and they were taken out of the room. The nurses bathed him with baby wash and put lotion on him; he smelled wonderful. There was no antiseptic or hospital odor present. They dressed him in the PJ's I had brought and swaddled him in his blanket, and they laid his stuffed animal beside him on the bed.

Someone went to labor and delivery to get a rocking chair for me, and they set it in the back-left corner of the PICU, just outside of the glass cubicle. The lights were dimmed, and I picked my baby up from the bed. I held him for the first time in almost three days. As soon as I sat down, I began to hum. I cradled my little one in my arms and drew him up toward my face. As I caressed him near my check, I rocked. My husband got on his knees in front of me and held both of us tightly; he was weeping.

I held Cameron in one arm and wrapped my other one across my spouse's shoulders. I do not know how long we sat there; but eventually, the hospital staff came and removed our baby from my arms, and then they escorted us to the front of the unit. I had a hard time leaving; it took a while, but no one rushed us. They hugged us as we left. All of us shed tears as we walked out of the PICU for the last time.

CHAPTER 10

Surviving

I Cannot Stay Here

My husband and I made our way into the exterior lobby of the Pediatric Intensive Care Unit; we found family and church friends waiting for us. The first face I searched for in the crowd was my dad's. He was standing in the right back area of the lobby where the elevators were located. I maneuvered through the cluster of people and made my way to him, and I put my arms around his neck. He held me securely and whispered in my ear, "Nora, please don't let this take whatever it is you have away."

I looked my dad straight in the eye and said, "Oh Dad, it is only because of what I have in Jesus Christ that I can even fathom getting through this." He cried, and so did I.

After speaking to several people and receiving hugs from many, my husband and I made our way to the elevator, preparing to make our final exit from this hospital. As we traveled to the main floor, the elevator stopped; a parent and toddler joined us. I had lost track of time at this point, so I was not sure what day it was, but it was around midnight. The toddler was fussy, and the adult was pulling on her arm, scolding her. I looked at the dad and begged him to cherish every moment with his precious one and not waste it with hateful words and actions. Of course, he looked at me like I was crazy or out of my mind. I was out of my mind— with grief.

We departed from the hospital through the ER entrance. I remember rounding the corner to head toward the door, and I just kept going. I failed to turn all the way; I ran into the wall, sliding to the floor and weeping. A voice somewhere around me said, "Boy, she's loaded." I think security came and escorted us to our car.

I don't remember the trip back to our apartment, but we got there safely. We were both in shock. I sat on the sofa staring aimlessly, not saying a word. I kept thinking: *This is not happening. Parents don't bury their children; children bury their parents. This can't be happening; it is not in the right order. I need to wake up so that this nightmare will be over. This is not real.* Suddenly, instead of thinking silently to myself, I blurted out loudly, "I can't stay here tonight. I don't want to stay here."

My mom packed an overnight bag for me, and our parents drove us to a hotel and dropped us off for the night. I was in constant physical pain because I had not nursed Cameron for several days. The pain was excruciating, and I had a slight temperature. I guess we slept. The alarm went off, so we got up and got moving. We had to take care of funeral arrangements.

Blessed in the Midst of Sorrow

The things that become crucial to us during the grief-loss process are strange. I emphatically insisted that our baby had to be buried back home, at the small country graveyard where my family had plots. My grandfather and other ancestors were already laid to rest there. Even though I knew Cameron was not there—it was his body, but he was in heaven—I didn't want him to be alone in a cemetery. I was going to be located several states away from his grave, in a place I may never reside in again once our school tenure ended. I couldn't bring myself to leave my child's body in a piece of ground where there was no family history. I wanted to take my baby home. This decision would cause me to face the second hardest thing I had ever done up to this point in my life.

Because we were transporting a child's body across state lines, we had to present a birth certificate and personal identification. One of us—me or my spouse—had to positively identify our baby at each end of the travel route, once at the parlor in Jamison and once at the funeral home in Dawson. My husband tried, but the stress was more than he could bear. My dad and my oldest brother stood on either side of me and escorted me into the viewing room.

As I stepped into the room, I began to shake. I got approximately halfway across the chamber before Cameron's body came into view. He was dressed in the same outfit he had worn the day we had the portraits made a few weeks earlier. He was swaddled in the quilt that my grandmother and I had made, and the stuffed dog puppet his daddy had purchased for him a few months earlier was tucked in beside him. My knees buckled beneath me; my dad and brother had to catch me for support. I made the identification required by law, signed the document, and collapsed against my dad. He and my brother carried me from the room.

The rest of that morning, the early afternoon, and the remaining time we spent making arrangements are a blur. Our parents were invaluable and instrumental in getting things accomplished. My in-laws took care of flight arrangements and the cost of transferring the body from state to state. My parents transported us back to our home state, contacted the funeral home which was located there, and allowed us to stay with them.

It was mid–afternoon when we left and headed south. Halfway through our journey, we stopped at a restaurant to eat. We were waiting for a table, and trying to be cordial the waitress asked me when my baby was due; I fell to pieces. While I was in the restroom collecting myself, my mom was in the restaurant consoling the server. When I returned to the table, she apologized profusely. We hugged, and everything was okay.

There was a family dining in the café that day. The group consisted of parents, a preschool-aged girl, and a baby boy. During the meal, the infant began to cry. I was embarrassed to find that the front of my dress became soaked with milk, but there was nothing I could do about it; my body was doing what it was designed to do. The waitress brought me an extra cloth napkin and laid it across the top of my garment. The owners of the establishment let me walk out wearing their property draped across the bodice of my dress. They hugged us when we left, praying God's peace over and around us. God incredibly blessed us even in our time of great sorrow; we were comforted and cared for by other believers, and our meal was free.

Endurance

Services were held within a few days of our arrival in our home state. As soon as we got to my parents' home, we began making arrangements. I had to buy something to wear because I didn't have appropriate clothes for a funeral. There was a dress shop in town named Tara's. The proprietor was a delightful lady and a dear friend of my mom's. She knew we were coming by the shop and why, so she picked out a dress for me. It was turquoise with a magenta and a taupe block on the bodice, austere and appropriate. It was perfect because I did not want to wear black or dark colors.

I was not sleeping well. My first morning back, I awakened exhausted. I was also anxious and nervous about the services. My fidgeting and taut nerves morphed into a major panic attack; I didn't think I could endure what I was facing. I called my doctor; he had taken care of me during my pregnancy, and he had delivered Cameron. I told him what was happening; he prescribed Valium.

We opted for a closed casket and placed the beautifully framed eleven by fourteen portrait of Cameron on top. Many from our church in Shelby played a part in the service. These people were special to us because they were from the church where my husband surrendered to preach; one of them sang *Amazing Grace* (John Newton, 1779). The church pianist played for the service, and our former pastor led. Friends and family came from all over the northern portion of the state and gathered at the small country church. The place where my husband preached his first sermon, and the sanctuary where we married, was now the place where we would face the final day of our greatest challenge. On September eighth, two days before Cameron should have been celebrating his nine-months-old birthday, we buried him instead.

I was in constant prayer to my Father, asking for strength and endurance; I am thankful I was led to ask for help to get through the day of the funeral. The grief was intense; I cannot even imagine what might have happened if I had not. The graveside setting was especially challenging. As the service came to a close and the last few words were spoken, I wanted to climb onto the casket and be buried with my child. I saw myself lying on top of the coffin, refusing to get up. I remember knowing I needed to leave the cemetery, but I couldn't make myself move; my feet felt as if they were cemented in the grass. I was frozen in place, and my gaze was fixed on the casket that housed my son's body. I do not remember who or how, but someone rescued me from that moment. I know the only way I did not succumb to the stress and sorrow of that day was the sustaining power of my Savior.

For the next few days, we walked around in a daze; I was still battling severe mastitis. A few days following the funeral, I got up to face the day and realized I had reached for the pill bottle without thinking; it was automatic. Just as I was about to take another dose so I could get through the day, I remembered the doctor's warning that this medication was highly addictive and habit forming. I realized what I was doing and stopped immediately. I fell to my knees and lifted a prayer to my Father, asking Him to help me get through this day and the ones to come. God granted me the courage and strength to flush the rest of the pills down the toilet.

Seminary classes were going to start on Thursday or Friday; we had to return to our middle–United States home so we could begin our course of study. When we got back to our state of residence, we arrived at a brand-new address. While we were gone to lay our baby's body to rest, our Sunday school class and new found friends moved us several blocks closer to the campus. Our new apartment was within walking distance of our church and the school; this would be a tremendous help because we were a one car family.

I walked into my new apartment and stood amazed at the wonders surrounding me; I had furniture. There was a washing machine; it hooked to the sink like a dishwasher. The accompanying dryer used regular household current. For the first time in my married life, I would not have to go to a laundromat to wash clothes. The bedroom set that was given to us was beautiful. Our church family had joined together to find, clean, paint, furnish, and decorate an apartment for us. They even stocked the refrigerator, the freezer, and the pantry. There was a living room, a small kitchen, and a bedroom with a small bathroom. It was a perfect home for us.

I didn't know where Cameron's items had been taken; they were gone, out of sight. Our Sunday school teacher explained that a dear couple we had met at church, and with whom we would become very close friends, had stored everything in their attic. They told us when we were ready we could come to their home and go through our baby's things; we could decide what to do with them when we were ready. Two years later, we would face that challenge.

Now What

After our return to seminary, my husband and I threw ourselves into our respective schools, jobs, and church. We concentrated on making and developing friendships, all while surviving our emotional ups, downs, and struggles. There were nights I was sound asleep only to be awakened by the sounds of a crying baby. Sleepily, I got up and moved toward the next room. Halfway there, I woke up realizing I had been dreaming and there was no baby. Days of zombie-like existence began to fade, and they slowly returned to some kind of normalcy.

The first year following our loss we just existed, taking one day at a time. I would deal with the reality of my baby's death during the first anniversary of his passing. I finally reached the point where

I could let go and cry enough tears that I could take a few steps forward each day, instead of staying stagnant or moving backward. Prayers, encouragement, and love carried us through the grief and healing process. We were blessed when we received God's best. He delivered it through those who choose to serve Him. Our new friends loved us the way Jesus commands us to love.

Time was a significant healer of my wounds. Only the peace and power of God can move one beyond the initial pain inflicted by this kind of loss. To this day there are certain times of the year—Labor Day, Christmas, Cameron's Birthday, Mother's Day—that are difficult for me. Sometimes dealing with the lack of memories (no first haircut, no first day of school, no first girlfriend, no college days, or no chosen career) is troubling. Smells, sounds, and certain events or people trigger flashback moments. At those times, I find myself needing to run to my Father for comfort. It is okay to grieve and seek solace in His presence.

Somewhere in God's boundless provision, all of the costs associated with Cameron's illness were paid, from funeral arrangements to medical expenses. I never received a single bill from the hospital or the funeral homes. When I called to ask about them, I was told that the accounts had zero balances; they had been paid in full. God did that for us.

CHAPTER 11

More Precious Gifts

Disney World and a Baby

The second year after Cameron's death was filled with continued readjustments, coping, and more mourning; we maintained our support of each other through the rough spots. It was emotionally painful to hear couples at seminary and church announce they were expecting a baby, but God helped me through those times of emotional tenderness. He allowed me to be human; He even listened in the night when I cried and asked Him, "Why?" Over time, things became more routine. I keenly remember the day that I realized I was happy again. Eventually, we talked about the possibility of another baby.

One Sunday in September, we were getting ready for church. I was not feeling well; I was nauseous and sick to my stomach. I went back to bed, and my husband went to church. When he returned home, I had severe pain in my abdomen; I thought it was just a painful cycle. We waited until morning and went to the doctor. We were told I had miscarried over the weekend. We lost our second child. It was a major emotional setback for us.

Fall arrived. *Anger and Rage* had not been in our home for many years, at least five or six. I was grateful and thankful, rejoicing that we had conquered these two elements in our lives. God was granting my petitions in this area, and I was excited and hopeful that we were going to be one of the couples who worked through these elements and gained victory over them.

My husband was preparing to graduate from seminary; only one semester remained, and then we would celebrate his accomplishment. We were happy, supportive of each other, and excited about the changes coming in our near future. In the looming year, we were busy seeking his first pastorate. We decided to take the retirement money from my teaching job and go on our first real vacation. I had never been anywhere famous. I was ecstatic when I discovered my husband was taking me to Disney World in Florida, for a whole week.

The day before we left, we learned I was six weeks pregnant. Four years after the death of our firstborn and two years after an early miscarriage, we found out baby number three was on its way. I only thought the trip was the best thing that had happened in a long time; boy, what a difference a day makes.

We enjoyed one day at Disney World, and then I was put on bedrest because of complications with the pregnancy. Limited walking, no rides, and no swimming were the orders given. The shows, shopping, Epcot, and the food were fabulous. We procured a wheelchair so I could continue to take pleasure in the allowed activities of the parks, and we enjoyed ourselves immensely.

When we returned home, we relished the activities of Thanksgiving and Christmas with my family. Then my husband went to work sending out resumes to churches and doing his last rounds of homework, while we waited for graduation. In late spring, a small rural church in a southern state issued a call for my spouse to come and be their pastor. We had been given our first church in which to serve. Fourteen years after I trusted in the voice of My Father, I was stepping into the fulfillment of His prompting in my life; I was becoming a pastor's wife. It's all in His timing.

Our baby was due in early June, so my husband traveled back and forth from our new post of service and me as we awaited the baby's arrival. Everyone agreed it would be best for me to stay where we had been living and under the care of my obstetrician until the baby was born; it would only be about six weeks. My brother and his family also resided in this town, and I would live with them for the duration. My husband would come see me early in the week and drive back to the church for the weekends. One Thursday before his return trip, we went to a doctor's appointment together. The doc said, "Why don't we have a baby tomorrow?"

"Really? A whole week early?" we asked.

We arrived at the hospital the next morning and did all of the paperwork. The nurse hooked me up to all the gadgets and started the medication that would begin labor; it didn't take long for the drugs to work. All of the staff and nurses said it would be late afternoon before I delivered. By ten o'clock, I knew it would be sooner than that; by eleven, I told them it would be before twelve. They said, "No way."

I said, "Wanna bet?"

Guess who won that one? That's right, I did. One minute before noon, our friend from church *ran* into the room. No gown, no mask, no gloves, and no time to scrub in, the doctor literally caught our beautiful baby girl. Lucy entered the world a sweet, seven-pound seven-ounce bundle of joy. The nurses handed her to my husband; he was thrilled and overcome with emotion. Once again, no one was in the waiting room anticipating news of the birth, but that did not stop the stream of joyful tears from running down his face. He whispered a word of thanksgiving for this precious gift; what a beautiful sight for this momma to behold.

Joy and Tragedy in the Same Season

Being a parent is an incredible experience. We decided early in our marriage we wanted six children. We wanted our last baby to be born when we were in our late thirties to early forties. Lucy brought us so much joy and fulfillment; we didn't want to wait too terribly long to do the baby thing again, and I wasn't getting any younger. We had been married for ten years, and I was already in my early thirties. We were hoping for a boy this time. We charted and planned, and I took my medication.

One moment in a day can change our emotions and temporary circumstances in an instant. During the same week that we discovered I had conceived, my dad suffered a heart attack and underwent quadruple bypass surgery. He went into kidney failure while in the recovery room; he never woke up. We went from doing splendidly to being greatly saddened in a matter of hours. Dad's heart attack, subsequent surgery, death, and funeral happened in early November. At Thanksgiving dinner, I announced to my family that I was expecting our fourth child. My dad was not there to hear the news. I was joyful and grieved at the same moment.

Things were different with this pregnancy. I was nauseous the first few weeks or so, but nothing like my other three pregnancies. After a few weeks of nausea, I had no morning sickness; it was ideal. I packed on weight super-fast, and by the time I began the fifth month of gestation, my abdomen was expanded to that of a woman seven months into the process. The doctor was suspicious twins were on board, so he ordered a sonogram.

The week before the ultrasound, I was teaching and discovered I was in trouble; I needed to get off of my feet. I went home and called the doctor; he ordered bedrest and instructed me to keep my feet elevated. Doing this helped alleviate my symptoms; by mid–morning of the next day, I thought things would be okay. Later that day, I noticed I was somewhat uncomfortable but not hurting. That evening, I realized my discomfort had become more painful, so I called the doctor. We were told to go to the hospital.

We arrived at the emergency room, and the staff took me to the back immediately. A nurse hooked me up to an IV, took my history, and recorded my vital signs. As I put on the hospital gown, I was feeling pretty rough; I noticed the indications of trouble and knew I was in labor. The attending doctor said he thought I was pregnant with twins, and my body was trying to abort one of them. He promised me he was going to do everything possible to save both babies if he could. If we lost one, he would try to rescue the other. My cramps were now contractions, and they were coming every twenty minutes.

I was admitted to the hospital that night and given medication, hoping to stop labor. The next day an ultrasound revealed I was pregnant but not with twins. It was a single fetus that had not developed properly, and there was no heartbeat. For some strange reason, my body did not abandon this pregnancy in its natural way, by early miscarriage. This was the reason my stomach had distended much further than normal. My body was nurturing and growing a mass of tissue and blood volume.

I had to go through full labor to deliver this bundle. It was the safest thing to do for my health; the pregnancy was too far advanced to chance any other procedure. I was given a drug to induce labor by IV, and the doctor broke my water. These two courses of action brought on full-force labor; several hours later it was all over.

We were told our baby did not resemble a child; therefore, we opted not to view the delivery. We did not know if this baby was a boy or girl, but that day in early February our fourth child was born; we suffered another significant loss. It was emotionally painful to listen to crying newborns being delivered to their mommies during feeding times. No joy or sweet gift waited at the end of this labor. It is most difficult to leave the hospital with empty arms, but I knew with every fiber of my being God is real, His design is perfect, and He works all things for my good (Romans 8:28). He has a plan, and I was going to be alright.

The day I left the hospital, I carried a suspicion and a secret away with me. Though I thought thc *Dastardly Duo* that had tormented our marriage in its beginning was gone for good, they reemerged after a long absence early in the first trimester of this pregnancy. It had been eight years since their last appearance. I have always wondered if the resulting kick across my lower back which forced my body to slam front-first into a solid-wood closet door was the reason for the events that unfolded in this pregnancy.

I have no answers for this, only speculation. I chose not to allow these thoughts to take up housekeeping in my mind, and I moved forward into life.

Out of My Hands

The miscarriage of my fourth child was very difficult for me. I have no clue how to explain the sustaining power of God, but I know it was only through Him that I was able to experience peace and perseverance. Time passed, and I found myself wanting another child.

It was July of the same year as the miscarriage, and a new school year would be starting soon. I was teaching fifth grade at a local elementary school. We figured by the time I conceived and got through the pregnancy, I would be out of school on summer break; thus, I would not have to take any time off from teaching when the baby came. Lucy was two, and we decided to start charting my temperature every morning. I began taking my medication to aid in this endeavor, and in mid–September we discovered we were expecting. Baby number five would be born sometime in May or early June.

We were excited and thrilled that we were going to have another child. I was praying this pregnancy would be uneventful, and all would go smoothly. I admit I was nervous and scared; I had to ask my Father in heaven to help me in the worry department on a daily basis. I must say it is incredible to experience the "peace of God that passes all understanding" (Philippians 4:7). It is available to us; and it is always present, even during times we should be falling apart. This peace faithfully does "keep our hearts and minds" (verse 7). This gift and promise are available through Christ Jesus, alone.

In late October, two of my students missed school for two days because they had contracted a stomach virus. They came back to class too soon. The day they returned, I had to send both of them home; their temperatures spiked and both experienced vomiting. They missed school for the rest of the week. The following week,

I experienced nausea; I had a severe headache and a slight temp. I left work early and went home.

My body tried to fight the virus and support the child that was growing inside of me, but the strain was too much; I could not sustain both. My body chose to nourish the baby. Because my system concentrated on supporting the fetus; it couldn't sufficiently attack the virus that had invaded my body. The infection turned into bronchitis, and then it developed into pneumonia; I became extremely ill.

My ribs ached from continuous, hard coughing. I knew I was in trouble when my cough was nonproductive. Every night, I slept upright in a chair because I could not breathe when lying down; I just couldn't get enough air. Eventually, I began coughing up bright red spittle. My temperature hovered in the 100 to 101-degree range. One morning I woke up and my eyes were matted shut; I soaked a washcloth in hot water and gently loosened the crusted substance that was preventing me from opening them. Many minutes after beginning this process, I finally got them opened; they throbbed with pain. I went into the bathroom to look at my eyes; my vision was blurred. I was terrified by what I saw. The whites of my eyes had turned bright red; the vessels inside were breaking.

I was frustrated because I had been to the doctor numerous times during this pregnancy, but I got ready and went again. This time, I landed in the hospital and stayed there for three weeks. I looked and sounded horrible. The orderly and aides didn't want to touch me; none of them were taking any chances. I don't blame them; I was scary looking, and I sounded ghastly. My medical team's first duty was to help me. For the first several days, I was pumped full of high powered drugs, hydrated, placed on oxygen, and given daily breathing treatments.

The illness did not improve with treatment, and my condition remained guarded. Steroids, antibiotics, and fluids were being fed to me intravenously. I knew heavy medications during pregnancy were not a good idea, but we had no choice. After being in the hospital for several days, my doctors wanted to check the condition of my unborn child, so an ultrasound was scheduled. My lab work and test results came back; the doctor was sitting in my room ready to talk. I could barely comprehend what he was saying to me, and there was no one else present to help me listen.

"Nora, I know you have been looking forward to another baby for a long time, but I don't think you can survive this. You are very ill, and you are not getting better. I want you to consider terminating this pregnancy for your health. I am afraid your lungs are going to continue to get worse; if that happens, then both you *and* the baby will be in danger. You have a little girl and a husband at home who need you; you can have another child." He told me to take a few days to think about it.

I had seen the ultrasound screen during the test, and our baby's heart was beating strongly; he was doing fine in the pictures. I asked the doctor if they could assess our son's health. He told me as far as they could tell, the fetus was okay for now. I was the one they were worried about and in the most danger. In a hoarse, barely audible voice I told the doctor I didn't have to think about anything. I said, "God is in control of how this would turn out, and I will not terminate the pregnancy; that is up to Him."

Two weeks later, just before Christmas, I went home—getting better and very pregnant.

Special Delivery

My health was improving; but every time doctors tried to decrease the antibiotics and steroid treatment, I immediately started to regress. I also suffered from extreme fatigue. I spent the remainder of my pregnancy on the drugs, using an inhaler, going to bi-monthly doctor's appointments, and sleeping in my recliner. Daily breathing treatments kept my lungs open and clear. I tried to return to school after Christmas break, but I didn't have the stamina to make it through a day; I had to relinquish my teaching position.

Spring rolled around, and it was time to have this baby. Labor was induced, and I received an epidural; all of my other deliveries had been by natural childbirth. This time the doctors were afraid my lungs were too compromised, and I wouldn't be able to handle all of the breathing, panting, and pushing involved with labor and delivery. They wanted this birth to be as stress-free as possible. Of course, I had to do things a tad differently than planned. The week before the induction was to take place my water broke, and I went into labor on my own; everything else went perfectly. On a gorgeous day in mid–May, I was admitted to the hospital, and I labored away.

This birth experience was totally different from the others. I discovered how some women can sleep through labor. The nurses had to wake me up and tell me it was time to get to work. I knew how to do this part exceedingly well; three pushes and Nathan James was born. Once again no one was in the waiting room, and Daddy was the first to hold our newborn. As the pediatric team examined my son and the doctor took care of me, I remember laughing and telling the doc, "I ought to sue you."

"Why?" he bantered back.

"Because. I went through regular labor all those other times, and I could have done it this way; labor without an epidural should be illegal." Everyone in the delivery room laughed.

Surprise, Surprise, Surprise

I loved being a mom; having a family was rewarding, demanding, fulfilling, and something I had prayed God would allow to come into my life. When Nathan was two, I decided it was not a sound idea for us to have any more children. My husband was not in agreement at the time I made this decision. No conundrum, I could handle this issue all by myself.

We had not used prevention measures for fifteen years. Fertility drugs and charts were needed for conception; so, why worry? All I had to do was stay away from these items, and I would never get pregnant; it was that simple. Once I made this decision, I literally put it out of my mind and believed we were done. Now that I think about it, this tactic does not exist on any legitimate pregnancy prevention list, anywhere.

In honor of this decision, I planned a massive yard sale. I sold all of our infant and baby stuff. I took the money and bought a big boy bed for Nathan. I had a grand time decorating, turning his room into a dinosaur den and creating a pink boutique for his sister, Lucy; both rooms turned out wonderfully. I was ready to move into the next stage of parenting—no babies, only children.

I began my second year as Education Consultant for Strong Beginnings, and I was preparing for a regional workshop. I had been given the opportunity to share my organizational and evaluation ideas with the entire region; I was honored and excited to be professionally recognized in this way. The first day of training arrived, and I was exhausted; I had not been feeling well for several days. As time passed, I felt increasingly worse. Of all days to wake up vomiting, this was the one on which it chose to happen.

I thought I was coming down with a stomach virus—again. I took some Tylenol and Pepto-Bismol and headed out to the conference. I was sick a few times throughout the morning and very fatigued by the end of the day. I finished out the week hoping I had done a suitable job, in spite of the fact that I felt so lousy. When I got home the last evening, I crashed; I slept the entire weekend. I even missed church—which was way out of character for me. A few more weeks passed, and I continued to fight extreme fatigue and nausea. If I called or went to the doctor, the first question asked would be, "Could you possibly be pregnant?"

I had been through the process so many times, I knew it by heart. I knew that before they would see me or schedule an appointment, they would tell me to do an at-home pregnancy test. I caved; I went to the store and bought a kit. I went into the bathroom, and performed the test; it turned pink immediately. I didn't have to wait the suggested three minutes. It was positive; I was stunned. I couldn't be pregnant; I wasn't *trying* to get that way.

My husband was thrilled. I was shocked but delighted about the news. I called and scheduled an appointment with my obstetrician. The doctor said the baby would be born sometime in early April; I was at the beginning of my second trimester. Other than the typical symptoms at the beginning, this pregnancy was uneventful; there was no drama or crisis involved.

This pregnancy was strange. I hated peanut butter, but it was the only thing that tasted good, and it stayed down when I ate it; it quickly became a favorite. Every night, I had two pieces of white bread with no crust. I spread the thinnest possible layer of peanut butter on one piece; then I placed the other slice on top and pinching the two pieces of bread tightly together. This created an ultra-thin peanut butter sandwich with no jelly. I downed it with a glass of Nestlé's Quick chocolate milk.

Clearly, this child was a miracle; after fifteen years of malfunctioning issues connected to pregnancy, my system decided to work properly. God was still showing me; He has a plan. No matter what I thought or decided my final decisions were, He managed to show me He has a design for my life. I'm so glad He does.

Though she was a beautiful wonder, this little cutie started out a stinker even in the womb—I mean this in the most endearing way. She refused to let us know her gender. We had to wait until the day she was born to find out we were blessed with another daughter. I had four ultrasounds during this pregnancy, and every time she presented sunny side up; she did not cooperate. Because of her lack of assistance during photo ops, we had to prepare for both name possibilities.

Flip a Coin

We agreed on a boy's name, Thomas Alexander; however, we were divided on the girl's. I leaned toward a combination of family names, but my husband wanted our second choice: Kara

Grace. I liked Kara Grace as well, but I had this thing about family names, respect, and honor. I didn't think it was going to be an issue anyway; this baby presented low and in front, just like my first child, Cameron. I knew it was going to be a boy. With a lack of evidence to the contrary, I determined Alex would be arriving in early April.

In the early hours of a March morning I went into labor, and around seven-thirty our wait was over. Three weeks before the estimated date of arrival, our little girl was born. She weighed in at seven pounds and seven ounces, exactly what her sister had weighed. It was time to name this baby.

Our moniker impasse was colossal, so we called in an expert. We decided to let big sister, six-year-old Lucy, help choose the baby's name. We called Lucy on the phone and said, "You have a sister, but we have two names to choose from, and we can't decide which one to use. Will you help us?"

"You mean I get to name the baby?" she said.

"Yes. You get to help us pick."

She listened intently to the choices. After a considerable pause and much consideration, she said, "We have to name her the one Mommy likes."

"Why?" we asked.

"Because, I really like the name Daddy picked; and when I grow up, I'm gonna name my baby Kara Grace."

We named the new baby, Naomi Ruth. As I held her in my arms, I realized God had given us our sixth child; the number my husband and I both had on our hearts individually, before we married. I smiled as I remembered the words of the Psalmist: "Behold, children are a heritage from the Lord, happy is the man who has his quiver full of them" (Psalm 127:3–4, selected sections).

CHAPTER 12

Trials and Errors

A Monstrous Mistake

There are times in our lives that we make choices we know are outside of God's will, but we make them anyway. I wish I could say I have never been guilty of this, but I would be lying. Preceding Naomi's birth, shortly after Nathan was born and Lucy was three, my husband resigned from his pastorate at our first church. He informed me that he was taking a secular job and moving us to the southeastern portion of a neighboring state. It didn't sound right, feel right, or look right when we went for our initial visit, and I was not happy about it.

On the way home from our trip to check things out, my husband got very upset with our daughter; this was a rarity. What patience he did possess, he reserved for his children. He also snapped at the babysitter who had come along to help with the kids. From the beginning of this entire segment of our life, I didn't like the prospects that lay before us.

The trip to relocate was a nightmare. Lucy rode in the moving van with her dad. I had Nathan who was barely three months of age with me in our family vehicle. He cried and screamed all the way to our new location. It was a seven-hour drive.

This move was the beginning of a season of discontent, stress, and extreme tension in our marriage. As a young couple, we made a multitude of wrong choices during the ten months we were in this situation; it was undeniably ten months too long. Many of our choices compromised the stability and security of our family. My husband's decision to take a secular job disappointed me greatly. I wanted to be a biblical wife: supportive of my spouse, choosing to follow his lead, and recognizing him as head of our home. I kept my feelings and concerns to myself, and I proceeded to play what I perceived to be the role of the submissive wife.

At this point in time, we had five kids; three of the five had not survived. The loss of more than half of our children had impressed upon me the short amount of time we have to teach, rear, and actively love our little ones. We decided we wanted to be around for all of the important events and teaching moments that come in the first five years of life. Early in our marriage, we determined one of us would be home with our kids, especially during the infant and toddler stages; this meant no daycare.

Contrary to everything we had discussed and against all we had decided in the area of rearing our children, we diverged from our childcare plan. I took a teaching job, and our babies went to daycare; this made me miserable. After two months of juggling, I finally got Lucy and Nathan into the same facility. Every day, I cried on my way to work.

During the long drive to my job, I had to fight the urge to turn around and go back home. More days than not, I played a game of *turnaround* in which I battled my emotions about leaving my little ones; most days I ended up at work. Three times I called the school and told them my children needed me; I spent those days with my kids. Those three occasions were the only times I won the game.

My spouse's job kept him away from home and family. He was the assistant manager at a store and was responsible for night auditing. He took the position knowing that after one year he would be promoted to manager. He seemed to be on call more than the other employees. In fact, he worked all of the time. He came home shortly after I left the house each day. Days he was not called back into work, he slept. He departed for work every evening before I got home from my job.

My day started at three-thirty in the morning. I got ready for school, gathered everything together and placed it by the front door. I fixed breakfast, got the kids ready, and loaded them and their stuff into our van. We had to be on the road no later than five, forty-five. I dropped my babies off at six o'clock and hit the road for my one-hour drive to work. The school day began at seven forty-five, and I stayed after the last bell rang so I could work. I knew I would not get anything done once I arrived home; that time was allocated to my little ones. I left work no later than four forty-five for the long trip home so I could pick up my children by the six o'clock deadline. My arrival time at home in the evening was determined by whether or not I had to go to the store after picking up my kids.

Most nights, I did drive-thru for dinner because I was too exhausted to cook. My evenings were spent doing domestic chores and taking care of my youngsters. By seven-thirty, my babies were bathed and in bed. Every day of the week looked the same. Monday through Friday I juggled daycare and work. Saturdays were for housecleaning, laundry, and shopping. Sunday the kids and I went to church. Most Sundays my spouse worked; he seldom attended services, and we never connected to the membership; we were friendless. We attended a small group meeting one time. This whole experience taught me the distinct difference between serving and being an active part of the body of Christ and just going to church.

Christmas break rolled around, and I was miserable. My misgivings and brave front turned to anger which I held inside. My personal displeasure over our situation turned into resentment, and secretly I blamed my husband for everything that was wrong. We didn't have to be near each other to feud; I was always confronting him in my head. Oh, the things I told him in the recesses of my mind.

Going Home

My spouse was required to attend the company Christmas party. I didn't want to go because I did not know anyone attending except my husband, and I was disgruntled with him. Another reason for my misgivings was the lack of knowledge about the babysitter we had hired. I was apprehensive and unsettled which leads to an unpleasant evening. When we arrived, I felt completely out of place, and I wanted to leave immediately. My spouse totally disregarded my feelings in this situation.

As the night inched forward, my anxiety level steadily increased. There was a lot of drinking and foul language present; smoke filled the room, and I sat at a table without my husband for most of the evening. I was in a room filled with people; yet, I felt isolated; it was awful. On our way home, I told my husband I was never going to another company gathering. We ended up having an atrocious verbal fight. I don't know how long we did not speak to each other after that. It was easy not to talk because we rarely saw each other.

Soon after this event, the kids and I went to my mom's house for the holidays. I never said a word about what was happening in our lives. No one back home knew how things truthfully were in our world. Then, spring break rolled around; I was frazzled, stressed, and exhausted. I was not getting much sleep; I was also furious with my spouse and lonely. The only positive, pleasant things in my life were my two children. I worried over them daily. I had heard a rumor that a neighbor in our eight-unit section of the apartment complex had a python snake. I checked on my babies repeatedly throughout the night because I was afraid that thing would get into the air conditioning duct and find its way into our apartment.

I had read about an infant in Florida being swallowed by one of these critters, and I couldn't let go of the images that had created in my mind. The scenes that played out in my imagination were frightening; I couldn't relax. My exaggerated unrest came from my horrendous fear of snakes which is almost paralyzing. I know

I should not have the spirit of fear, but it's a snake! I neglected to access the peace of God available to me in such circumstances.

One night after I had put the kids to bed, I was cleaning the kitchen. I opened the dishwasher and jumped back against the refrigerator screaming. I was so obsessed with that stupid snake, I thought I saw it curled up in the bottom of the machine. It didn't take long for me to realize that what I saw was a piece of black foam that had come loose from somewhere inside of the unit. After that, I had nightmares for weeks.

Weeks turned to months, and my spiritual battle intensified. I felt abandoned by my spouse even though he was still in the picture. Our marriage relationship was non-existent because we were no longer a team, and we seldom saw each other. I felt he had turned away from his position as spiritual head of our home. I desperately clung to God, crying out and praying, admitting I didn't understand what was happening in our lives. I just knew it was bad and not pleasing to the Lord.

Sometime in April, I reached my limit. The children were sleeping, and I decided to clean the kitchen. I dropped a casserole dish; it shattered when it hit the floor. It was not the only thing that fell to pieces that night. I slid down the cabinet and sank to the tile beneath me. I broke emotionally. I cried, and I cried, and I cried. I called my husband at work and told him I needed to talk; I asked him if he could squeeze in a lunch or dinner date. He couldn't check his schedule or talk at that moment, and he hung up. I ended the call on my end and cried some more. He never got back to me on the subject of making a date.

Our track record of communicating and spending time together was subzero while living in this foreign state; it was apparent we were never going to get around to talking. Thoughts of leaving, taking my kids, and moving to my mom's house had been jumping in and out of my head since late February. I tried especially hard not to entertain them, but as the school year went on, they entered my mind more frequently and finally established residency.

Spring break was coming; and after that, there would be four weeks of school left. I was sick of dealing with everything and decided I had wrestled with this dilemma for the last time. It was the extreme rarity, but my husband was home. He finally had a few days off; he had taken Lucy to the city zoo in a neighboring metropolitan area while I was at work, and Nathan was in daycare. We were both quiet that evening, now the norm for us. I could tell something was bugging him. I was bugged, too.

I finally hashed things out in my mind and prayed them through. I loved my husband, but I hated the direction our lives had taken. I was no longer willing to tolerate the conditions of living here and what they were doing to us individually, as a couple, and as a family. I felt the entire experience had been negative. If we stayed, our marriage would be over anyway. I began referring to his place of employment as Satan Place. I was getting away from the evil influences of this city. He could come with us or stay; it was up to him. The children and I were leaving in May.

I gathered the strength and courage to tell him that I would be turning in my resignation the next day. I had decided that when the school year was over, I was packing up the kids and moving to my mom's. I was not leaving him; I simply wasn't returning to this city. I would be in our home state. If he wanted us, he knew where to find us. I rounded the corner into the living room and started to say, "I have something to say to you." At the exact same moment, he said the same thing to me; I let him go first.

This man who rarely shows emotion got teary eyed, and his voice became broken as he recounted the experience he had as he and his baby girl exited the zoo that day. Lucy was exhausted from her active day, and she fell asleep shortly after they got in the car to head home. As tears streamed down his face, he recounted the marvelous day they had spent together. He said they were stopped at a red light, waiting to exit the compound. He looked over at his daughter curled up on the seat next to him; she was sound asleep.

I intently listened as he told me that reality hit him like a ton of bricks. He said he realized how much his little girl had changed, and he had not witnessed any of it. She was completely different, and he had missed it. As he traveled from the metro area to our home, he reflected on the past several months. He became markedly upset before he finished telling me all of his thoughts that night. I could hear the sincerity in his voice, and he was very beloved in my sight at that moment.

It was one of the rare times my spouse allowed himself to be emotionally intimate and vulnerable. Listening to him tell how much he loved his children and nothing was going to get in the way of his being with them ever again was pleasing. Hearing him say he missed me was what I needed to hear. His last statement on the matter was, "When I get back to work on Monday, I'm turning in my resignation. Do you think your mom will let us stay with her until we get back on our feet?"

I never said the things I meant to divulge that night. I only told him I would turn in my resignation as well, and I was confident Mom would welcome us. He didn't need to know I had already planned to talk with her about living in her home. The scenario I presented to her would just be slightly altered. Besides, there were no incidents of abuse since just before the loss of our fourth child, and there had been none during our tenure here in our desert place; that was approximately a three-year time span.

Our talk that night is a treasured moment. The next day, I called my mom and conversed with her for a long time. I told her that my spouse and I mutually agreed our move to this place was an enormous mistake; it resulted in multiple trials and hardships, and we needed time to regroup. I asked her if we could come home. Her response, "Well, it's about time."

CHAPTER 13

Intrusions

Here They Come Again

Shortly after Nathan's first birthday, we moved back to our home state. I was thrilled and happy that we were moving. My plight in our desert place was over. For the first time in almost a year, I could look at my husband and smile. We were getting back on the right track; and hopefully, we were going to be okay. After our return to my mom's house, I had to have my appendix removed. The stress from our horrible year in limbo also took its toll; I had developed two stomach ulcers and required hospitalization and treatment for this condition as well. We were living with my mom, and the stress continued to mount.

Upon our return home, my husband immediately hit the church circuit and sent out resumes in search of a pastorate. He took a secular job in the interim, and I looked for a teaching position. The county where we were living is a much sought after district, making it a challenging market in which to procure employment. In addition to registering with all of the school systems that were within driving distance of my mom's house, I searched the want ads. One day, I found a notice listing need of an Education Consultant for the Strong Beginnings Preschool Program in a local city. I called and scheduled an interview, and I got the job. I enjoyed my work at this establishment.

I cannot say what set him off; I have no recall of what we argued about, or why we had an altercation. Frankly, I just don't remember. I do know it was the first time anyone in my family ever witnessed his wrestler treatment of me—he had been a valued member of his high school wrestling team. *Anger and Rage* returned and made an unwelcomed appearance in my mother's home; it had been almost four years since their last visit.

My mom did not appreciate the event one bit. We started it, but she finished it. In a tone that meant business, she told my husband, "I better not ever see you touch my daughter that way again. If I do, you will be sorry." I never told my mom it had happened before. I convinced her it was a build-up of stress from the past year-and-half. I apologized to her for our behavior and told her it would never happen in her home again; it didn't.

A few more months passed and my husband received a call from a church located in the same city in which I had found employment. The pulpit committee was interested in speaking with him about becoming their new pastor. After a series of meetings and sermons, he received a call from this congregation to be their new preacher. We started the journey in our second pastorate. A house came with our salary package. We settled in, and life started running somewhat smoothly. We developed routines, and life was much improved.

Interlopers

Over the next year, we worked hard and concentrated on our faith and family. Things seemed to be going well. We were excited when we discovered I was pregnant with baby number six, Naomi. This pregnancy was uneventful which was highly unusual for me; physically I was fine.

Though it would be short-lived, this was one of the better seasons in our union. Approximately one month before the baby was due, the *Dastardly Duo* of *Anger and Rage* butted into our lives, again. It had been two years since they invaded my mom's home, and they decided it was time to make another appearance. I don't know what triggered this episode. It occurred around my birthday, and it was a bad one. We ended up in one of those marital discussions that people next-door can hear; good thing we didn't have any close neighbors.

One thing led to another; words and actions escalated, and he grabbed me. He placed me in one of those dreaded wrestling holds that ended in a takedown. Nathan was hiding in the corner rocking, and Lucy went to battle for her unborn sister and me. She jumped off of the desk chair and yelled, "Stop it Daddy; you're hurting Mommy and the baby!" He let go and walked out of the room. I grabbed the sixteen-by-twenty family portrait from the end table and threw it on the concrete outside of the back door, smashing it on the carport. I was crying, and I roared, "We're such a farce; some Christian family we are."

My actions made him even angrier; he grabbed me again. Lucy continued to shout at him to stop hurting us. He walked away. I silently started gathering my things together, my usual routine; only this time, I was taking my children with me. This time, I said I wasn't coming back. True to pattern, he went out and disabled our car; we were repeating our cycle.

I was determined not to allow him the power to stop me from leaving. I put on my tennis shoes, repacked the diaper bag and my purse, put a blanket in the bottom of our Little Tikes wagon, and placed my daughter in the back of the buggy with her brother in front of her. I told them to hold on, and I started to walk the seventeen-mile jaunt to my mother's house. It was a cold rainy day, so I opened an umbrella for the kids, pulled up my hood, and headed out. I barely got out of the driveway and down the street before my husband pulled up behind us. He jumped out of the car and grabbed me by the arm. He told me to stop.

In a flat toned and emphatic voice, I said: "Let me go." He did. Then he asked me to come back. "Why?" I asked as I stared him down.

"Just come home and bring the kids back." he said.

Then I heard: "Please Mommy." My Lucy was crying and scared. I turned the wagon around and went home.

I slept in the recliner for the next several nights. After a few days, I apologized to my husband for creating a situation that caused him to become so angry, and I promised I would diligently work at not making him so mad. We were okay, and we started over. A week later Naomi Ruth was born.

Little Boy Blue

Our menacing visitors were not the only things intruding in our lives. A major eruption was about to take place; it centered on our precious son, Nathan. At the time of his birth, I was ecstatic and filled with joy because we had trusted God for the outcome of that pregnancy. The baby I was advised to abort was perfect, and my lungs were just fine. At the time of his birth, I did not know Nathan came to us in very special wrapping, tied with a unique bow. His exceptionality would not be revealed to us for several years.

In the beginning, it appeared Nathan was going to be a sleep fighter or a fussy baby. I was not used to that because my other children were snugglers, and they calmed down quickly, especially when I rocked them and sang. I had been rocking and singing babies to sleep since I was ten years old; it had never failed, until now. It simply didn't work with my sweet boy.

One frustrating day I needed a break, but no one else was home. Nathan had been irritable all morning. I was rocking him trying to get him to stop crying, relax, and go to sleep. I placed him in the center of my bed, barricaded him with pillows, and ran to the bathroom which was located off of our bedroom. Before I got to the door, he stopped squirming and screaming. Only a few minutes had passed by the time I got back, and he was fast asleep. I discovered Nathan didn't want to be held or cradled, and my singing seemed to annoy him. From that point on I merely put my baby in his bed, and he was just fine.

Regardless of my bruised emotions, I knew I was blessed. I could not forget God's hand in the birth of this child. I plunged into my life as a wife and mother trying to remember my blessings. I had a seemingly solid marriage, two precious daughters, and God had given me another son; I thought I was happy.

Over time I began to noticing red flags in Nathan's behavior. He did not like books. He didn't make eye contact with me like my other babies did. He always seemed to be looking off somewhere; his gaze drifted past me, and it was impossible to link our vision. He showed zero interest in interactive games like patty-cake or sing-song learning activities in which most babies participate, and he didn't point to or repeat patterns or actions over time. He seemed to be acutely affected by sudden changes in volume and pitch of sounds. I attributed all of these characteristics to the fact that Nathan had an unusual learning style.

No Labels Allowed

I was right, but I had no idea what was coming. As time went by, Nathan's special needs became more and more apparent. He advanced pretty much on target, but he developed the habit of rocking in his crib and playpen; he banged his head on the sides. He continued to avoid my gaze, and it was most difficult to get him to interact. The real danger signal surfaced at his eighteen-month check-up, he had lost a couple of developmental skills and gained none. He grew increasingly uncontrollable over the next year. As his second birthday approached, my concern escalated; distressed would be a good way to describe how I was feeling.

His twenty-four-month appointment revealed he had lost more skills and still made no gains; my distress became apprehension. I knew for sure we were facing a learning disability of some kind. By age three, Nathan still made no attempt to communicate, and potty training was nowhere in sight. His three-year exam was marked with even more delays in his development; now I am alarmed, but I refuse to worry and panic.

During this time, I began the practice of going to my large walk-in closet to pray. I took a pillow, some water, and my Bible with me. I would pray until I fell asleep. I was not about to make the same mistake I had made when we lived in our desert place. I knew I needed the peace, comfort, and wisdom only God possesses, and I was not going to repeat history; I went to my Father in prayer. I wish I could say my husband and I did this together, but we didn't. It was tough getting my husband to see a need for this prayer vigil. He decided that Nathan's issues were solely based on him being a boy, and most boys develop slower than girls. His son would outgrow it, plain and simple.

My husband was sure I was making a big deal out of nothing. At this point, I had been working as the Education Consultant at Strong Beginnings for almost two years. I had issued many developmental tests to preschoolers. I screened them for at-risk behaviors, looking for indicators and early detection of learning disabilities. I had a gut feeling my son had special needs; I was suspicious he was autistic or had a disorder similar to it, as well as some other issues. I discussed this situation with Nathan's pediatrician; she agreed with my assessment. Dr. Dryer and I spent the third year of my son's life trying to convince my husband something was wrong. The sooner we intervened, the better things would be for our son.

My spouse was vehemently opposed to any kind of labeling. He recounted to me how he was tagged early in his school career, and teachers never let him get out from under the stigma of those markers. He told me it was one of the reasons he eventually dropped out of school. "I'm a high school dropout with a master's degree. I'm not going to let that happen to my boy." My husband would not discuss the topic, nor would he allow me to explain the effects of autism. It was a closed subject as far as he was concerned.

An Ultimatum

I cannot begin to imagine the turmoil and hurt my husband was facing during this time of trial in our lives. I know the emotional toll had to be tremendous. I really did understand his side of the issue concerning labels. Here, too, was a man whose first son had been required of him in death; two children did not make it into this world. This father was blessed with two daughters whom he absolutely adored, and he was ecstatic when given the gift of a second son; his joy was so intense, he glowed. He was looking forward to all of the things he had planned to do the first time around. Now, this opportunity seemed to be evading his grasp as well. I am sure this was most difficult for him to handle.

I remember a poignant sermon my husband preached, several years after the death of our son, Cameron. He said that because of the tragedy God had allowed us to experience, he had a greater respect for God's love. Never again would the words: "For God so loved the world that He gave His only begotten Son, that whoever believes in Him should not perish but have everlasting life" (John 3:16) simply be one of the most well-known passages in scripture. My husband stated that our experience helped him realize the sacrifice God made in offering His Only Son to death. He said he couldn't fathom the depth of love it took, or the strength of character it mandated, to sacrifice His Only Son for the benefit of all others in the world. This is one of my all-time favorite sermons.

I cannot comprehend the emotional toll taken on this man when his second son was required of him; it had to be excruciating. Though the conditions of surrender were different, the sacrifice was still being required. It was being demanded of me as well, but there is something unique about a father-son relationship; I know he was crushed and hurt beyond measure. He never could bring himself to share any of his emotional wounds concerning Nathan with me.

My heart grieved for my husband during this time, and I prayed for him every day; I was not sure if it was humanly possible for him to deal with the significant loss of another child. I gave my husband to God, requesting that He heal his heart and bring this man to a place where he could deal with the issues concerning our son. I asked Him to bring this father to the point where he could walk beside me on the journey of taking care of our child.

I marched forward and dealt with the doctors and tests without him. At Nathan's four-year check-up, his pediatrician and I decided it was time to get a precise diagnosis of his problems. It was the only way to help him and the best way to prepare for his future. At this point, Nathan was pretty much an unruly child. Not because he was bad, but because of his brain garbling information; when things were absorbed, many registered incorrectly. He babbled incessantly and made perpetual noise. He showed his displeasure by throwing tantrums and destroying things. We made zero progress in toilet training, and he didn't try to count or say letters of the alphabet; no standard developmental milestones were being met.

Dr. Dryer decided to send us to a specialist at a well-known medical center in a nearby metropolis; he was an expert in his field. I scheduled the appointment and faced the daunting task of telling Nathan's dad what was going to take place. Knowing I was going to hear about the non-necessity of this action and the argument of labeling would be brought up again, I was not looking forward to what I was facing. That night after Nathan's check-up, I broached the subject. Let's just say it did not end well, and there was much tension between us.

The night before we were to leave for the appointment with the specialist, I went into the den where my husband was working on his computer. I was nervous and close to tears, but I laid the truth on the line. I did not enter that room to discuss anything; I went to deliver an ultimatum, and I did not mince words. I said, "I have no clue what this is doing to you as a father. I know it is hard. That does not change the fact that we can't keep putting off intervention for our son. We've already waited way too long. He's four; two years ago, we should have intervened. I have respected your position on labeling and school, and I've waited to see if he would outgrow this. We can't wait any longer; we've run out of time. I'm leaving at three-thirty in the morning to go to the medical center. I don't want to go by myself, but I will if I have to; Nathan and I are going, with or without you. I'd love to have you by my side going through this with me. If you can't, I'll accept that; I'll deal with it."

I was crying before I finished my statements. I said what I had to say, turned, and left the room. I went back to our bedroom to lie down for a few hours before I had to rise to head out on this journey. I was resting when I felt the bed move.

My husband laid his chin in the crook of my neck and put his arm over me; he gathered me close. I could feel his warm tears on my neck as he whispered into my ear, "What time are we leaving?"

We laid there and cried for a while, just holding each other. I prayed for us as a family, our position as parents, and safety during our trip. I asked God to help us with whatever we were going to hear the next day concerning the issues we would be facing in Nathan's future. This is another of my most treasured moments with this man.

CHAPTER 14

Beyond Medical Advice

Process of Elimination

We both knew neither of us would sleep, so we decided to get up and hit the road. I had taken the girls to my mom's house the evening before, nothing hindered us from leaving when we wanted. We decided to stop and eat breakfast somewhere along the way. Our only criterion was being at the medical center by nine-thirty that morning.

It was chilly outside, and the inner city was still waking up when we arrived. We took a wrong exit and got lost downtown. I convinced my husband to stop and ask for directions, only to discover the more directions we got, the more lost and confused we became. We finally found a place to purchase a city map. (This was before the days of GPS). Eventually, we found our way to the medical center. It was a beneficial thing that we left early.

When we got to the hospital, we went through the admissions paperwork; then a bunch of lab work was drawn. Blood tests and a brain scan were completed. A major part of getting a developmental disability diagnosis is weeding through and ruling out what is not wrong. In other words, it is a process of elimination. Tests ruled out things such as poison or toxins in the blood, Fragile-X syndrome, hormone malfunctions, and several other disorders that have mimicking characteristics. Other steps in diagnosis involve behavioral specialists watching the child and documenting how he interacts and plays or relates in differing situations; this measures his interactive social skills. A physical is done, and a developmental milestone survey is completed. All of the information is compiled; and after an exhausting day of tests and waiting, we finally get to see the doctor.

I will never forget what transpired next. To this day, I cannot comprehend how a physician can deliver devastating news with such cold callousness and lack of concern for the family involved. By the time the doctor came into the exam room, Nathan was restless; wild would be very descriptive. He was literally climbing the walls, and I appeared to be in an endless struggle with him, trying to keep him out of and off of things. Nate was everywhere all at once, and he jabbered and screeched non-stop.

The doctor was telling us our son's condition classified as a pervasive developmental disorder, and forms of autism fell in this spectrum. He also said that there were mental developmental delays. After a lengthy explanation, he informed us that at this stage Nathan was considered to be in the severe levels of the autism and retardation spectrums. He went on to explain several things about autism, and the dismal future our son faced. Then he told us that we had some tough decisions to make.

The doctor's next statements—though mostly true and I understood them—hurt, and they made me angry. He told us Nathan would never be normal—of that I was already aware. "Your issues will intensify and worsen as he ages." I could see how that might be true. "You have two daughters to care for, and you need to concentrate on them." I agreed. He told us we needed to make sure the girls' needs were being met. Again, I agreed. "You two," he said as he looked at my husband and me, "need to try and create as normal a life as possible for everyone involved. Nathan's level of functioning is limited and challenging." This, too, was true.

His next proclamation is the one I could not wrap my brain around. "It would probably be best to institutionalize him now (He handed us a list of facilities located in our state as he said this.)

and try to get on with your lives." I sat in total disbelief; I was dumbfounded and stunned. My husband and I had tears running down our faces, and Nathan was still trying to scale the walls. We gathered our things together preparing to leave.

I don't know what possessed me to voice what I said next. As we were exiting, I turned to the physician and said, "May I ask you a personal question?"

"Yes." he said.

"Do you have children?"

"I do. I have two daughters."

"Are they okay? Do they do well in school?"

"Yes; they do fine."

As he stepped away from us to head down the hall, my final statement was, "Boy, aren't they lucky; good thing they're normal. They'd be living in an institution somewhere, locked up and forgotten if they weren't."

Those were my last words to the specialist who saw our son that one and only time. I found myself wondering how many parents have followed his professional advice over the years; this thought saddens me greatly. I left absolutely certain of one thing that day; I would find a way to move beyond this doctor's "expert" opinion.

We spent the night in a hotel on the outskirts of the metro area; we were too drained to drive home. We held each other and cried a lot as we watched Nate play on the floor. Then we talked. As long as we could, we were going to keep our son with us, in our home, and in our family unit. We realized that the day might come when we would have to visit the possibility of placing him under the supervision of an institution that specializes in caring for older children and adults like him, just like the doctor we had seen that day had told us. We agreed that as a developing child, we were to be the major influence in his life for as long as possible.

Potty Attack

During our drive home, we developed a plan of attack for Nathan's future. Those plans included teaching and lots of it. We were going to teach him to hug; we were going to continue to give kisses and hugs, whether he wanted them or not. We were determined to teach him to share, no matter how difficult the task. We were going to show him what "love" looks like. We were going to weather the storms ahead, choose our battles, and work with him as much as possible. Our goal for him was the same as our goals for the girls. We were going to love, guide, teach, and direct him while praying that he would become as successful as he possibly could.

Our first decision was to register Nathan as being homeschooled by me, a certified teacher; this was temporary. When he learned a system of communication, gained some self-control, and mastered toileting we would examine school attendance. Until then, I would do everything I knew as an educator to help him learn as much as possible.

The first item we chose to confront was toilet training. Not knowing this endeavor would take almost two years, and he would be six before we could claim success, we dove in and started. As I embarked on this venture, I gained a new appreciation for the meaning of "girding one's self for battle." No matter what, I had to have more determination and stamina to win the fight than anyone else involved. I had to be tenacious; for only then, would we be victorious. I also knew to pick my battles wisely. I confronted the ones I felt we had to win; toileting was absolutely one of them.

We had a portable potty, and I used it exactly as its name describes. I toted it around the house with me everywhere I went. No more allowing him to hide behind or under furniture to do a job. No more letting him get up before he finished. No matter what kind of tantrum we had to endure, once he was on the potty, he remained on the potty until there was some result. We adhered to a strict schedule. Wake up in the morning; sit on the potty. Eat breakfast; sit on the potty. Play, sit on the potty. I had to pay close attention to signs of need. We set a timer; and every hour and a half, he sat on the potty. He did not get up until he experienced some kind of success. Every time he started to search for a hiding place, we put him on the potty.

Rewards were given for every successful event. Day after day we adhered to a strict regime; repetition over time solved our problem. We applied the same principles as with our other children; it just took more opportunities across a much longer timeframe. Every day, it seemed as if everything he had learned was erased when he slept. Each morning was like the first day of training all over again. We never knew when mastery would come, but it seemed instantaneous when it did. Magically, one day, the information registered, and he made the connection. He literally potty trained overnight. Once he grasped the concept, he never forgot it. Nathan was six when we won this victory.

Deciphering the Code

Language usage was a major area we were determined to develop. Nathan made plenty of noises, and he babbled, but no dialect or communication took place; at least that is what we thought. Nate engaged in what is known as parroting; he mimicked sounds and noises, but he did not process words. My husband and I were desperately trying to pick up on anything that seemed like he was trying to talk. We had no clue that our son developed his own lingo; one that we did not understand. The sounds we heard which we interpreted as babbling were his valiant efforts to repeat the jargon he heard going on around him on a daily basis.

The silent connections siblings have between themselves amazes me. One seems to have the ability to read the other and interpret what is going on with them. Parents remain clueless as to their secret link. Nathan's older sister, Lucy, would unravel his ramblings and discover what he was saying. Because of her incredible listening skills, keen observations, and willingness to interact with her brother—even though he was very different from her friend's siblings—she was able to decipher his code.

Nathan was four and Lucy was in first grade. She got off the school bus, came into the house, and asked for her afternoon snack. Lucy asked for Sprite with a straw and graham crackers. We had a conversation about "Sprite with a straw" and what kind of treat she wanted. As I gathered her snack together, her brother started to spin around the kitchen table, flapping his arms and squawking like a bird saying, "Strawp, strawp, strawp."

I knew my sweet boy wanted something, but I had no clue what. When I finished taking care of Lucy and baby sister Naomi, I turned my attention to my son. I took him to the refrigerator and cabinets trying to figure out what he wanted. The whole time he continued to squawk that sound: "Strawp, strawp, strawp." The more he jabbered, and the more times I guessed incorrectly, the more frustrated he became.

Lucy was naming off items and all of a sudden, she said, "Momma, I know what he wants." She got down on his level, got him to come to her, and as she held out her Sprite with a straw she asked him, "Nate, you want Sprite with a straw?"

Instead of whining and squirming in frustration, he grinned and chirped, "Strawp, strawp, strawp." He happily helped himself to some of her soda. She took the can away, and when she did he screeched, "Strawp, strawp, strawp." She gave it back to him. My brilliant seven-year-old exclaimed, "Momma! He's saying, 'Sprite with a straw.'"

My son's brain had processed a phrase and turned it into a single word. This information entered his mind the same way it does everyone else's; only it came out in encrypted code. I cannot explain to you the amount of celebrating that went on at our home that evening.

The following weekend I went to town to shop, and I took all three of my darlings with me. We were walking through a department store; and again, sounding very much like a bird squawking, Nathan was swinging his head around and saying, "Shem, shem, shem."

People frequently stared at us; I must admit, we did create quite a scene. Nathan looked toward Lucy and repeated the same sounds. She walked over to an associate in the store and said, "Nate, who is this?"

His reply was, "Shem, shem, shem." We continued to shop. Our little wonder, Lucy, notice that her brother was using his head to point at people. Every time a person walked by us, he swung his head toward them and said that series of words: "Shem, shem, shem." My exceptional daughter looked at me and declared, "Mom! He's naming the people; they are she and him, *shem*." I was utterly amazed.

The discovery of two deciphered phrases led to the process of substituting every Cameron expression this incredible girl could distinguish with the real words. Eventually, my husband and I became pretty astute at figuring out which words and phrases our son had combined to create a new word. We made our way into his world, and we were beginning to speak his language. Our seven-year-old had deciphered her brother's babbling and discovered he was talking; we just couldn't understand him. He was saying exactly what his brain had processed. This quaint child gave our family the remarkable gift of communication and the ability to talk with her brother; she is the reason we were able to unlock Nathan's language. Move over Einstein!

Nathan was almost five when we first started word replacements. He was seven before he spoke in understandable phrases, and communication became easier. We finally arrived at a point where we didn't have to make constant substitutions. Around age seven, Nathan somehow started hearing the words individually, instead of collectively. Twelve years later as long as we discuss a topic that is of great interest to him—*Transformers, Bumblebee, Optimist Prime, Jack Sparrow,* the *Black Pearl,* or the newest action hero movie released—he is quite the conversationalist. He recreates sound effects from movies, and he imitates them with fascinating accuracy. His ability to remember the sequence of events and dialogue in a film amazes me.

Conquering Self

Our third battlefield was self-control and discipline. I went to meetings and training to acquire some of the most efficient ways to help calm Nathan when he lost control of himself. I learned the best forms of discipline to use when necessary. They were somewhat complicated solutions, but they were helpful in the long run. The crab-cradle (which involves the parent wrapping their arms and legs around a child and holding them tightly during a tantrum or meltdown) and the pressure press (which uses the cushions from the couch to assist with boundaries and control) and one-two-three magic changed our lives. The hardest part to learn was the rigid consistency necessary in their usage.

Over time these tools became second nature to us. After several years, Nathan started requesting the cushion pressure press because he could identify times when he was losing control and needed help. Nate would say, "Mom, lay on me Mom; I need help!" Then my son would lay on the floor in front of the couch; I would follow right behind him. Nathan even got to the point where he would pull the cushions off and crawl under them and call for me to come. These behaviors were huge steps in developing Nate's ability to manage himself in a situation that was uncomfortable or trying for him.

I have since turned this into teaching him how to place himself in time-out. This is a space away from others, where he can concentrate on breathing and talking to himself, not yelling or striking out at others. All of this is with the intent of helping him to learn how to maintain or gain self-control. Is he one hundred percent triumphant? No. Are any of us when it comes to controlling our tempers? It is a work in process and progress.

We opted to keep Nathan off medication for as long as possible. However, by the time he was six, we realized he was having severe issues with self-control, visual anomalies, and defiance. I found a child psychiatrist in a neighboring large city who specialized in children with disabilities and control issues. Dr. Green was impressive; with his guidance, help, and the right medications Nathan's behavior improved rapidly.

The September following his seventh birthday, Nathan attended school for the first time. At the age of twenty-two, he earned his certificate of completion. Though in reality, the following scenario will never happen, it thrills me when Nate tells me he wants to go to college to study science, his favorite subject; and, he aspires to graduate like his sisters did.

CHAPTER 15

Divine Intervention

Watch 'Em Like a Hawk

We had returned home from our trip to the medical metro-plaza with Nathan, devastated but determined. Things were satisfactory and pleasant for about a year. Then my husband decided to resign his position as pastor of the church. The part-time, secondary job he worked making him a bi-vocational pastor was turning into a full-time management position. I thought our days of transitioning and moving were over; I was wrong. The church wanted us to vacate the premises immediately upon resignation. It would be six weeks or more before we got our assigned position with the other company, so we had to find a place we could rent for the interim.

My dear friend Melissa Jane, the owner of the daycare whom I meet my sophomore year in college, and I had remained friends over the years; I was working for her in the capacity of a preschool teacher during this time. We worked out a deal for a decent salary, and my two youngest children, Nathan and Naomi, went to work with me every day. We were in our second year of this arrangement, and it was successful. I told her about our dilemma concerning my husband's job and housing for the short-term. She graciously invited us to stay in her home until the company told us where we were being placed.

It had only been a few months since we received the news that our son would be challenged cognitively, developmentally, mentally, and emotionally for the remainder of his life. I was always trying to out-think him for safety purposes; he was fearless. Nothing scared him, and he was a daredevil. I was always trying to stay one step ahead of him; he managed to stay three paces in front of me.

I had only one misgiving about staying at my friend's house. Our room was right next to the entry of a hallway that led to an exterior door, and there was a doggie exit cut in it. This door led to the patio and built-in swimming pool area. My biggest concern was that Nathan would find his way out of the doggie door, make his way to the pool slide, go down it, and drown. I asked my friend if we could put a locking bolt up high on the interior exit so my son wouldn't have access to the exterior door; she said we could.

I didn't sleep well the first week we were in the house. I had to make sure Nathan couldn't get out of our room in the middle of the night and find his way to the pool access door, located immediately outside of the suite in which we were staying. After three nights of scarcely any sleep, we decided to place a chest of drawers in front of the bedroom door. We secured this barrier every night until the lock was installed.

During the lapse between our move-in and installation of the safety latch, I watched my four-year-old and eighteen-month-old like a hawk. I wanted to know where my kids were and what they were doing every minute. I tried to remain keenly aware of their presence at all times. We had been in the house for several weeks, and the pool was closed for winter; it was mid–October.

Lighten Up

One night, I made dinner for everyone. My friend's daughter, Miranda, who lived next door came over to eat with us. She had a daughter the same age as my youngest, Naomi. Miranda and I had an interesting conversation near the end of the meal. My children had finished eating, and they were somewhere in the house playing. I persistently checked their whereabouts, probably every two to three minutes since they left the table. This was a habit I developed so I could monitor the doggie door during the times we didn't have our bedroom door barricaded.

We had finished eating, and I was clearing the table. It had been about five minutes since I checked the locations of all three of my kids. At my last check, Lucy was in our room doing homework. Nathan was playing with some cars, lining them up one behind the other in a long line in the hallway a few feet from me. Both of them were to my immediate right. Naomi was playing on the stairwell that led downstairs to the daycare center. She was in the room to the left of the kitchen, known as the den or office area. Miranda had just finished telling me that I needed to lighten up and relax a little. She said, "Give your kids some space."

In turn, I told her she didn't understand the extent of caring for a child that was like Nathan; and when the latch was installed, maybe I could relax. I promised her I would try. I jokingly said something to her like, "When did the baby get big enough to tell the babysitter how to deal with children?" (I used to babysit Miranda and her brothers when they were little; now, she was a mom with a toddler giving me advice.)

When Miranda and I finished our bantering exchange, she left to go home. There was no one else in the house, and I continued clearing the table. Only a few minutes had passed since Miranda left to walk across the driveway to her house. I picked up the third plate and was scraping it when I heard: "Check on your children, now!"

A Brick Wall

It was not an audible voice, but I heard it loud and clear in my head. It was so startling; I fumbled the plate I was holding and dropped it. I turned to look in the hallway for Nate; he wasn't there. I ran to my left to see if he had joined his sister on the stairwell, and I was calling their names as I went. When I arrived at the passageway, I didn't see either one of them. I went back to the room where Lucy was doing her homework and asked her if she had seen her brother or sister. I was hoping they were watching the cartoons that happened to be playing on the television in our room; they were not there. I asked Lucy to stop what she was doing and help me find her brother and sister. I went back up the hallway, through the dining room, and into the living room to see if they were hiding behind the couch or chair—something they loved to do. I yelled out, "Mommy is not playing; answer me now. I need to know where you are!"

I turned in sheer panic because I couldn't hear anything; I was scared. It had been at least five minutes since I'd seen my two youngest children. Lucy was right behind me, and in my worry, I lashed out at her. "Why weren't you watching them?" I scolded. I immediately stopped and apologized to her for that remark. I took a second to tell her I was sorry, and that it was not her responsibility to watch them. I told her I should never have said that; it was my worry talking. I asked her to forgive me, and I gave her a quick hug. I can still hear her reply, "It's okay Mommy, you're nervous."—Kids are so smart.

I turned from my apology to my oldest daughter and continued searching. I was about to go down the back hallway to see if they had ventured into the first bedroom on the right or into the bedroom on the left which was further down the hall. As I rounded the corner to do this check, Nathan was walking up the hallway. He was soaking wet, spitting and sputtering as he said, "Nah-me, Nah-me!"

I was frozen with fright. I knew Nate had been in the pool, and I didn't know the location of my youngest child. I told Lucy to hold her brother and not let him out of her sight. I raced toward the pool exit, terrified that I was about to face my greatest fear. Only it was not Nathan for whom I was looking; it was my eighteen-month-old baby girl, Naomi.

I tore out of the back door and stepped toward the pool; there were no signs of my child. I stopped and scanned the surface of the water for a body; I didn't see one. I turned around and headed back up the stairs; I was going to see if she had found her way back to the stairwell on the other side of the house. When I arrived at the door that I had left standing wide opened, I attempted to whip through it at high speed. It felt like I ran into a brick wall. I tried to go through the opening again; I was stopped cold in my tracks. It felt as if a source of power spun me around, and the same voice I had heard in my head a few moments earlier was now booming forth, "Turn around, she's in the pool."

I planted my gaze at the far end of the swimming pool. I began methodically scanning the water's surface left to right, from the deep end toward the shallow. At the same time, I was removing my shoes and sweater, preparing to jump into the cold concrete pond. My eyes made several passes across the surface of the murky water, and I reached the area beyond the diving board with my search; I was looking in the direction of the left side of the pool. Several inches below the surface of the water, I barely saw the red poke-a-dot, ruffled bloomer bottoms of the playsuit I had dressed Naomi in that morning; they were barely visible in the green hues of the stagnant pool. She had already sunk a significant distance. Everything I had learned in lifesaving during my college days came rushing back to me with great clarity. As I jumped into the water, I screamed, "I found her! I found her; she's in the pool!"

Lucy had followed me outside, and she was dutifully holding onto her younger brother. I made it through the cold water to Naomi. I lifted her up and turned her over, pulling a few strong strokes at the same time. I was trying to get her into shallower water where my feet could touch the ground; we were about a third of the way from the far side of the pool. All of these things happened in one continuous motion. I yelled out to Lucy to get the phone, and call 911.

Naomi was not breathing; she was dark purple. I immediately started CPR on my toddler as I waded toward the side of the pool. I got her to the side and lifted her up to the concrete slab. I pulled myself up out of the water, and Lucy handed me the phone on which the 911 operator was waiting. She informed me that an ambulance and rescue team were in route. I checked my baby's eyes as the operator had instructed; they were rolled back in her head. She was still purple and cold; she was not breathing. I continued CPR. (Being a daycare employee, I had to renew my CPR certification every year. Never in a million years did I dream I would be using this technique on one of my children.)

Unknown to me, my husband arrived home from work just as I hollered, "She's in the pool!" He heard me yell and saw my friend's daughter take off like lightning coming toward the house; he thought it was Miranda's daughter, Hanna, I had found. He climbed an eight-foot fence to get to us quickly so he could help. He scaled that barrier in one crawling leap; and by the time he landed on the other side of the fence, I saw the ambulance coming down the circular drive. Miranda had arrived and took over CPR. My husband headed toward us. I sat back on my heels and began to cry out, "Please God, no; not again." I looked over to see my husband fall to his knees, as he realized this was his baby girl lying there, not Miranda's.

As the EMT's got to my daughter's side, she coughed up a vast amount of green water and cried. I could tell she was disoriented and frightened, but she was making glorious noises. I reached out and pulled her into my arms, and the rescuers took care of her while I held her. They wrapped blankets around us and placed us on a gurney; then they wheeled us to the ambulance. Sirens blared as we were transported to the local emergency room.

I Can't Do This

We got to the hospital quickly, and things happened at breakneck speed. We had revived her, but now the hard part started. It was determined Naomi had been underwater between five to ten minutes. The medical professionals attending us in the ER did not mince words. There would be brain damage; we just didn't know how much. We would also be fighting major infection because she had ingested large amounts of the germy, bacteria-ridden water from the pool. We would have to wait and see how things developed.

The doctor told me to plan on staying at the hospital for several days.

We were finally ushered into a room where they placed Naomi in a hospital crib; we were located directly across the hall from the nurse's station. I received clean, dry clothes, and the staff brought in a rocking chair for me. It was about ten-thirty that evening before everyone was notified of what had happened and things began to settle down for the night.

Naomi would occasionally cry out and whimper; she sounded horse. It was evident she was not coherent or oriented; she was not out of the woods by a long shot. She was restless, but she didn't open her eyes. It was eleven-thirty before I was able to rock her back to sleep. A nurse came in and adjusted my baby's oxygen; things finally became peaceful, and it was quiet.

From the first "Check on your children now" that I heard ring through my head, I had been crying out to God from within my soul. I put my little girl gently in her bed and walked over to the corner of the hospital room. I started out on my knees with my face to the wall. I began praying out loud. It took me awhile to get passed just being able to cry out saying, "Oh, God. Oh, God. Oh, God." Eventually, I was able to enter a season of prayer.

> Oh God, I know You have a reason for everything You allow; but I don't understand this. Please do not require another child of me. I'm just not strong enough; I can't do this again.
>
> You have no obligation to grant my petition, but I am asking, begging You to reach down and divinely intervene in this. The doctors are telling me there will be brain damage; they do not know how much at this time. I'm really scared.

I continued to talk to my Father in heaven for a long time. At some point during my pilgrimage, I sprawled out on the floor, flat on my face before my Holy Creator and said:

> Father, I will not be skeptical of You; nor will I blame You. Please help me trust You through this, no matter what happens. I put Naomi in Your hands, and I'm letting go. You have proven Your existence to me beyond all doubt. I will not question that.
>
> I cannot think of anything that is standing between You and me at this moment. If there is, please reveal it to me; so, I can bring it to You and beg Your forgiveness.
>
> Oh God, with every fiber of my being, I am asking You to spare my daughter. Please reach down and heal her. Touch her and kill the bacteria that is in her body. You created all that is, and it is under Your control and command. Help me where my faith is weak.
>
> I lay before You now proclaiming that I know You are the one true God of the universe, and all things are under Your power. I know You have a plan for my life, and I know You are still the God of miracles. Please God, come here tonight and deliver my child.
>
> Father, if You choose to work in another manner, help me to trust You. Oh God, I am begging for mercy and a miracle.

I was silent for a bit, and then I started to sing: I Love You, Lord (Laurie Klein, 1974).

I sang this song over and over again. Eventually, the singing faded to a hum. Finally, I fell asleep in sweet comfort and peace. Just before two in the morning, I was awakened by a nurse who entered the room to check on my daughter. She had come in to monitor the oxygen count in Naomi's blood; it was holding at seventy-three percent. She took the rest of Naomi's vital signs, recorded them, and left the room.

Miracles Still Happen

I pulled myself up from the cold floor where I had petitioned God. I checked on Naomi and rubbed my hand gently across her sweet head. Then I stepped across the hall and asked the nurses to keep watch over my baby; I needed to take a small break. I went for a walk and spent the time thanking God for His comfort. I asked Him again to help me remain steadfast and calm. I got a bite to eat and drink, took a bathroom break, and then headed back to my daughter's room. The nurses said she had not stirred.

I fixed my rocker with some pillows, placed a blanket where it would be within my reach once I was seated, and gathered my little one into my arms to cradle her. I looked into her sweet sleeping face and smiled. I was distinctly aware that I wasn't worried; I was peacefully calm. I wiggled around quietly until we both seemed comfortable, and I started to rock gently. I was humming *Amazing Grace* (John Newton, 1779), and that turned into singing *Thank You, Lord* (Seth and Bessie Sykes; 1940, New Spring).

I nodded off. In the early hours of the morning, shortly before five o'clock, I felt a light pat on my cheek. I opened my eyes and looked into the face of my sweet baby girl. I heard: "Momma, Momma."

I sat my little treasure up in my lap and looked into her eyes; she was back. I cried out, "Thank You, God," as tears of joy splashed down my face. I smiled at her; she smiled back. I hugged her; she hugged me back. I gave her little kisses, and she giggled.

We went home that morning. The doctors couldn't believe it. I did. Oh, I did!

She never got a sniffle. To this day, I am careful to thank Him for sparing and healing my child. I will never cease to thank God for the miracle He granted me that day.

The speculation of the rescue team was that Naomi had crawled off of the diving board and had fallen into the deep end of the pool. A few days after we returned home from the hospital, I was thinking about what had happened. To be perfectly honest, I was reliving the whole event. I reached the part where Nathan was coming up the hallway sopping wet, and I had rounded the corner to head toward the back door. When I saw him, he was soaked from head to toe; it was obvious he had gone under the water.

During this replay, I found myself wondering how Nate had gotten out of the pool. He was four years old, and he didn't know how to swim. His favorite part of the pool is the slide. I found myself wondering if he had gone down it. If he did, there was no way for him to get out by himself. The water was over his head at the entry point of the slide. To this day, I dare to speculate that the same angel who stood in the doorway blocking my reentry into the house guided him safely out of the water. I believe this is a very real possibility.

CHAPTER 16

Beginning of the End

Fly Away

Almost a decade had passed since we almost lost Naomi. We continued to face the challenges of family, marriage, and life changes during that time. *Anger and Rage*, our menacing duo, sought opportunities to reappeared on many occasions. Time elapsed quickly; and before I knew it, my kids were leaving childhood. Nathan was a preteen stuck in the emotional realm of a toddler, Naomi was nine going on sixteen—quite the norm for this age, and Lucy was in high school. On top of everything else, I was sinking further into a pit of emotional, physical, and spiritual illness.

I am not sure when this next experience took place in the timeline of events. I do know that I was still married and at home, and driving my white van. I'm not positive if Nathan was still residing with us or not. I vividly remember this episode concerning my mother, and it was during the fall season. It also unfolded within the last year or two of our marriage.

A few short years and a series of strokes brought my mom to her final moments; she succumbed to the ravages of Alzheimer's. In her last days, she confused faces of the present with people from her past. She thought my daughter, Lucy, was my sister Jane. She called my son Nathan, Donnie-boy; this was her pet name for my youngest brother when he was a child. One of my brothers appeared to her as her handsome soldier-groom, Martin. My little brother seemed to be her spouse from later years; she did not remember her husband had died fifteen years earlier.

One of the greatest blessings throughout Mom's illness was the fact that she never reached the cold-hearted, mean stage that often accompanies Alzheimer's. She remained in a child-like, giggly-girl state, being silly and playful most of the time. I attributed this to the wit and wisdom of my older brother; he was terrific at joking around with Mom and keeping things light and upbeat. She always looked forward to family visits, even though she did not know most of us in our current roles. She loved to hear scripture being read and have songs sung to her; these were my responsibility when I was around; I was thrilled to deliver.

When I was twenty, God granted me the distinct privilege of leading my mom to an authentic relationship with Jesus Christ. She and I were on our way to visit my maternal grandmother, and I as driving. During the trip, Mom shared with me an ongoing personal struggle. She told me that she had lingering doubts about her salvation. Mom remembered walking the aisle at age eleven, but she wasn't sure about what took place. She asked me why I was so confident and sure of my relationship with Christ. We stopped along the way at our favorite pizza place for lunch.

We continued to talk, and I shared scripture with her. Finally, I declared a solution to her dilemma. I shared the simple truth that if she was not sure of her salvation, we could make sure and settle the question once and for all. I told her I didn't think God would mind if she asked Him to dispel any doubts she had, for He wants us to know we are His and be confident in that knowledge (1 John 5:13). I told her we could claim that day, that very hour, as the point in time when she made sure her relationship with Jesus Christ was right. We prayed right there in the middle of Pizza Hut, and we wrote down the date and time on a napkin. We shed tears of joy, and we left that place arm in arm with huge smiles of thanksgiving and rejoicing on our faces.

When the call came stating that Mom had been taken to the hospital and things didn't look hopeful, it was evening around five o'clock. I made arrangements concerning my children and spoke with my husband about a plan. After making sure everything at home was covered, I loaded my van and headed out. It was dark when I arrived. As soon as I walked into her hospital room, I knew she was in her final hours. She was feverishly picking at the sheets when I entered; the nurse said she had been doing this since her arrival. I walked over and took my mom in my arms. I bent down and softly called her name as I gently caressed her face. "Momma, it's okay; I'm here. I'm here, just like I promised. I love you, Mom."

Amazingly, Mom always knew me. Her illness had advanced to the point where it was difficult for her to say much. Her hazel eyes always lit up when I came into the room, and occasionally she managed to say, "Nor," or "My Nor." She always called me Norrie; unless I was in trouble, then it was *Nora Jean*!

She moved her head slightly to one side and lifted her eyes a little. "Nor" was formed with her mouth, but the word pelted against the oxygen mask she was wearing. When her breath hit the hard plastic, it disappeared into a vapor. I caught a glimpse of her blurred eyes. She knew I was there, and she gave me a faint frail smile.

I crawled into the bed with her and cradled her in my arms. I laid her head against my chest and started to sing. I sang one hymn after another, as many verses as I could remember. After a few songs, she calmed down and stopped fidgeting; she no longer picked at the bedding. Throughout the night, I sang as I softly stroked her hair. Song after song, verse after verse, I comforted Mom with some of her favorite words, words about her Savior. As dawn broke the morning skies, the nurses came in to do their morning duties. For the first time since I had arrived, I stopped singing and got up from my semi-reclined position.

They straightened Mom in the bed, brushed her hair, and made her as comfortable as possible. I stepped over to the side of the bed and gathered her hands in mine. As I drew close, she sat upright and looked straight at me with those sparkling hazel eyes that had been so clouded with illness and fever a few moments earlier. There was glory radiating from her face. She whispered, "Love, Norrie." Then, she fell against my chest and breathed out her last breath. I held her tightly and cried into her hair, "I love you too, Mom; I love you, too."

I left the hospital in tears, humming one of her favorite tunes: *I'll Fly Away* (Albert E. Brumley, 1929). I will never forget the day my mom passed from this life into eternity. I will treasure it always.

Physical Destruction

It was March, and it was my birthday; I had made it to forty-six—I think this was approximately six months after losing my mother, but I'm not positively certain of the time frame. I know I was exhausted, and I dreaded my future, hated the past, and bitter in the present. For many consecutive months, I experienced debilitating migraines so severe I was hospitalized for weeks at a time. More neurological symptoms developed and intensified in coming days. My hands were drawn in pain, and I couldn't use them. My extremities were numb and tingly; pins and needles pricked all over my body. My blood pressure was dropping to dangerous lows; I was passing out and growing weaker by the day. I was severely depressed. I began to withdraw, isolate, and alienate myself from all of my relationships.

Eventually, my entire body became numb. Needles, IV's, and other procedures didn't bother me because I couldn't feel them. Over time, my vision became severely distorted. I could no longer read, and things became difficult to distinguish; everything was blurry and unfocused. My cognition became impaired; reading and simple math computations became impossible, and my speech was slurred. I was not sleeping. I finally retreated to my bed; it was the only place I felt safe.

On top of the everyday issues we were dealing with, I was parenting an autistic son headed toward puberty and dealing with the government, trying to make arrangements for Nathan's future care. Add a defiant, strong-willed preteen and the existence of a spouse who worked hard and spent all of his spare time with his kids, one finds a marriage that was sicker than I. Feeling as if my husband could care less about me just added more stress and hurt to an already troublesome situation.

Medications and bills began to pile into my life. Avoidance, seclusion, and prescription drugs became preferred tools for problem-solving and coping. I spent the majority of my days secretly hoping there would not be many sunrises left for me. All through the day and night, I fought the constant barrage of negative emotions, destructive thoughts, and visions of death. My life became a jumbled web of twisted, ugly mess. My biggest error and omission in all of this, I gradually left God out; I stopped turning to my only hope and source of comfort. I opened myself up to the flagrant attacks of evil.

A week after my birthday, my health had deteriorated even more; I was very sick. I felt terrible, and I had no energy or strength. The kids were in school, and I was home alone—in bed as usual. Walking was difficult because my legs wouldn't do what my brain was telling them to do. I held on to furniture and walls to prevent a fall. I made it to the bathroom and looked in the mirror; I was terrified when I saw my reflection. I had dark circles under my eyes, and my face was distorted; it looked like it was falling. The entire right side drooped and sagged. I was gray in color. My mouth was twisted, and I was drooling; I could not stop it or control it. I couldn't speak. I felt like I was going to vomit; I shook all over, and I started to cry.

I let go of the sink and turned to go back to bed; as I tried to step through the doorway, I fell. I do not know who found me or how long I laid there. The next thing I clearly recall is my husband taking me to the hospital. I was admitted for what I understood to be a stroke. I remember something being said about a blood clot hitting my brainstem and hormone medication possibly being the culprit. There is hospital documentation that states this, but I don't remember much of what was said about it. My husband stayed by my side throughout the ER portion of this ordeal. After that, he was at the hospital some; but, most of his time was spent taking care of our children and working.

Test results were inconclusive as to what really happened, but something was very wrong. I was paralyzed; I couldn't move upon command, and my entire body was numb. I could not feel painful stimuli at all. The ER doctor took his car keys and scraped the bottom of my feet from heel to toe. My toes didn't move, and I felt nothing when he scratched me. We looked later; there were long, red streaks running the length of my feet where he had taken off skin in the process of checking for reactions; I have scars on the bottom of my feet caused by this. I could not speak; I was aware of my surroundings, but I couldn't communicate. Having suffered what appeared to be a stroke, I would have to learn to walk, talk, and function all over again.

An interesting diagnosis of this event surfaced during later years in my recovery. There is the possibility I was suffering from something known as conversion disorder. This condition is mental and emotional in nature, and the brain becomes highly stressed and distraught. Emotional traumas create anxiety that remains at high-intensity levels for an extended time, and it morphs into physical symptoms. Many times, this manifestation mimics a neurological illness. The person appears to be physically ill, but the ailment is emotionally induced and fueled by severe anxiety. It looks real, affects the person as if it is real, and one must recover as if it is real. This is the extent of my knowledge about this disorder. I experienced something that left me physically incapacitated, but I do not thoroughly understand what happened.

Pieces of a small clot were removed from an artery in my head, during a procedure associated with this episode. One doctor stated he was suspicious that both diagnoses were in play, a small blood clot hitting my brainstem and conversion disorder. Whatever the cause, I was severely debilitated and very ill. I spent several weeks in the hospital and approximately six weeks in a rehabilitation facility; physically, I got better. At some juncture during all of this, my husband took me to a mental health center in a distant city to see a psychiatric specialist. I cannot recall where in the timeline of events this visit took place or even if it happened at this point in my journey, but I remember going.

I never knew why I had to go, and I still don't. I took a bunch of written tests; answers were marked by filling in bubbles. The only other thing I remember about this event is getting into the truck to go home. This visit is possibly the first time I received information of my severe emotional and mental states. I have never been able to get my ex-husband to talk to me about any of this, so I can only guess and speculate. I cannot report any of the findings, results of tests, or recount discussions concerning this particular event. I have a generalized feeling this is about the time my spouse seriously gave up on me.

In August, I suffered a relapse; I was hospitalized for eight days. There is only one thing I recall from this episode. The neurologist in charge of my case came to my room one evening to talk with me; I was alone as usual. He told me gently, but quite bluntly he didn't think there was anything physically wrong with me. He did think I was devastated and psychologically wounded; he felt I was suffering from severe emotional trauma. This doctor told me I needed professional, psychiatric intervention. I listened as tears ran down my face, and I cried myself to sleep after he left. I do not know if I told my spouse about this conversation.

Insult and Injury

In March, when the first stroke episode occurred, my in-laws decided it was the appropriate time to send their other son to stay with us and help out around the house while I was recuperating and working my way through rehab. I was always nervous and uncomfortable in my brother-in-law's presence. I did not like the fact that he had come to live with us, and I didn't want him there; he was a problem. I will not share the details of our entire time together for it would take too long. I will tell you this; I put an end to his stay pretty quickly.

The day I asked him to leave was traumatic for everyone involved. I was in my room getting ready for the day. I heard a major disturbance taking place in the living room. I stopped attaching my leg braces, dropped to the floor, and dragged myself down the hall to the living room to see why Nathan was screeching hysterically. I arrived just in time to witness my brother-in-law flinging my child's plate and drink against the wall. He shoved Nathan onto the couch and grabbed him by the neck; he was cursing my son vehemently, poised and ready to throw a punch. I screamed as loudly as I could and commanded Joe to get out of my house, demanding that he not come back. I told him his brother would bring his things to him later.

I had armed myself with the telephone, and I was ready to call the police if necessary. I was insulted and outraged that more physical and emotional unrest had entered my home. That was Joe's last day in our house. I hated that things ended as they did, but I could not take any more. One man in my abode with a volatile temper was enough; I was not going to allow the second one to stay. I wasn't married to him.

One of The Hardest Things I Have Ever Done

In the midst of this chaos, we had to make a decision about our son and the girls' safety. Nathan's tantrums and strength were more than we could handle. He was able to hurt me, and he was becoming masterful at escaping his dad; it was evident things were escalating out of control. I was in a wheelchair at the time, trying to learn to walk again; this put everyone at risk, and we could not allow anything horrible to happen. The day Nate pointed a knife at me and said, "I kill you 'fir' now," I knew we had to do something.

The decision to place a child outside of one's personal care is beyond excruciating. This decision is the one that the specialist had spoken to us about years earlier; the one we hoped we would never have to face. We knew the time had come to place Nathan in a facility. He was twelve.

Over the next few months, his behavior became increasingly erratic and unpredictable. We were told that when puberty hit, we would experience major self-control issues. He was bigger than me, and he was getting to the point where he could take me down. He had the ability to hurt others physically when he lost control; he had a superhero, Herculean strength. Nathan was no longer safe, neither were the people around him at the time of a major melt-down.

The combination of his behavioral issues and my physical condition forced us to face an excruciatingly painful reality. Though it took a few months and mountains of paperwork, our day of unimaginable emotional pain arrived. It ripped me apart when I signed the contract making Nathan a resident at a local state facility. I cried for weeks before taking him to his new residence, and I cried for many months after we placed him there. I felt like the worst parent in the world the day we walked away and left Nathan at his new place of abode. Even now, there are times when I take him back after a visit that I shed tears. These emotions and feelings still run deeply.

The Final Visit

Months later, I knew the pressure in our household was about to explode; it was purely a matter of when. We were in crisis, and things were coming to a head. I didn't realize until years later that my marriage, therefore my entire family, was in serious trouble. My relationship with my husband was beyond strained, and he was overworked. We were both stressed out, and we were not communicating.

Just to be clear, you need to know, I was not guiltless in adding stressors to our marriage. Unfortunately, I am not perfect. The things I did were never intentional. When I became aware of problems that I had created, I admitted them. Then, I would seek forgiveness, trying to make things right. I will be perfectly honest; there were a few habits I developed over time, especially in the last two to three years of our relationship, that were damaging to our family. One was my mouth; it had become increasingly toxic, an indication of the pained and ill condition of my heart. The other was financial infidelity; I was spending money we did not have. I did not understand a fundamental principle of bookkeeping: *Just because the checkbook says I have eighty-nine dollars, it doesn't mean I can spend it.* I did not comprehend the concept of earmarked funds.

This particular sin plagued me on and off throughout our marriage. I've been able to trace it's beginning back to the time we were "in the desert place" when Lucy and Nathan were young, and neither my spouse nor I was doing marriage or practicing our faith very well. I'm sure this had roots further back, but the halfway marker in our relationship is the point at which I personally became aware of it and identified it as a major issue; something I needed to work on and get under control.

I discovered through my journey in therapy that the spending habits I developed were efforts to fill emotional voids in my marriage. The act of buying "stuff" created a euphoria that gave me a temporary high and feelings of control and contentment. The consequences did not register until after the deed was done. Thinking through to possible results was irrelevant at the moment. Over time, I became proficient at "robbing Peter to pay Paul."

I tried to repent for my money mismanagement fiascos in our marriage. One Christmas just before the end of our union, I asked my husband for forgiveness concerning the financial follies I had thrown into our relationship. His gift that year was a small box filled with the slivers of every credit card I possessed. I wrote him an apology which included a list of the cards with balances. I wrote out a promissory statement declaring I would make better monetary choices in the future. I said I would always talk about large purchases with him, and we would make them together. I also voluntarily relinquished my checkbook. He proceeded to go a step further by removing my name from all of our accounts. Make no mistake; my spouse had every right to be upset, concerned, and angry over my spending habits. He ***DID NOT*** have any reason, ***EVER***, to use harmful physical force and restraint against me.

About a year before our final visit from *Anger and Rage,* the two most unwelcome elements in our marriage, my husband pounced yet again. The results caused me to land in a closet, and I sustain a bump on my head. I dug myself out of the shoes and clothes that had fallen in on me. I got to my feet and steadied myself. I put my hands out in front of me, looked my menacing spouse in the eye, and said in a flat, biting tone, "You better listen to, and remember, what I am about to say. You will not hurt me again. I don't know what I'll do about it, but it's not going to happen anymore. I don't want a divorce, but I will not get hurt anymore. It's going to stop!"

I thought he was going to "punch my lights out." As he swung in my direction, he diverted his clenched fist downward, turned, and headed for the back door. I should have just let him go, but I followed him demanding to know where he was going. He walked out of the door that led to the carport, and he walked down the passenger side of our van toward the driveway and street. He lifted his fist, still clenched from the bedroom scene, and punched the center of the rear side window. It shattered into a million tiny pieces with one blow. If that had been my face, I don't think I would be sitting here writing my story.

Things remained chilled between us from that point on. I totally disconnected from him. My feelings toward him were frozen. This chilly silent season lasted for many months. I knew we had drifted dangerously far apart. I do not remember the month or time of year in which the final abusive episode in our marriage took place, but Nathan was home visiting. I remember he and his dad had been watching movies all day. The surround-sound system bugged me; it hurt my ears. They had watched *The Lord of the Rings Trilogy.* Nathan and his dad went to bed around nine or ten o'clock.

Physical therapy associated with the stroke issues was paying off. I had graduated from my leg braces, walker, and cane, and I was able to maneuver my way around the house unassisted. My girls and I were going to camp-out in the living room and have a girl's night, the first one in a long while. We planned to watch a movie Lucy had picked.

My daughters went to the kitchen to prepare snacks, and I went to the living room to put the DVD in the player. By the time the disc came on, I had made my way to the dining area of the kitchen. The surround-sound system had been left on and was set at a very loud level. It kicked in; and before I could turn around to go deal with the volume, I heard my husband yell from the back bedroom, "Get quiet, I need to sleep." His tone frightened me; I knew he was really mad.

I turned around in the kitchen to head back to the living room to take care of the sound problem. However, I wasn't fast enough; I saw my spouse coming down the hall toward me. He had that look, and I knew I was in trouble. I could tell I was not going to be able to stop him this time. He was yelling something about the volume and sleep. I think I told my girls to get out of the way, to go to their rooms and stay there. I didn't want them to witness what I knew was about to take place. Intruders *Anger and Rage* were on the scene, and it was not going to be pretty.

I don't recall my next actions in the midst of this conflict. My daughters have told me that as my angry spouse made his way down the hall to deal with me, I was throwing shoes and objects at him. I do remember trying to stay out of his grasp. I knew if he caught me in a wrestling hold, I'd be finished. I hated being trapped in those maneuvers; I dreaded them terribly. My only thought was to deter and avoid him long enough to get my keys, grab my purse, get out of the back door, and escape to the car; this was my usual course of action.

My keys were hanging on a hook by the carport door. I reached for them, got them in my hand, and managed to unlock the back door. I opened it, intending to leave. The next thing I knew, I was lying face down on the floor, and I was crying. I have no idea what I was saying, but my words fueled his anger.

Just as I knew he would if he ever caught me, he began tossing me around using wrestling maneuvers. I don't know how I got away from my angry husband. Maybe he just finally let go of me, possibly thinking he had subdued me, and I was under control. I got up and headed for the back door. All I could think about was getting out of danger and getting away.

Any time one of our arguments led to a physical altercation, I would run away to collect myself. I had to disconnect from the episode to defuse and think; this time was no different. My spouse hurt me pretty badly; I needed to escape so I could reflect upon what had happened. Because I was still trying to run, he tried to stop me again. A karate kick and another wrestling hold came into play. I didn't know where my girls were during all of this.

For the first time, ever, I knew for sure my girls saw their dad physically hurting me, and they were old enough to remember it. These things were usually played out behind closed doors or when the kids were not home. I was not sure if Lucy had any memory of the episode concerning her unborn sister, but she was definitely old enough to recall all of this. I couldn't let my daughters think that this behavior was acceptable or excusable. Though things were very much the same as the times before, this event differed in that I knew my girls were aware of what was happening; they were eyewitnesses.

Somehow, I managed to get away. The back door had been an unsuccessful escape route, so I headed for the front door. I got to my car, only to find him standing there with the hood up disconnecting everything; this was typical. I desperately wanted to get away, I grabbed an object from the top of his toolbox and threatened him with it. He reconnected the wires and let me go; this had never happened before when the detachment of car parts was involved.

I peeled out of the driveway intending to follow my usual plan of action. I would hurry down the road for many miles and head toward the next town. I would follow a major highway and then aim toward the interstate; I would drive for hours. I would yell and cry the entire way. I would say whatever I needed to voice while he was not present, to get it all out of my system. Eventually, I would arrive at a rest stop somewhere along the interstate. I would stop to rest, and sometimes I would sleep there. I would war within myself and struggle with what my part had been in the situation.

Over time, I would calm down. I would come to the conclusion I had dealt with everything that had happened, and it was time for me to head back to the house. I would arrive home before dawn and apologize to him for my part in the scuffle, pretty much taking on all of the blame for creating an explosive situation. The cycle was always the same.

This round began in usual fashion. I hit the lonely, dark state highway that led to a neighboring town. Halfway there, I rolled down my window and threw my wedding rings out onto the road. That thought and action had never crossed my mind before that moment. The rings were lost, gone forever. I continued to drive, uncontrollably crying the whole while. I was also talking to God, out loud. The gas indicator came on to warn me that I would be running out of fuel soon; I needed to stop for gas.

As I drove, I became acutely aware that my face was stinging bitterly, and my right side was aching. I tried to look in the mirror to see my face, but there wasn't enough light; it was too dark to see details. When I arrived at the gas station my face was hurting terribly, and breathing made my side ache. I filled my car with gas and paid at the pump.

I decided to run into the store to get two cold bottles of water; one was to hold on my face and side to help alleviate the pain, and the other was to drink. I grabbed a couple of dollars from my purse so I could throw them onto the counter to pay for the drinks; then I wouldn't have to wait for change. I would tell them to keep the money, and I would just keep moving. I walked in quickly, turned toward the cold case, and didn't make eye contact with anyone. I noticed a stocky man sitting on a stool facing the door; as I walked by him, he said, "Good evening." I didn't answer.

I ducked my head downward and headed toward the refrigerated section. I got my icy bottles of water, walked up front, threw the money on the counter, told them to keep the change, and kept walking; I never stopped or hesitated. I hurried to my car. As I opened the driver's door, I heard a man behind me say, "Ma'am are you alright?" I didn't look at him and raised my hand, waving it in an answer that I was okay.

"Ma'am, I don't think you're okay; you don't look like you need to be driving," he said. I told him I was fine. I shut the door and started my car. When I looked up to pull away, two Sheriff's Deputy cars pulled in and blocked my front and rear bumpers at the pump; I couldn't move. I sat back stunned. The man who followed me outside grabbed the door handle. I rolled down my window for more air.

The man and the deputies proceeded to ask me a series of questions. The guy who followed me to my car apologized for calling his buddies. He identified himself as an off-duty officer. He informed me that I was hurt, and it looked like I was in trouble. He wanted to know what had happened; I didn't answer. The deputies concluded I had not been in a wreck because my car was not damaged; they began to ask questions, trying to determine how I had gotten hurt. They did their best to convince me that what had happened was wrong in every way, and whoever inflicted my injuries needed to answer for their actions.

CHAPTER 17

The Final Curtain

Change of Plans

When I left home that night, it was never my intention for the story to unfold as it did. I fully intended to follow my regular game plan and arrive home some time before dawn the next morning. The reconnection of the car wires and ditching of the rings was only the beginning of twists to my customary pattern of dealing with these events.

The abuse incident happened in my home township. The officers who stopped me at the pump were not able to do much because I had crossed jurisdiction lines. They said they were not going to let me drive any further by myself, due to my fragile emotional state. They offered to escort me back to my home county. I didn't want to go back, but I had no choice. Once there, the deputies escorted me to my small-town police department where officers were awaiting my arrival.

I was led into the station; three officers waiting inside. One was at the desk filling out a report; another was milling around in a desk straightening things; the third stood behind my right shoulder after I was seated. All three asked questions about what had happened; they pretty much figured out the story. I listened but remained mostly silent and crying.

I was trying not to make a massive deal out of everything. I wanted to get out of there so I could go deal with my situation the way I always had. The female officer got perturbed with me because I wouldn't sign a formal complaint against my husband. The officers wanted to arrest him; they did everything they could to convince me to sign assault and battery charges. I couldn't bring myself to do that. The lady officer finally got so irritated, she bent down in front of me and in a stern voice asked if I had seen my face. I shook my head, *NO*.

The policewoman told me as soon as they were finished questioning me, they were sending me to the hospital to get checked out to make sure I was okay; I could have hidden injuries. She grabbed my elbow and escorted me to the restroom. The female officer placed me in front of the mirror so I could see what my face really looked like. She asked me if I realized what my husband had done to me. She moved me closer to the mirror, raised my chin, and made me look.

I was shocked and shaken when I saw the extent of my injuries. I burst into a new fit of tears. My face was distorted; I did not recognize myself. My entire face was multiple colors, swollen, and it was stinging badly. I looked like I had been in a fight or a car wreck. She examined my throbbing side. There was a massive bruise across my right, lower rib area, and it hurt like crazy when she barely touched it. She said I would be lucky if some of my ribs weren't broken.

As soon as I left the house that night, I knew this was the worst beating my spouse had ever given me; but, I was clueless as to the extent of my injuries; he had never before hurt me this severely. I was appalled when I saw my face. This time his rage had escalated beyond anything I could imagine. It was absolutely unbelievable; yet, it had happened. The officer took me back out to the main office. The man at the desk put the paperwork in front of me and placed an ink pen in my hand. I sat there crying; I still could not bring myself to sign that document.

Then one of the officers asked the magic questions. "Are you going to sit there and let this end like this? You mean to tell me that you are going to send your girls the message that it's okay to let their boyfriend or husband do this and get away with it? Are you going to let your daughters believe the lie that someone who is supposed to love and care about them has the right to hurt them this severely? You're going to tell them this is okay?" As tears coursed down my face and memories of my prayers asking that the cycle of abuse would end with me raced through my mind, I signed the papers. This was the first time I ever made the abuse public, and I officially pressed charges of assault and battery against my spouse.

The officers escorted me home, and we entered through the front door. They went into the bedroom and got my husband out of bed; they brought him to the kitchen. They handcuffed him and sat him in a chair. They began to question him to hear his explanation of the night's events. He acted like he was sleepy and disoriented, and he glanced in my direction. I was standing against the wall in the hallway just outside of the kitchen door. He looked at me sleepily and said, "Oh, Nora, sweetie, what happened to you? Are you okay?"

Anger flashed over me in that second. My husband took no responsibility for what he had done. I had spent the last several hours going over and over what had happened; agonizing, trying to figure out what I had done to tick him off so terribly. He had the audacity to sit there and act like he didn't have a clue about what happened. I recognized that my spouse was more awake than he was pretending. I discerned as I caught his eye in that instant, he knew beyond a doubt what he was doing and saying; he was acting clueless on purpose. I screamed at him, "You know what happened to me. You did this." (pointing to my face) "You hit me!"

He didn't say another word. The officers arrested him and hauled him off to jail. They escorted me to the hospital. I left the medical center in the wee hours of the morning with instructions for taking care of my facial injuries and three cracked ribs, at least they weren't broken. I carried a prescription for pain medication home with me as well.

What About the Kids

The police told me I would have a few days to decide what to do about living arrangements because my husband would be incarcerated. They warned me that it wasn't a wise idea to reside with him at this point because of the level of anger and rage involved in the conflict; his rage had escalated to a new height of extreme force and violence. I could be in danger, particularly if he hadn't cooled down. One of the officers pointed out the fact that stewing in jail for a few days would *not* have a cooling-off effect.

I spent those days gathering some of my things and putting them in my car. I knew I had to leave. Why? Why did I not put his things out and demand he depart? I struggled with this portion of the situation. I had no money nor access to any; all I had was a gas credit card and twenty dollars in cash. I had nowhere to go. I couldn't drag my kids away from their home. My spouse didn't have issues with his children; he had major problems with me. The kids would be safe with him; I was not leaving them in danger. Depending on what happened, I could regroup and have them with me at a later date. My health and safety were at stake, and these were my immediate concerns and dilemma.

My spouse had income, a job, and a way to provide for our children. My kids needed to stay in the same school and surroundings with which they were familiar. They had grown up in this town; their friends and lives were here. All of these factors made it clear to me that my children should stay at the house, their home. Things were not going to be normal, but they needed to remain as close to routine as possible. The fewer changes that took place, the better it would be for them.

I wasn't sure I could deal with what was happening. As I faced the issue of what to do about my children, I felt like I was running in overdrive and my mind kept saying, "They'll be okay with him, but you're not. They'll be safe; you are not. You have to get out, get out now. You told him you were leaving if it ever happened again." I was conflicted and confused.

I explained to my kids that either their dad or I had to leave. I told them it wouldn't hurt my feelings, and I would understand if they wanted their father to stay at the house instead of me—I totally lied. This was the right thing because I could not take care of them properly at that moment. I did not have access to any resources; for now, my kids would be better off with their dad. This decision is up there in the top ten of the hardest things I've ever done, walking away from my children.

A Fish Out of Water

My husband was scheduled to be released from jail, and it was time for me to leave. I went to stay with a dear friend of mine in a neighboring town. It had been twenty-six years since Melissa Jane arranged my wedding dress and veil as I got ready to walk the aisle; ten years had passed since Naomi almost drowned in her pool. Melissa Jane and her husband were gracious enough to invite me to stay in their home for the duration of whatever was about to happen in my life. I can never thank them enough for helping me when I had nowhere to turn.

My memories of the next six to eight months are vague, cloudy, and few. I remember my sister's anger when she saw my injuries. I remember Melissa Jane provided me a place to live, and she helped me in many ways. I got a job, and I went to the domestic violence counseling center. After a few months, I moved into a cute cottage-type house and searched for a place to connect to a church.

I was trying to identify myself and figure out what I was going to do with the rest of my life; I literally could not figure out who I was. Everything I ever possessed, accomplished, or poured my efforts into no longer existed; I didn't fit anywhere. I wasn't Nora Alexander; she ceased to exist twenty-six years ago when she married. My married-self no longer existed because my marriage was over, and my husband was seeking a divorce. Because my marriage had disintegrated, I was no longer a wife. I was not a teacher; I'd been out of the classroom way too long, fifteen years. I wasn't a mom; my children were not in my care. I was no longer a successful beauty consultant; I left that behind when I ran. I was not a preacher's wife; it had been quite some time since I served in that capacity. I was not a daughter; both of my parents were deceased. In my head, I relentlessly asked myself, "Who am I?" I heard, "You're *NOBODY*."

I was confused and completely lost, floundering like a fish out of water. I was in a position where I could neither offer nor receive love. My emotions were stone cold, and I was spiritually frozen. I tried to connect with my estranged spouse a few times during our separation. I wanted to talk about and work through our situation, but he was not interested. I did everything I could think of to stay married. I even went to the district attorney's office to drop the charges I had filed against him—I learned later that this is a typical, textbook behavior of an abused spouse.

One day, I woke up and prepared for work. I walked outside to get in my car; it wasn't there. Sometime in the night, my alienated spouse had come to my home and confiscated my vehicle. I immediately knew where it had gone, but there was nothing I could do. The car was registered in both of our names; he had the legal right to drive it.

The "D" Word

Months after we separated, I received a form of communication from my husband. I got a certified letter in the mail; it was the legal notification stating he had filed for divorce. In our home state, once the six-month separation marker passes, one of the parties involved in the separation can legally sue for divorce. If both individuals sign the request, the proceedings can move forward. If one party refuses to agree, six more months must pass with no attempt at reconciliation. After that period, the individual seeking the divorce may proceed without the cooperation of the spouse. The date for our hearing was set, and the papers advised me to get representation.

When I received this letter, I made a phone call to my estranged husband. I asked him if we could meet for dinner or coffee to discuss things and a possible future. "I can't discuss the case with you," was his only reply. I pleaded with him again to meet with me. I told him I thought our years together were worth fighting to save; I didn't want a divorce. I asked him if the passage of a few short months could diminish all of the pleasant memories and "us" to a case file. I felt we were worth at least a chance to salvage all the "good" from our twenty-six-year union. His response, "I can't discuss the case." Then, I heard CLICK.

Those were the only words spoken, and the last thing I've heard from my husband concerning our marriage. We have never discussed the events; he refused then and still refuses. I signed a piece of paper from the initial notification and returned it in the enclosed envelope. My signature at the bottom of that document was the only active part I played in the actual divorce proceedings.

I tried to procure a lawyer, but I had no money. I got the phone book out and tried to find someone with special rates. I picked a number, called, and made an appointment. The advertisement in the *Yellow Pages* said something about special rates for special circumstances. When I arrived, the attorney sat me down and listened to my story; he asked questions as I shared. I told him I didn't want the divorce, but it looked like I had no choice; my spouse told me to accept it. His exact words were, "Do it now, or I'll do it in six months without you."

I specified I was not going to use my children as pawns or bargaining tools in power plays; they had been hurt enough. I made it clear that I would surrender whatever was necessary to guarantee provision for my kids. I didn't want to procure anything that would aid in their care, welfare, and education. I wanted us to have joint custody with equal say in what would take place in our children's lives and equivalent time to spend with them. I wanted an arrangement where neither of us could make a one-sided decision about our kids against the other parent's choice. These children are not his, and they are not mine; they are ours, and we should both be present and influential in their lives.

I left the lawyer's office dazed, devastated, and fifty dollars poorer—borrowed from my friend against my next paycheck. He told me as soon as I brought him five hundred dollars as a retainer, he would get started. He may as well have asked for a million; it would have been the same difference. I never went back, and I never sought further legal counsel. I had no clue when our court date was scheduled, and I never went. The official date is stamped at the top of the final notification of the divorce that was sent to me by the court.

The decree gave me nothing in the settlement, and it awarded my husband sole custody of our two daughters. Their visitation schedule would be left to his discretion. I don't know why I was granted joint custody of Nathan, but I am thankful. Our marriage legally ended twenty-four days short of our twenty-seventh wedding anniversary. A day that should have dawned in triumph and joyous celebration faded into the dismal dark, carrying with it a casualty—my heart. It would be years before I would be able to detach myself from our union emotionally.

I was defeated. I merely existed, dreading and hating every minute of life. It hurt to breathe. I felt like everything in my life had piled in on top of me, and I was being crushed under the weight. At every turn, it seemed that more and more things were being added to the heap. Though I had been pushed into the pit, and cave-ins happened over and over again, I allowed the spiritual issues in my life to multiply which in turn piled in more dirt, causing me to slowly suffocate. I kept digging a deeper hole. Solomon was such a wise man; he said it this way: "Whoever digs a pit will fall into it" (Proverbs 26:27). He was right.

CHAPTER 18

Wandering in the Wilderness

Depressive Encounters

Nine-eleven, Katrina, Rita and other significant historical events had taken place in recent years, adding more instability and fear to my personal existence. The world around me was a scary place, at home and in my country. Every minute of every day, I was sad and frightened; I lived in terror. Life became so challenging I couldn't face it, and all I wanted to do was escape.

When my final divorce papers arrived, my world had become so horrible I didn't want to exist. I did not want to feel anything; it was all confusing, and it hurt too much. Every situation had become a panic place, and I was alone. Something as simple as going to the grocery store became so uncomfortable, I could hardly breathe. My anxiety levels skyrocketed at the thought of meeting someone I knew. I would have to talk to them, and I might say something wrong, and they might ask questions, and— — —.

One of the hardest things I struggled with was the fact that I knew the Bible says: "God hates divorce" (Malachi 2:16). Truth be told, I didn't like the thought or idea of it either. I firmly believed in the bonds of holy matrimony—I still do. I found myself in the midst of an internal war, as I faced the conflict between what was happening in reality and what I truly believed to be the sacred truth; they contradicted each other.

Finding myself divorced was extremely problematic for me. The demise of my marriage was as devastating of a loss as if my spouse had died, leaving me a widow. (Given the emotions associated with my feelings of abandonment and worthiness, his physical death may have been easier to deal with; though I realize that would have been extremely difficult as well.) I lost my entire family in the events of one night. I found myself labeled, tagged as being shameful and wrong; and, it was permanent. I was wearing it, whether I wanted to or not; this added to my already overloaded brain, and it magnified my emotional instability.

A Hidden Monster

Depression can be a serious condition, and it can become life-threatening. Left unchecked, it is a destructive life-disintegrating disorder. Divorce, abuse, being on my own and alone, and various health issues were only a portion of the reasons for my severely diminished state. There was something far more sinister and frightening present in my life; I was caught in its clutches, yet unaware of its presence. It was devouring me, and I didn't even know it. I had found a way to survive, but it led me to death's door. Unknowingly, I stepped into the lair of evil; I discovered the monster known as *addiction*.

Prescription drugs are brilliant inventions, created to help us in times of crisis and need. Many people have benefited from some pretty potent pills available on the market these days. There is nothing wrong with taking medication when it is needed and necessary. However, when physical necessity becomes an emotional dependency, the real problems begin. I stepped into the world of addiction when I chose to alter the directions on the pill bottles. I no longer used the medication to treat a problem; I took the pills because I thought I needed them to survive.

Nagging questions and statements ate away at me, daily tormenting me with doubt and destroying my self-image. *What had I done that was so horribly unforgivable? Why didn't my husband love me enough to fight for our marriage? Isn't it shameful and wrong to be divorced? Isn't it against God? I can never get married again. My kids don't want to live with me; they don't even like me. Nobody cares about me anymore; they don't even pretend to be concerned. I'm too much trouble to deal with. My depression issues made me miserable to be around; he had every reason to divorce me. I had become the wife and woman no man wanted; no wonder he wanted out.* These thoughts and others haunted me day and night, slowly driving me further into mental illness.

Over time my medication list changed often and continued to grow in number; the dosages changed, continually increasing in strength and amount. In the beginning, the label read: "Take one at night to help sleep." Now it said: "Take one tablet *up to three times per day to control anxiety, and take two at night to help with sleep.*" A new element had been introduced into the administration of my meds; now, I had control over the number of pills I could take in a day. This freedom was the catalyst that fueled my addictive life.

You're A Christian

The depression worsened over time, and several of the medications prescribed to me altered my personality. Before this depression saga that plagued the last few years of my marriage ended in calamity, I would be on twenty-one different prescription drugs. Not twenty-one collectively over time, I would be taking all of them concurrently on a daily basis. This regime continued over the course of a few years, but I never got better; I just kept sinking deeper into depression. I realize my spouse dealt with some very challenging hardships because of this; it is still not a reason for abuse.

To my knowledge, I never went out and purchased drugs illegally, but I learned how to get what I wanted from doctors. A neighbor who had illicit drug use behaviors pursued me as a friend; she sought me out, wanting access to my personal prescriptions. We drug swapped a few times—bad idea. Even in my debilitated state, God convicted me about this; I knew it was wrong, and I put a stop to it. After I refused to participate in this behavior anymore, my neighbor never spoke to me again. By the time I was divorced, I had become the shell of a person; an individual who was bodily present but otherwise absent. I felt nothing, and I existed in a zombie-like state.

My behaviors at this time, driven by outside influences and drugs, were indicative of a life without Christ. However, I had been a Christian since the age of fourteen. Christ was the only speck of goodness and light that remained in my life. I sank so far down into the pit of darkness, everything around me appeared as gloomy shadows. My failure came because I stopped looking to Jesus for my strength and comfort. His glow and illuminating power had almost been extinguished. However, because I was a believer and still breathing, there was *a flicker of hope* remaining somewhere within me; once ours, it can *never* be taken away.

Why would a believer in Jesus Christ, in a relationship with God, ever fall victim to addiction or any other sin? The answer is simple, yet complicated at the same time. I can speak only from my personal experience with this matter and what I believe to be truth.

I needed to remember that there is no situation too big for God to handle. He knows everything that is going on in our lives, and He is sovereign over all of it. Satan had attacked my mind, and I fell captive to his lies and twisted truth. I stopped running to the only source that could protect me and deliver me from this hell. I needed to act on the knowledge that there is absolutely nothing we bring to our Savior that He will not forgive. He died to take on the very sins we choose to keep, and only He can conquer those that are so difficult to release. There is not a place where He can't find us, even if we think we are at the ends of the earth. He knows where they are; He created them.

"Hear my cry, O God; attend to my prayer. From the end of the earth I will cry to You when my heart is overwhelmed; lead me to the rock that is higher than I" (Psalm 61:1–2). Every relationship with God is salvageable in Christ Jesus. Ignoring the conviction of His Holy Spirit is the only thing that will keep us from His presence, and that will steal our joy.

Every time I chose to ignore the still small voice within me that said, "Pick up My word and find comfort," I placed a barrier in my relationship with God. Every time I turned to pills instead of prayer, I strengthened the strongholds of evil in my life. Every time I stayed away from other believers, I weakened my ability to defend myself. The answers I needed, and the help I longed for, would come when I cried out, "Oh, God, hear my cry."

Errors in Judgment

Sometime after my divorce was final, and during fall session at the local university, my friend's daughter was issued a college assignment to check out online dating sites. She was supposed to sign up, play with the system, and write a comparison paper on the modern way to meet and date via the internet; this was a new phenomenon that had become more widely accepted in our era of modern technology and advanced communication systems. She was married and didn't want to go online to talk with men. She asked me if I would "get connected" in her place. She wanted me to investigate the ins and outs of the processes on three different sites. At first, I emphatically said, "No."

Her final argument and appeal got to me. She didn't want to have to explain to her children why she was visiting a dating site and messaging men she did not know, while their daddy sat in the other room. She was also running out of time to get the project done. I surrendered and decided to help her with the assignment.

Agreeing was my first step toward trouble. My second mistake was making a choice to remain on these sites after the task was completed. My third error in judgment was deciding to meet with some of the members from these posts. My final move into danger was leaping headlong into a search for someone to care about me; I wanted to be loved.

I made several acquaintances during this project. While there are some men of respect, honor, and good intentions who use these sites as a legitimate avenue to meet women, there are those who are unscrupulous. The member from two towns over was great, and a man from the state just north of me was kind; they were courteous, non-threatening, and respectful. I enjoyed my subsequent dinners with them. Even though I had no defenses and emotionally I was an easy mark, they chose not take advantage; they were gentlemen. I appreciate their courteous treatment.

Of the three local men with whom I had interacted, only one was reprehensible. We had returned from dinner, and he walked me to the porch of my cottage. I didn't invite him in, and I said good night. As I tried to close the door, he placed his foot across the threshold. He pushed his way into my living room. He felt he was entitled to a "reward" for taking me out to eat. He did not understand the meaning of the word "No." He forcefully took what he thought he deserved.

I resisted and struggled at first, but then my self-doubt and loathing surfaced. Why should I care? I was worthless anyway. After a few minutes, I stopped fighting and closed my eyes, praying it would be over soon. He finally left. I got up and locked the door. I got my pillow and blanket from the bed, took a handful of pills, and slept in the bathtub that night.

My fourth internet encounter was from a distant state. By this point, my world had spun completely out of control; I wasn't thinking rationally. I let each day happen as it may, and I said, "Yes," "why not," or "who cares," to whatever happened. I think a hidden part of me was trying to prove something. What? I have no clue. I had no purpose in life, and I didn't care about anything. I told God I would rather be dead than living in my messed-up world. My daily prayer was: "God, can you just take me home, so it will all be over?" As each new day dawned, I found myself hoping and wishing it would be my last.

I continued to chat with my newfound internet contact for several weeks. He finally decided to come and visit me; we were going to meet in person. He made this trip twice during our time of correspondence. I have few memories of him and the events that took place at this junction in my life. Here is the account of my cyber acquaintance.

> I didn't remember him, his name, or the extent of our relationship until I had been out of the hospital for a few weeks. I was at my brother's house recuperating when a faint recollection surfaced. The remembrance emerged the morning my brother introduced me to his best friend. When he called his friend's name, I was thrown back into a memory that was in my amnesic past. All of a sudden, I felt panicky and unsafe.
>
> My brother's friend possessed the same name as a mysterious person with whom I had some kind of encounter, and the introduction triggered the recall. I excused myself after the initial dialogue and went to my room to deal with my shadowed memory.
>
> The feelings that accompanied this event were troubling. At this point in my recovery, I was having dreams about a man, a dog, and an elderly woman; they had been reoccurring since my hospitalization, but they made no sense to me. The people involved were faceless. The day my brother introduced me to his friend ignited a season of nightmares about these featureless personalities, and that name kept resurfacing in my sleep.
>
> I told my therapist what happened at my brothers and that I knew my reaction was tied to the dreams in some way. During appointments, we embarked on a search to discover who these characters were and

what this missing portion of my past contained so I could leave them behind and move forward. Over time, I worked my way through this mystery and found a few answers.

My therapist told me to ask my sister what she knew about this man, if anything, so we could use the data during our sessions. She said that I had spent a few months with this internet friend. I left my small cottage and went to live with him in his hometown and state.

I had no remembrance of marrying him, but documented evidence indicates I did. The only reason I can think of as to why I wed is because of my belief and stance on physical relationships outside of marriage. I would not and could not just live with him.

My sister stated that environment was not safe, and this man was not kind. When I finally did remember parts of the story, they revealed that the man had pushed his elderly mother to the ground because she had let the dog out of the house, and the dog had run away; this scene led to a major altercation at Ms. Sue's house. A loaded pistol was involved in the ensuing drama. I discovered I had managed to find another man who thought it was okay to handle the women in his life with physical force and fear. My internet contact's actions led to the police being called, and he was escorted from the premises in handcuffs; a restraining order was issued against him at that time.

In the midst of recovering some details of this memory, another surfaced. One of the deputies who responded to the domestic call that day ended up being a foe, not a friend. He returned to our house

> nine hours after writing the report and arresting Ms. Sue's son. When he got off duty that evening, he called me and asked if he could come by to make sure we, the ladies in the house, were okay and safe. Before his courtesy call ended, I was another notch on his belt. He crossed professional lines, giving new meaning to "above and beyond the call of duty."

This relationship and events associated with it ended with a culminating episode that would leave me homeless. A few days after the dog, man, and deputy episode I was legally banned from the property and barred from seeing Ms. Sue. I was put in a cab and driven to a local shelter. Official documents indicate that within three days of my arrival at this center, I was served legal papers; four or five weeks after marrying, another man decided I wasn't worth his efforts.

I forfeited most of my remaining earthly goods when I left this man and his home. I did manage to keep some of my clothes, shoes, and a few personal belongings. For the first time in all that had happened in my life, I was alone with no place to go. I had no friends, no family, no home, no car, no church, and no money. Technically, I was homeless and cut off from any source of support or help. I didn't know who or where I was or what my next step would be, and I didn't possess the presence of mind to contact anyone from my past. I had separated so far from that world I couldn't think of anyone who might remotely care. In my thoughts, they had already proven to me that they were too busy and burdened with issues of their own to take on me and mine.

The Lost Sheep is Found

My sister, Jane, can be tenacious at times. *Do not* get in her way when she is determined to accomplish something. She will bowl you down, roll over you, and keep searching until she finds that for which she has been looking. I am blessed to have a sister like her.

God used her and her dogged determination to bring me to a place where I could get the help I needed. I am here today because she refused to stop looking and caring for me.

Do not ask me who Suzie Somebody was; I can't tell you. I had become her, both in my mind and in my private world of survival. She was my new identity; I was lost in another existence. After the drama of the man, the woman, the dog, and the gun I went silent and disappeared for several weeks. No one knew where I was, and I was clueless.

My sister somehow managed to track me down. She found me at the Salvation Army center under an assumed name. She drove to the state where the center was located, packed me up, and brought me back to her home. (Jane told me this portion of the story; I do not remember it.)

I stayed at her house one night. I don't know what I did, but I scared her and her family pretty badly. My behavior was too bizarre; I was not her sister Nora, whom she knew and loved. I was *Suzie Looney Somebody.* I looked like her sister, but I was a stranger, a person she did not know. She connected me with the local Domestic Violence Center because she didn't know where else to turn. I was given a room at one of the local safe houses.

I look back at this time, and I can tell you that I was constantly in and out of reality, more out than in. My greatest realism: *I wanted out of this world.* I concluded it was time for me to leave this planet. In my mind and according to my truth, I was useless, worthless, unnecessary, and in the way. I was tired, and I wanted it all to end. I was tired of searching for things I was never going to find. I was tired of being confused. I was tired of being lost. I was tired of being unwanted. I was tired of being unloved. I was tired of being lonely. I was tired of being in constant physical pain. I was tired of being sick. I was tired of being tired. I was tired of being sick and tired.

One night at the women's shelter, I went to my locker and got my medications. I had recently renewed them, so all of the bottles were full. I took my bath and fixed myself a Coke, a big one. I took seven bottles of what I thought were the most potent of my meds from the locker and carried them to my room. The manager of the house was watching a movie in the den which was located at the back of the house. There were no other clients in the shelter at that time, so I had a private room.

I set up the CD player and pulled my Michael W. Smith disc and a recording of *The Prayer*, performed by Heather Headley and Andrea Bocelli, out of the case. I inserted the music, got my soda and meds, went to my room, and lowered the lights. I turned on the Bocelli CD and paused at *The Prayer*. This song is so beautiful; it is about finding rest, shelter, and peace in the place where we belong. For me, that place was heaven with Jesus, and I desperately wanted to go there. I was not going to wait any longer. God was not answering my daily, hourly, minute to minute request to be removed from this world; so, I was going to do it for Him.

I poured the medications out onto my bed, started the music, and began to implement my plan. When I finished consuming one item from each of the seven rows I had created, I went back to the first and started again. I determined I would not be waking up on earth the next morning. It took the whole time the song played for me to work through this process. I don't know how many of the tablets I consumed; I stopped counting at thirty.

When the song was over, I turned on Michael's CD and took a handful of the remaining pills that were laid out and topped off my consumption with more soda. I fluffed my pillows, pulled the blanket over me, got comfortable, and lay there listening; I was ready to drift off to sleep and step into God's eternal presence. Michael's song *Let It Rain* began to play. He was asking God to pour out His power from heaven, and let it rain; God open the floodgates of heaven and let it rain.

Then *Agnus Dei* broke forth; I was transcended. I had no earthly desire to do what I did next, but I got up—Do not ask me how with the number of foreign substances in my system—and staggered through the dining room and kitchen. Then I made my way down the long back hall that led to the den at the rear of the house. I held my right hand out in front of me and opened my clenched fist to reveal a mound of meds. I showed the manager the evidence of what I had done, as I slid down the wall to the floor.

I believe God, through the power of His Holy Spirit, moved me through the length of that house to find the attendant on duty. She called 911; shortly afterward, an ambulance and the police arrived. I was shipped off to the emergency room. They pumped my stomach and made arrangements to send me by ambulance to a behavioral hospital for an extended stay; it was two and one-half hours away. This hospitalization was my first confinement for psychiatric evaluation.

I cannot recall much from my time there. I think I was there for two weeks. I never had a visitor during my stay. I remember how shocked I was when I saw my hospital entry photo. I didn't recognize myself. One day while in line waiting for meds, the patient behind me laughingly said, "You look like an eighty-seven-year-old crack-head w—." She was right; I did, and I didn't think it was funny. It was frightening.

I listened a lot during my stay there, but I did not speak much. I became aware that I was having seizures and experiencing blackouts. The most notable thing I remember is the *Master of Disguise* speech; I could relate. I had spent most of my life in that mode, and I excelled in it. I remember making a comment, "I deserve an Academy Award in that department."

The staff at this hospital stabilized my condition. It was time for me to be release, but I had nowhere to go. My family (my brothers and sister) did not need the burden of taking care of me, and I had no one else in my life. I had no other connections, and I felt like no one cared. Why should they? I didn't. I was nowhere near well, but I was being discharged anyway.

I was released into my sister's custody and care. She found a nursing home in a town near where she resided that was willing to take me as a resident, and for the next seven months this would be my home. By definition I was homeless, but I had a roof over my head and food to eat. Shortly after my arrival at this facility, my mental health deteriorated even further. I managed to escape to another realm that was far away from reality, and I stayed there, ninety-eight percent of the time.

CHAPTER 19

End of My Rope

Hanging by a Thread

My sister became my personal warrior. She fought for me when I could not fend for myself. I had no strength or cognition left, and I was in a severely altered mental state. God used her to set into motion events that were necessary for me to experience. These incidences would bring me to the place where I could finally hear and listen to my Heavenly Father. Jane took care of everything for me. I have no idea the monstrous undertaking she took upon herself when she decided to handle all of the medical and legal details of my illness. I do know the task had to be daunting, but I am thankful she loved me enough to handle the tough stuff, including the hatefulness and anger I dished out in her direction.

I don't remember much about the seven months I spent in the nursing home. I recall that a group of young people from a church came and sang for us. I clung to my music and my Michael W. Smith CD; I played it every day, multiple times per day. It was the one thing I connected with that kept me grounded to my only reality; I belonged to God because of Jesus.

After being at this center for a time, I began hallucinating. Toward the end of my confinement in this facility, I was transferred from a private room to a semi-private one. I saw a demon, a monster if you will, every time I looked at my roommate. I could hear adults screaming day and night. I was afraid and miserable, and there were spiders and bats everywhere.

I would tell you I had no faith or hope, and I had lost all interest in church, and that I was the worst example of a child of God you could ever see. A subsequent visit to this facility, after my deliverance, revealed a different story. I am told that I attended church services almost every week while residing here, and I sang a solo or two. I remember none of this.

It was early September, and I had just finished going through the process of reliving the death of my first child; it was the twenty-third anniversary of this event. The anniversary of my brother's death had passed a few months before this, and it was also the first anniversary of the date my husband had legally cut me out of his and my children's lives. Just a few weeks in the future, the anniversary of my mother's death hovered on the horizon. I had not seen my three children for two years. I could not get to them, and they were not allowed to come to me.

Once again, I made the decision that it was time for me to exit this world. Only this time, I was determined to be successful. I took one of the pictures of my babies down from a shelf in my room and removed the glass from the frame. I broke off a shard and threw the rest of the glass into the trash. Then I put the picture back together and placed the framed photo back on the shelf so no one would notice anything amiss. I had a burgundy velour robe which I laid over my lap so I could hide the results of what I was about to do. I laid two bath towels over my knees, and I put the robe over the top of them; next, I draped the rest of it down the front of my legs. I placed the jagged glass in my hand, hiding my weapon and hands under the covering. Then, I proceeded to implement my plan.

I asked God to let my family know this was not about hurting them; it was about relieving them of having to deal with me and my care. They did not need the burden of a crazy needy sister. It was about my desire to destroy myself and remove myself from life; I was nothing but trouble for everyone who knew me. I was thoroughly convinced of the lies Satan unrelentingly threw my way. Lies that said I had ruined my witness as a believer, and God could never use me for His glory or kingdom ever again; I begged God not to be mad at me. I asked Him to forgive me for what I was doing and beseeched Him to let me come home, never doubting for a moment that Heaven was my destination. I worked diligently at my endeavor, and I never felt a thing.

I was completely broken and shattered inside; I was beyond miserable and despondent. I had zero hope that the rest of my life would be any different than it was right then at that very moment. I was forty-eight, in a nursing home, wearing diapers, being bathed, not eating, and homeless with no immediate family or possessions; I was alone and had been floundering and wondering for two years. I was tired of crying myself to sleep every night, and I wanted out. It hurt terribly to feel like no one loved me; thinking that no one ever would drove the heartache even deeper. I had botched and ruined everything in my life, and I had made too many impetuous and foolish decisions. I entered a state of complete and utter hopelessness. Nothing short of a death sentence would do; therefore, I pronounced it.

I was talking to God the entire time I worked on my project. In the middle of my efforts, my sister and niece walked into the room to visit. I stopped what I was doing and quickly searched for a way to get them to leave. I think I managed to make my sister angry. Whatever I did or said worked; Jane and her daughter gathered their things and left. I rolled my chair over to the door and pushed it closed. I left it barely cracked, and then I resumed my final task.

A nursing home worker interrupted my progress and brought my dinner tray. She sat it down on a small table in my room and left; I continued with my plan. The damage became quite pronounced, and I was feeling weak. My robe was a dark red color, so I was able to conceal what was happening pretty well; I was hoping no one would notice what I was doing. I rolled my chair over to the bed and crawled on top of the covers. A couple of aides came into the room and said something to me. I got mad and yelled at them—hissed and spewed would be more descriptive. I demanded they leave. They were laughing as they exited, and I remember screaming: "You won't be laughing tomorrow!"

I hunkered down in my bed and took one final stroke. I was successful. I could tell I was sinking fast. The charge nurse entered my room; I thought she was there to read me the riot act for yelling at the assistants. I was barely conscious. The only words and last thing I remember was hearing the nurse say, "Not on my watch you don't!"

Four years would pass before I knew the real reason the nurse had entered my room that evening. My sister told me that I pulled the call cord and activated the signal at the nurse's station; she had come in answer to my call button. I must have unknowingly triggered it when I flung myself back in the bed after screaming at the assistants. That was not in *my* plan, but I believe it was in God's.

I do not know how long I was in the intensive care unit. I have learned through conversations with my sister and older brother that the nursing home where I resided had signed me over to be a ward of the state. Upon my release from the hospital, authorities would be transporting me to a behavioral management facility. I was being shipped to a metro area three hundred miles away for permanent placement in a psychiatric hospital, where I would stay for the remainder of my life.

The paperwork was already completed; I just had to heal enough to travel safely. The nursing home supervisor and staff made this decision because of my almost successful suicide attempt and continued decline in health. Had my brother not arrived and rescued me on that mid-September morning, I would be somewhere in the southern portion of that state living out my life in an institution, merely existing in an altered state; the prognosis was I would not live long anyway.

The Place I Needed to Be

Two things I ponder concerning what I thought would be my last night at the nursing home and my last moments of life. First, of the five framed photos in my room, four had real glass and one held Plexiglass which is a hardened clear plastic; this was unknown to me. I thought they were all glass, but only four of the five pieces were what I needed for my plan to triumph. I had chosen *the only one* that made my task less likely to succeed. Secondly, I had planned everything perfectly. There would be no opportunities for rescue, and I wasn't asking anyone for help this time around. So, how did I get tangled in the pull cord of the call button? That was the last thing I wanted. I usually draped it over the left headboard post of my bed. This particular day, it was lying free in the bedcovers waiting to be snagged. If either of these elements had been absent from the scenario, I would not be sitting here writing my story.

Some things that touched my life do not have clarity, and it is okay if I never understand them; however, many are crystal clear. I know beyond any doubt there are dark things in existence that seek to destroy us, or at the very least trap us in a defeated, damaged state. Emotional abuse, cruel discipline, molestation, and rape are all horrific events to get through and overcome. Physical abuse and emotional neglect in a marriage, and miscarriages are terrible experiences. Constant degrading, fear of people who should be providing safety, ridicule, and depression are brutal encounters. The death of a child, rearing a special needs child, and loss of both parents are excruciating events. The unexpected death of a sibling, the demise of a long marriage, and the premature separation from one's children are cruel occurrences. Drug abuse and addiction, stroke, and extreme emotional distress are devastating in and of themselves. The trauma that mounted and built from the presence of all these circumstances in my life transported me into the harrowing world of mental illness. "For evils beyond number have surrounded me; my iniquities have overtaken me, so that I am not able to see; they are more numerous than the hairs of my head, and my heart has failed me" (Psalm 40:12). This scripture is an exact description of what happened over the course of my journey through life.

These issues caused scars and baggage to accumulate along my pathway. Their assault caused extreme difficulties in my ability to navigate through my days. They worked away at my mind, eventually destroying my spiritual peace. Because of this, all kinds of unhealthy, reactionary behaviors began to develop and grow within me and take over my life. Eventually, I consciously chose to make a final stroke in this world.

This vessel once a beautiful piece of pottery, molded personally by the Master's hand, had been smashed against the rocky places of life. I was shattered, and the pieces of my life were being scattered among the jagged edges of cruelty. The parts that had been ground to powder were being carried away by the winds of destruction. The dust was being delivered to oblivion, assisted by the ruler of deception, Satan.

There I lay, crumbled and in a heap on the cold tile floor of the psychiatric ward at a prominent hospital; the place my brother had chosen to take me. Insanity and craziness filtered through the air as I beat the floor with my fists, begging these would be my final moments on earth. Maybe now, God would grant the desire of my heart and allow me to dwell with Him; finally, I was where I needed to be.

Facing the Truth

I was broken and poured out before my Father who resides in heaven. God and I were in full agreement, as I lay on that floor thinking I was headed to my eternal home. We were in complete harmony, yet we were on two entirely different pages; I just didn't know it at the time. I thought I was facing death and relieved because of it. He was pleased because He finally had me at the point where He could help me live. God had dealt with me many times about the poisons that had built up within me. If I did not relinquish the toxins this time around, spiritual pride and stubbornness would be my final sins; I would die physically.

There is nothing wrong with reacting to trials and hardships that come into our lives; however, when we allow the anguish and anxiety to take root and dominate, they can grow to crisis levels and become deadly. When that happens, it is time to seek God's divine intervention. I was at that final pivot point. I would agree with God that resentment, jealousy, bitterness, selfishness, animosity, envy, anger, self-reliance, and addiction had taken control of my life causing massive decay in every facet of it, or I would cease to breathe. I would repent and surrender all of these malignancies to Him and be delivered from the hold they had on my life, or I would ignore Him again and die physically.

If I had not cried out and chosen repentance and help, I believe my life's journey would have come to an end that day, as I laid on the icy floors of the hospital psychiatric unit. God met me in that moment. In that defining instant, as I lay there thinking all was coming to an end, He revealed a simple truth: *I had to stop blaming everything and everyone else for what was wrong in my spiritual life, and I had to stop trying to handle everything by myself.* It was time for me to face some cold, hard facts and own up to the things for which I was directly responsible.

Illness, both physical and emotional, had infiltrated my life and taken a tremendous toll. Traumas and tragedies had bombarded me with unrelenting cruelty. I had been the victim of many of life's ills; there was no denying that. Now, the most difficult thing with which I had to deal was facing the unrelenting truth. I had allowed sin to permeate my life and take root; it fermented in my soul and grew in deadly strength. My spiritual life had withered away because of neglect, and it was stagnant. I no longer had the internal fortitude to carry on, nor did I possess the will to forge ahead; I was halted in my journey. I was decaying and dying in every facet of my existence; this was the merciless truth confronting me.

Hurt, bitterness, and anger are all natural reactions to things and events that touch us, and they can cause damage. When I allowed the bitterness to embed and take control of me and my reactions, it turned into a deadly deterrent; it became a shackle that grew stronger over time, binding my heart and refuting everything sustaining and nurturing in my spirit. I was starving and spiritually malnourished. The internal battle created by this infiltration, magnified and complicated the physical and emotional problems that were manifesting in my life. I needed to ask God to help me deal with the legitimate hurts that were present in my life. I wanted to be set free from the bondage of bitterness that had me so tightly bound that I could not move. Anger ran deeply; it twisted and distorted everything else in my life as it slowly ate away at me, eroding my heart.

Deliverance

I was at the place of transition, the line between life and physical death; it was the place for which I had been praying. Lightning peeled through my hospital room. (There was no earthly storm brewing outside of my window, but I saw lightening just the same.) This storm was transpiring within the walls of my confinement. My spirit was fighting its way back into the land of the living, caught in the passageway between the exodus from this life and the transition back into the realm of reality. In those moments, I had a distinct vision; I felt like I was living it as I saw it.

> I saw myself suspended over a deep dark chasm, so black I could see nothing. An ebony sea stretched across the vastness that lay before me. With each flash of light, I saw my surroundings: thick, gray slabs of jagged rocks. The gorge was steep, and it was windy and cold.
>
> The weather was brutal, harsh, and stormy. Rain poured down, bombarding my flesh like tiny

needles. Lightning flashed relentlessly, and thunder crashed ruthlessly all around me. The echo was profound, and I couldn't make sense of anything. Words were not distinguishable, and I could not comprehend what was happening. Everything was loud, obnoxious noise, and it was chaotic.

I teetered on a slippery slope in total confusion. I surrendered. I gave up. I couldn't hold on for another second. I succumbed to the war that had been waging around me and raged within me for years. In a split second, I made the distinctive decision to go limp and let go. As I leaned into the dark abyss for my final fall, I lost my footing in this world.

At that moment, I saw a hand reach down and grab the back of my garment, between my shoulder blades. It drew me back into strong arms, where I was cradled, protected, and safe. God had gathered me into His arms, and He held me there securely. I experienced a comfort and peace that I had not felt in a long time; possibly years, maybe even a decade or more. I let go of the string, but God caught the last fiber of thread in his fingertips.

Instantly, He shed light into the pool of darkness; not revealing a cavern, pit or dead end, but exposing the path of my unfinished life. I had been brought back into the Light. The area behind me and that on both sides of me looked like a combat zone. As far as I could see into these arenas, I witnessed the ravages of war. When I turned my gaze to the land stretched before me, the smoke was gone, the terrain was even, and I could see far into the distance. It was bright, crystal clear, blue and fresh. It was pristine and peaceful.

I heard a quiet, gentle voice in my spirit. It said, "You are not alone; you are loved. Nora, I am so glad you are here; I am not finished with you. The journey back will not be easy. At times, it will be frightening, but I will be with you every step of the way. Forgiveness is given when it is actively pursued. You learned that the day you asked Me to be Lord and Savior of your life. You have sought forgiveness now, and you have surely found it. Welcome home My child, 'For I know the plans that I have for you; plans for welfare and not for calamity to give you a future and a hope'" (Jeremiah 29:11, selected sections). Remember Nora, "the joy of the LORD is your strength" (Nehemiah 8:10).

Whiter than Snow

God does not want us to air our dirty laundry and then walk away with the filth and stench still lingering around us. He wants possession of the laundry so He can wash it, making it crisp, clean, and fresh. The sin of addiction and the neglect of my relationship with God had stifled my Father's voice. It is not that He would not deliver me; it was the fact that I had not come to the point where I could admit, I needed to be rescued. I had to admit that part of my problem was wrong choices I had made. Being a victim was a major part of what had brought me to this place, but my personal and private decisions had pushed me to the deepest recesses of the pit. The more I tried to fix things my way, the worse they became. I needed God's help, His design, and His way; that meant total surrender.

I discovered a parallel from the account of the children of Israel found in the Book of Judges. God sent a deliverer or leader, called a judge, every time the Israelites goofed and did what He told them not to do. They found themselves in the midst of calamity because of their disobedience. Therefore, as God said He would, He removed His protective power from their lives; they walked away from His protection. In turn, they found themselves facing and dealing with the hardships and evils of this world, all alone.

We all face difficulties; but there is a distinct difference in facing trials and hardships with God's presence as opposed to facing them without Him, relying on our own strength. If we do not belong to God, we should be terrified; for there is a place of sure death and eternity without Him. Because I am His, I knew I had reached the scariest place there is for a believer on this side of heaven. I had withdrawn from His power, presence, strength, and peace. Therefore, all of the things I had dealt with for so long could now move in close, and Satan could use them to cause havoc in my life. The evil of this world was moving in, trying to take over and make me ineffective.

It is vital to understand Christians cannot be possessed by demons, but they can be demonized, or harassed by demonic forces. I did not start out with the intention of becoming a drug addict. I ended up there because of evil influences and bad choices. I was acting like the children of Israel; I was disobedient, moving away from God and His protection. I was doing things my way, instead of His way.

Each and every time things got bad and unbearable for God's chosen people, they verbally "Cried out" to God. He was always faithful to return them to His presence and help in their time of trouble. They came to a point where they recognized Him for who He is, admitted their sin, identified it, and sought forgiveness. God, in turn, showered love and compassion on His own, offering His mercy and grace. He then granted deliverance. After deliverance, He bestowed peace and rest which stayed in their possession as long as they remained obedient to His ways. (The Book of Judges)

I had finally reached the place I needed to be, total brokenness and dependency. I came to the point where I was ready to confront the whole truth and nothing but the truth. It was on God's terms and on His turf. Facing God was the only way I would ever be completely well; if I wasn't honest in seeking spiritual healing, I was not going to make it physically or emotionally. I just wasn't strong enough. I had arrived at 2 Corinthians 7:1, "Therefore, having these promises, beloved, ***let us cleanse ourselves from all defilement of***

flesh and spirit, perfecting holiness in the fear of God" (bold italics are mine). After this revelation, I cried out in song.

Lord Jesus, I long to be perfectly whole;
I want Thee forever to ransom my soul;
Break down every idol, cast out every foe;
Now wash me, and I shall be whiter than snow.
Whiter than snow, yes, whiter than snow;
Now wash me, and I shall be whiter than snow.
(Whiter Than Snow, James Nicholson, 1872; Public Domain)

I had been in the behavioral unit of this hospital for more than a week, clueless as to who or where I was. As I lay crumpled on the floor, the words from *Whiter Than Snow* drifted from my lips and floated to the ears of my waiting Savior. He had planted the words from Second Corinthians and the lyrics to this magnificent hymn in my head and heart. They made their way through my brain and pierced my soul; this, in turn, caused me to utter a life-changing prayer of deliverance. Lying flat on my face before God, I cried out.

> Oh, Sovereign God of the universe, Yahweh. Hear my cry; please allow me entrance into Your Holy presence.
>
> I do not deserve Your ear or Your lovingkindness. I lie broken before You. I am Your child; yet I come to You ashamed, for I have sought wisdom and comfort in the things of men and this world instead of asking You to be my Deliverer.
>
> I should have been praying and seeking You in all of my troubles. I should have been searching Your Word for the comfort and wisdom that You have for me there. Instead, I have strayed from Your Word and the shelter of Your presence.
>
> I should have been going to church and worshipping You, recognizing that You are God

Almighty, Creator, and Master of ALL things. You are Ruler over everything, even the hardships in life.

Oh God, I have sought escape and comfort in medications and earthly advice. I searched out the counselors of this world first, leaving You behind in my quest. I pursued and used the remedies of men and science before I ever looked for guidance from You. I trusted in the things I could see in this world, instead of turning to You first.

These things have become my world. I looked to them for deliverance from my physical and emotional pain. They have become my idols, and they have taken over as gods in my life; they control everything about me.

In their proper places, these things that You have allowed to come into existence are not wrong. You created them for my benefit. Oh, dear God, right here, right now, I give these drugs to You. Please forgive me for seeking solace in them. I acknowledge You are the only source of Comfort that I need in life.

You, oh God, are the Highest Counselor. It is to You, I run. I have made choices based on selfishness, bitterness, anger, and hurt. Father, I surrender these to You right now. I have snubbed You and lamented my existence. I have questioned and blamed You because of all that is wrong in my life, and I have turned my back on You.

I lost sight of the power of Your Word. I forgot that You are sufficient in all things, and I have neglected to draw my strength from You. Oh God, please, please, please forgive me for these failures.

God, I have completely messed up my life. I give this heap of muddled mess to You. Lord, please take these things and bury them in the deepest part of the ocean, and I ask that You remember them no more.

I bow before You and proclaim that You are God, my Creator. You are the Great Physician and Healer of my body, mind, emotions, and soul. You are the Ruler of life and death; to You, I look for my healing and deliverance.

It is with a repentant heart I am asking You to forgive me for all the ways I have wronged You. Please forgive me for hurting those You have given to me to love. I am begging You to forgive me of the actions I chose; the ones that have taken my life in the direction of evil.

I should have surrendered to the moving of Your Spirit on my life when You revealed to me the things that were separating me from Your abundance, peace, and love. I should have admitted them and given them to You then. I am willfully and intentionally surrendering them to You now.

Father, guide me to the promises You have for me in Your Word. Help me adhere to what You have written to me there. I desire to be obedient, to walk in Your will and in Your ways.

Sustain me in the battles of this life as I face the real hurts that have touched me, for only in You will I be victorious over them. Right now, at this moment, I beseech You to heal my life, every facet of it.

Please be with me and help the doctors as I make my journey toward health. Please put fellow believers who are wise in this world's medicine, in charge of my care. Help me seek and cling to Your leading and wisdom in all future decisions I make.

I have touched the edge of death, and You have pulled me from its grasp. There is a reason for this, though I have no idea what it is. Please help me find my purpose, and give me the strength and courage to live it out for the remainder of my days.

The only thing that can restore my life and transform this pile of broken pieces into a useful vessel is the atoning and healing power of the cross. By the authority of Your Holy Name, I claim that power and ask You to heal and redeem my life for Your honor and glory.

Father, when Satan tries to trick me with his lies or causes me to turn with his deceptive schemes bring them into the Light, so I can accurately identify them for what they are. Help me stand firmly in the knowledge that this enemy has no power over me, though he will try to prove to me that he does.

Thank You, LORD, for Your mercy and grace.

Thank You for forgiving me.

Thank You for showering me with Your kindness.

Thank You for sending healing to me.

Thank You for allowing me into Your presence.

Thank You for saving me for a purpose.

Thank You for the knowledge that You can still use me.

Keep me beside You, behind You, or cradled in Your arms.

Never let me roam ahead of, or away from You again.

Oh, most Holy God of Heaven and earth, I love You.

Thank You for loving me first.

It is in the precious, mighty, awesome,

And most wonderful name of Your Son, Jesus, I pray.

AMEN.

When God put me on my face in that hospital room, I would make a choice. I would listen to what I believe was God's final attempt to get my attention to do things His way, or He would grant my petition and take me home to be with Him. To survive, I had to do what He was telling me. I had to repent of the disobedience and disrespect that took place when I didn't trust Him, and I turned to other things instead of Him. I had to admit my part in the failures of my life and ask for His help in dealing with the real tragedies. If I had not, I believe my life would have ended right there, exactly then. At that moment, God etched and cemented another of His promises on my life. No matter which choice I made, I belonged to Him. I stood in accountability for the things that were amiss in my personal and spiritual life because of my doing. He was waiting for me to surrender.

My sin of addiction would have consequences; I had already experienced many of them, and some penalties would be waiting for me in the future. This path of repentance and forgiveness brought restoration. Healing and freedom from the dark things that had held me captive were granted in those moments. Now, I had to step into the task of regaining my overall health: physically, mentally, emotionally, and spiritually. I was not alone; God would be right there with me in the midst of it all. He would afford me the strength and courage to cope with whatever my future held.

PART 3

Blessed

CHAPTER 20

Reconnect

Do Not Forsake

Those precious moments with God were the last time I awoke on the icy, cold floors of the hospital. The remainder of my days there, I found peaceful sleep under the warm covers of my bed. God brought me back to sanity, reality, and living. More importantly, He drew me back to Himself. He chose to leave me on earth, and I know He has a purpose for my life. He loved me and released me from bondage. My desire is to spend the remainder of my days seeking out that which He has for me to do and share accounts of the incredible ways He has worked in my life.

Approximately one month after attempting to take my life at the nursing home and two weeks after my encounter with God, I ***walked*** out of the hospital into my restored life. I was weak and taking baby steps, knowing I was moving in strength that was not my own. I was headed in the right direction, His way.

One of my top personal priorities upon release from the hospital was to connect with a congregation of believers of the same faith. I had determined in my heart that I would never again forsake the gathering together of myself with other believers. My prayer from that day forward was that God would grant me another opportunity to serve Him and that I would be willing to do exactly that. I determined nothing would wedge its way in and create the vast chasm of emptiness that had formed between my Lord and me, ever again.

My brother who lived one state away from the hospital and his wife invited me to live with them. I am thankful they offered me a home. When we got to their house, and I settled in, I asked if we could go to church somewhere on Sunday. Their response was: "Depending on my brother's work schedule; we might go." We didn't attend a church that weekend. The next week, I asked the same thing. Once again, we didn't go. I watched church services on television as a substitute, and I prayed often. I told God my desire was to be actively in service somewhere; and when I could, I would. I did not ask to go to church anymore. I continued to watch services on television, pray, and read my Bible.

My brother and sister-in-law had taken on a daunting task when they agreed to be the ones to open their home and watch over my initial release. I was not allowed to handle my medications, and I had to keep a rigid routine, similar to the one I had followed at the hospital. I had doctor visits, programs, and therapies to sign up for and meetings and appointments that required scheduling and attendance. I was not allowed to manage my social security money; it was to be controlled by someone else.

All of these tasks fell to my sister-in-law. It took some juggling, but she managed it well. She ensured I went to every appointment. She tracked my medications and guaranteed the dosages were correct. She made sure I connected with everyone with whom I was to be established. She included me in her social activities and introduced me to her friends. She and my brother were instrumental in God's plan for me. I can never thank them enough for the role they played in my recovery.

Things were going on in their lives at this time of which I was not aware. They did not need the stress of dealing with me and my issues; it added too much to their load. About four weeks after moving into their home, we filled out paperwork for housing assistance in the local and neighboring towns. Whichever one became available first would be my new home.

Look out Ashville, here I come. An apartment became available shortly before Thanksgiving. I turned in all of the documentation, qualified, and passed the interview process. My brother decided he wanted me to stay at his house through Christmas; so instead of going back and forth, I stayed. I took the apartment a month before moving in because I did not want to get placed at the bottom of the waiting list and forfeit the unit that was available.

Just short of three months into recovery, on December twenty-seventh, I stepped into my single life; I was on my own. It was time to fly solo, and I was genuinely scared. I continued to read my Bible for comfort, and I talked to God daily. In the beginning, survival was minute by minute, then quarter-hour by quarter-hour, then half-hour by half-hour, and so on; until I reached the day-by-day stage. Day-to-day was my place in the process of healing when I moved to Ashville.

I received a back payment from Social Security. It was enough to cover the deposit and first month's rent on the apartment. There was a little money left over; with that, I bought a refurbished mattress and boxed springs from Salvation Army and purchased a couch from Big Lots. My brother gave me a television and rocking chair. With these four pieces of furniture, two suitcases, and a box of personal items, I moved into my new home. The move, though beneficial for me, caused a temporary setback. My existence was no longer day-to-day; I reverted to minute-by-minute survival.

January dawned bringing a new year, and my new life lay before me. I moved into my apartment on a Friday evening. I spent the first Saturday cleaning and organizing my few possessions. On Sunday I sang, read my Bible, and prayed. I walked through my apartment and prayed over it. During my time with God, I let Him know I had not forgotten about worship. I was going to find a church ASAP (*as soon as possible*). Not one more Sunday would pass without me being in a pew, in a house of worship, somewhere in this city.

I did not have a telephone; so, first thing Monday morning I went to the office of the apartment building in which I resided and asked the manager if she had a phone book I could borrow. I made a list of five churches I could call. Two of them were churches of my faith, and each had a bus ministry. I discovered few churches offer this assistance anymore; this is sad and unfortunate. God has used a bus ministry two times in my life to meet my need for transportation to a place of worship.

I also had in my possession the names and number of a young couple who lived in Ashville. It had been given to me by the man who had brought a group of young people to the nursing home where I had resided. I told him that I had a brother who lived near his town, and I would like to contact the couple if I ever got to go there to visit. I decided to call this couple first. While I was in the office, I asked if I could use the phone. The manager said it would cost me a quarter; I paid up and made the call. I went to church with that young family the following Sunday. The teaching appeared to be biblically based, but the atmosphere was too hectic and loud for me. It was not an acceptable fit.

I had two priority church possibilities on the list I had made from the phone book. The next Monday, I went back to the office and asked if I could use the phone to make another call. It would cost me a quarter, but I was determined to get connected to a local body of believers. I knew if I didn't, it would be my first giant step back into a messed-up life of disobedience. I had purposed in my heart, like Daniel, not to sin against God (Daniel 1:8). God's Word tells me not to forsake the gathering of myself with other believers; therefore, I was determined to find a church home and a place to worship (Hebrews 10:25).

The following Sunday, I visited a local church that provided transportation. No one spoke to me. In turn, I did not speak. When a church filled with fellow believers does not take the time to notice there is a stranger in their midst, it creates an uncomfortable place. I went home and cried. I told God, "Starting over is so hard." It was difficult for me to socialize, and I was still in the stage of forcing myself to interact; it didn't come on its own or easily. I heard in my heart: *I know Nora, but I am with you, and I love you.* I fell asleep.

The next day, I went back to the office and asked if I could use the phone, yet again. I gave the manager another quarter, and she allowed me to make the call. The following Sunday a bus from First Baptist Church came to my home and transported me to church. I felt an instant calm when I entered the facilities. My first thought was: *I can serve here; it's within walking distance of my place. I don't need a car to be involved, and I'm not dependent on anyone for transportation.* Of course, Satan had to throw a dart: *What if no one speaks to you today,* rang through my head. Audibly I said, "I don't care; I will serve God anyway." I smiled; I think Satan tucked his tail and ran.

There was not one person in this congregation who knew me or knew of me. There was no one in the entire city to whom these people could go to get information about me. What they saw was what they got. I knew that no matter how difficult socializing was, I had to give my fears to the Lord and ask Him to help me get connected. It was my responsibility to get "plugged in"; no one else could do it for me.

I had learned my lesson. I am accountable for the choices I make; therefore, no matter what, I was linking myself to this body of believers. I would grow and serve God along with them, whether they wanted me to or not. Three weeks later, I walked the aisle of the sanctuary. Pastor Watts took my hand, and I told him I wanted to move my letter to this church; I wanted to become a member. The congregation chimed a unanimous "Amen"; then they chose to love me.

The Sunday I joined this body of believers, the life group (*Sunday school class*) I attended was having a fish fry. I was invited and offered a ride to the assembly. No one knew I was terrified. I was far outside of my comfort zone. I was in constant prayer the whole evening, asking God to quiet my trembling and help me trust

Him in this portion of my journey. I was embarking on the avenue of friendship. I was frightened because I had not been there for a long time. I had to learn to trust people. I couldn't do that on my own. I needed God's power to face this issue. He granted it, and immediately people within the class began to reach out to me.

The Lullaby Singer

I auditioned for my first choir when I was in the sixth grade. I sang *America the Beautiful* as my tryout song, and I was selected. I have been singing in a choir, ensemble, or some other group ever since. I grew up listening to country music albums which my parents played on their RCA turntable. I spent many Saturdays listening to famous musicians sing and play. During the roughest portion of my illness, I lost my voice. I barely whispered when I spoke, and songs seemed to stick in my throat when I tried to sing. I would tell you I was voiceless for several months; that is how I remember this portion of my life.

Visits back to places where I spent time during my illness brought knowledge that the opposite is true. I discovered that I was known as the "Lullaby Singer" at the nursing home where I had spent several months of my life. Apparently, I rolled from room to room in my wheelchair every night, asking the residents to name their favorite hymn, and then I proceeded to sing it for them. I am told it was a favorite activity of the patients. They looked forward to my visits. I wish I could remember doing this. I am sure I was more blessed than those who listened.

My love for music and songs and their ability to speak to my soul is more alive than ever. I was so excited when God granted me the opportunity, privilege, and courage to step back into a choir. First Baptist had one, and I joined. My first time to stand in the loft was the July Fourth celebration service; this was a gigantic victory in my life. I am thankful God has restored my voice; once again, I can lift it to Him in song. I do not miss many opportunities to do so: "*It is* good to sing praises to our God; for *it is* pleasant, *and* praise is beautiful" (Psalm 147:1, NKJV).

Bible Study, Choir, Servant Hands (a needlework circle, making products for missions), The ROC (Recreation Outreach Center), Life Point (Wednesday Lunch and Prayer), Together (Ladies Keeping in Touch), and visits to the church library filled many moments of my weeks. God introduced me to some delightful, loving Christian friends through these groups at my new church. I simply had to say "*yes,*" when they invited me to participate in activities.

Some of these friendships would be incredibly fantastic. One, in particular, would grow to surpass "remarkable." It was a blessing beyond anything I could have imagined, asked, or thought for myself. It came straight from the heart of God to me, just for me; "For of Him and through Him and to Him *are* all things" (Romans 11:36, NKJV).

Thinking of Others

At the beginning of my recovery, there was no way I could work a job. I had to focus all of my energy on getting physically and mentally healthy and strong. I also concentrated on remaining renewed, spiritually. I recognized the fact that I needed to "get out" during the day and do something, interact with people, and get some fresh air. Part of my recovery was relearning to socialize and connect with others. I came to remember that life is not about my existence only; it is about those around me as well. I asked God to help me look beyond myself and see where I could help others who were hurting or in need. He opened the world of volunteerism to fill all of these needs in my life. I received many blessing through this gift.

My new church worked in cooperation with the local Brandon Group facility which was located in my new town of residence, and it was within walking distance of my home. They had a well-established community clothes closet. I volunteered two days a week to run the front desk, answer phones, accept applications, and pull the records of returning clients. I helped with seasonal swap outs and stocking of the racks. I loved having an opportunity to help families get clothing they needed, at no cost to them. Through this association, God also took care of me personally. He provided me with clothes, shoes, and household items through this ministry. I didn't have to worry about "needing" or buying anything. These items may have come from someone else's closet, but they were new to mine.

Another volunteer group in which I was able to be of assistance was Church Food Ministries. It was offered through my new church as well. The program helped provide one hundred dollars of groceries at the personal cost of only thirty-two. This box of food helped me stretch my thirty-five dollars of food stamps, and I was able to eat for an entire month using the combination. The ministry provided a menu of what would be in the box for the following month. By using that list and picking specific items on which to spend my food stamps, I was able to plan three meals a day and snacks. Things got lean toward the end of the month. I would consume the last of the food on the final day, but I never went hungry, and I always had food.

It thrills my spirit to know God keeps His promises. Through these two community programs, organized through my church, God provided for my food and clothing needs. His Word says: "Therefore, I say to you, do not worry about your life, what you will eat or what you will drink; nor about your body, what you will put on. Now if God so clothes the grass of the field which today is, and tomorrow is thrown into the oven, *will He* not much more *clothe* you? Therefore, do not worry. For your heavenly Father knows that you need all these things. Therefore, do not worry about tomorrow" (Matthew 6:25–34; NKJV, selected sections). "My God will supply all your needs according to His riches in glory in Christ Jesus" (Philippians 4:19). God's word is true; He does not lie.

God combined the work of these two organizations, and they joined efforts to accomplish one purpose, to serve the community.

I was granted the privilege of helping them with their district-wide community Thanksgiving Dinner Box and Christmas Drive. They provided the fixings and all of the trimmings for both holiday meals, and they gave Christmas gifts to families who could not afford the pleasures of the season. Once again, God would bless me far more than the amount of effort I put into these worthy causes.

God tells us we are to look to the needs of others. Through Paul, He says, "Regard one another as more important than yourselves; do not *merely* look out for your own personal concerns, but also for the interests of others" (Philippians 2:3–4). Meeting needs is a huge part of our faith walk. We love because we were loved (1 John 4:19); we seek because we were sought (Isaiah 65:1); we teach because we were taught (2 Timothy 3:14), and we serve because we have been served (Galatians 5:13).

A Safety Net

Once established on the road to recovery, I dealt with my next highest personal goal, second only to staying in a right relationship with God. That goal was to get as healthy and well as possible and stay that way. I needed to get established with doctors, counselors, and therapists; and I needed to remain in their care. Where do I start? There are so many professionals from which to choose.

I love what my pastor says, "There are no coincidences in life." I agree; my pastor is right. God had his hand on everything in my life in my new city of residence. No one will ever convince me otherwise. How else can one explain a social worker, in a hospital several states away, who appeared to "care less" about the patient with whom she was working, setting up an appointment in a distant state with the counselor who would understand the strange combination of addiction and faith? These services were found in the very city in which I would come to reside. (In the beginning, no one knew I would end up in Ashville.) I don't think it can be explained any other way; it was Divine intervention.

This counselor was working at a Dual Diagnosis Center, where I had been mandatorily placed; this was a requirement of my release from the hospital. She understood me because she had been me at one point in her life. I had to go through a twelve-step plan to deal with my addiction to prescription drugs, and I had to learn about the diagnosis and treatment of my newly discovered disability. She was the person who would guide me through that process.

I was uncomfortable with the group discussion portion of the curriculum. I was afraid of the atmosphere into which I would be placing myself. I wanted to participate in the program, but I was exceptionally nervous about the meeting places. I also had a bad experience with group therapy in the past, when I lost my first child. I shared my concerns with my dual diagnosis counselor. She agreed to be my sponsor, and I worked the program with her assistance.

During this time, God presented into my life a special, new friend with whom I could discuss private issues. She is a fantastic listener, and she is wise. She took everything I said in stride. No matter what I shared, she never judged me. Through her, God taught me how to trust again; she is of vital importance to me. With God's guidance, the counselor, this new friend's help, and a year of hard work, I graduated from this twelve-step program. There was lunch, cake, and hugs galore. There were plenty of happy tears and smiles, too.

The next intricate part of my network was the medical doctors who would agree to take care of me. Finding a non-specialty, general care physician who seemed to care was difficult. It has been my experience that the medical field has a small number of professionals who are willing to take new low-income patients, especially those who have been diagnosed with a mental/emotional disorder accompanied by addiction issues. There are some, but they are few. I understand the reasoning behind these feelings and reactions, but it does not make it easier to be on the receiving end of them. I am so thankful and grateful for the compassionate ones God has provided for me along the way.

The two doctors who cared for me in my new town of abode always let me know they were not making any money from the care they were giving me. I felt like I was on a short time limit when I went to their offices. It was like "hurry up and get out." The first physician I had chosen, walked into the exam room one day and said, "You've got ten minutes that's all I get paid for." I know this is a true statement because the government does pay for a ten-minute visit.

Personally, I do not think that message needed to be presented to me in the way it was vocalized. After that statement, I found a new physician; this one did not fare much better. After several visits, I began to questioned her competency; apparently, the state did as well. Unfortunately, these two physicians were the only choices available to me because of my health coverage. Having exhausted my options, I remained in the second doctor's care.

I maintained my basic health while in the care of these two professionals, and I was able to get medications for infections and my thyroid issues as needed. By this criterion, they did their jobs, and for that I am thankful. These physicians were responsible for referring me for specialty services. Hats off to those specialists; they were all great, and they treated me like I mattered. I thank them for this kindness.

I must take this opportunity to brag on my psychiatrist. His responsibility was to monitor my overall mental, emotional health and manage my meds. (It is important to remember that when I entered the hospital, I was ingesting twenty-one different medications, plus over-the-counter substances. By the time my journey brought me to him, I was taking seven prescriptions.) This doctor's health management philosophy was perfect for me, minimum meds with optimum results.

During treatment under his supervision, I started losing substantial amounts of my hair. It started coming out during the night. I would awaken to clumps of hair on my pillow. Then it started coming out in handfuls when I brushed it. Eventually, I lost all but a few sprigs. Surprisingly, I never cried over this. (This is fascinating, due to the fact I have always been super picky about my hair.) I remember knowing God was with me in this. My sister-in-law took me shopping, and we bought a wig. I became a dark shade of brunette.

My psychiatrist determined my hair loss was caused by the medication I was taking for seizure control. He decided to evaluate the length of time since my last seizure; and because it had been over a year, he opted to discontinue the drug. It was the right call; my hair began to grow back, and the seizures never returned. That decision meant I was down to six meds per day.

Over the next four years while under Dr. Johnson's care, I would wean down to low doses of just two prescriptions. A third med I take is a "must have" for hypothyroidism. Having the correct medications that help manage my issues has been an enormous victory for me. This medication regime is working marvelously, and I am more emotionally healthy than I have been in a very long time. I am being monitored closely, and I have superb care in the city in which I now reside.

The last thread in my web of professional connections was my therapist. Of all the therapists in this sizeable new town, and of the four located within that particular office, God put me in the care of the most fantastic professional counselor I have ever met, and she is a believer. I wish I could shout her name to you, but professional courtesy will not allow it. She went through the grueling hard stuff with me, and a lot of it was not pretty. However, the end results are beautiful.

My first visit to her was in October, one week after my release from the hospital. My journey toward emotional renewal began and continued for the next four and a half years. This was the toughest portion of my recovery; up to this point, the drug withdrawal had been the worst. Now it was time for me to begin the grueling process of dealing with all of the "baggage" I had collected throughout my life. I had to investigate and sort through the traumatic events that had infiltrated my world. I would deal with the damage that had been inflicted across my lifespan. It was time to scrutinize these and leave everything possible at the "baggage claim counter," never to be picked up for hurtful purposes again.

This portion of my recovery was not only mentally and emotionally exhausting; it was physically draining as well. The things that had rotted away inside of me for so long had to be dissected and resolved. I became physically ill the first few weeks of therapy. I left my sessions exhausted, going home to spend my afternoons hugging the toilet. We started out meeting three times per week for two-hour sessions. After a while, we went to two days per week for two hours, then one day per week for the same hours, and finally we moved to a one-hour session once a week. We stayed at this level for a long time, a bit over three years to be exact. Eventually, we went to every other week, then once a month. I have been released from treatment, and I do not see her professionally anymore. She's there if I need her.

God used wonderful people across my new city of residence as instruments to touch my life and bring me to full restoration. The hospital floor is where God performed the supernatural surgery that saved my life, and Ashville is where God placed me for the time it would take to heal and rehabilitate.

CHAPTER 21

The Jerusalem Project

A Few Buckets of Paint

I had been attending FBC (First Baptist Church) for three months, and I joined a Sunday school class. People reached out to me, and I was asking God for the continued courage to say "yes" to their invitations and generosity; this is not as effortless as it sounds. Saying "yes" placed me in situations that made me vulnerable and accountable, situations way out of my comfort zone. God gave me the courage to say "yes" and then granted me power to overcome my fears. Little did I know that the early steps in my journey toward wellness and knowing my life had started over would begin with a home improvement project and a few buckets of paint.

I developed the practice of putting back a few dollars at every opportunity, so I could purchase paint and redo my apartment. After several months, I collected enough money to buy three gallons of paint. My dwelling was small, and I thought this would be plenty; I didn't know at the time, I miscalculated the amount needed.

I was sitting in life group one Sunday morning listened as our teacher shared about the class's most recent "Jerusalem Project." They had met the day before to help a widow in the church with some handiwork around her house. To help offset the cost of hiring someone to do the work, fellow believers gathered together to help their sister-in-Christ with a specific need. Several who were present in class that morning shared, and I remember thinking: *What a great ministry idea.*

When the time arrived to begin my apartment project, I asked my teacher if there was anyone at the church or in our class who might be willing to help. I told her I could not afford to pay them, but I am an exceptional cook. I would love to feed everyone in exchange for their help. I also told her I had been planning to do this job myself, but I was still under climb restrictions. I had not been free of seizure activity for a full year, and I was told not to do anything that involved climbing. I explained to the leader why I wanted to paint and what had been done to prepare for the event.

Before receiving help with this undertaking, I was asked a series of questions. I'm sure it was to see what my actual needs and motivations were. I think this is a wise thing for an organization to do when helping those in need. It cuts down on abuse of the system by those who continually take, thus hurting the whole purpose of a program. The first question asked of me was: "Why do you need to paint?" The second was: "Isn't the apartment complex responsible for taking care of that?"

The simple answer to the second question was: "Yes, they were supposed to paint." The management team told me they would do this, clean the carpets, and sanitize my unit before move-in. They didn't. There were streaks of something on the walls, and the ceilings were yellow and stained. Stale cigarette odors hung in the air and seeped from the dirty carpet. It may have been clean by their standards, but it was certainly not by mine. It was obvious it had not been painted. I embarked on an expedition to rejuvenate my apartment. I started with a stint of thorough cleaning and disinfecting which included steam cleaning the carpets. I had to scrimp and save over time to do this, but it was important to me and oh so worth it.

The answer to the first question was personal, but I took a step toward trust and responded to it. Up to this point, no one in this city knew anything about me or my past. I was about to share something private with a stranger. I told my group leader that I wanted and *needed* to cover the walls in my apartment because they were depressing. Even though they were white, they were dingy, and they looked filthy. I had been in a hospital or facility of some kind for seven months, and I had seen plenty of white, dirty, shabby walls. I had come to call the color in my apartment "institutional white" because that is what it reminded me of every time I entered. It was like stepping into institutionalization every time I walked through the door. I was spending much of my time here, and I needed the atmosphere to enhance my mood, not increase the possibility that I would have to deal with more uninvited depression.

I wanted my unit to feel like home; I wanted an apartment that enhanced living, promoted peacefulness, and housed tranquility. I wanted it to be more than just a place to stay; I needed it to be my home. My group leader took the information back to a small group within the class, and I was placed on the Jerusalem Project agenda. I had no clue what God was about to accomplish in my life, but what a blessing it would be.

It was an awesome Saturday. Early that morning, fifteen people who barely knew me showed up at my tiny apartment of five hundred and twenty-five square feet to paint. We ordered lunch, and someone went to pick it up. By seven-thirty that evening, the last person packed their tools and headed home. My entire space was covered in a beautiful soft shade of yellow with white accents and trim.

The class discovered that I had very little furniture, household goods, and no decorative items. My cabinets and fridge were practically empty. These incredible people chose to bless my life even further. When they were finished putting everything back into my apartment and setting up my home, I had a completely furnished flat. Upon completion, I had a space that looked like it came straight from the pages of a *Better Homes and Gardens* magazine.

My pantry and refrigerator-freezer were stocked, and household items were in ample supply. These kind people even paid for the paint which afforded me the money to replace the thirty-five-year-old wallpaper in my kitchen. The end results were phenomenal. I cried tears of joy and offered up a prayer of thanksgiving; because once again, God reminded me of His presence and provision. "Now to Him who is able to do exceedingly abundantly above all that we ask or think, according to the power that works in us, to Him be glory in the church by Christ Jesus to all generations, forever and ever. Amen" (Ephesians 3:20–21, NKJV).

I had asked God to send a few people, two maybe three, who would be willing to help me paint. He sent fifteen! I planned to compensate these willing workers with a meal; instead, they bought and served me lunch. My clothes were no longer stored in cardboard boxes placed on the built-in shelving units in the closet; now, I had a real dresser and night tables. My bedroom floor no longer served as my desk; I had been provided one, including the chair. Books that had been stacked in the corner of my living room were now nestled on the shelves of a bookcase. Even the minuscule things were taken care of; from lamps and pictures to special soaps, knick-knacks, dishes, and towels; nothing was omitted. There was even a vase of fresh cut flowers to grace my brand-new café table and chairs.

God had done "*exceedingly abundantly*" above all I had asked, and He had gone way beyond anything I dared imagine. He worked through His people, my new friends, to bless my life. I believe God smiled that day as His children listened to His prompting and did what He desired of them. He was glorified, and I was blessed. God's Word does not lie. When we do that which we are supposed to do, He works in a mighty way through His people.

F. R. O. G.

Nell, one of my new friends, offered to let me stay at her home for a few days while the paint fumes died down in my apartment. She was the driving force behind the creation of my gorgeously decorated home. This project was also an opportunity through which God would grant me the chance to grow in friendships. He used this group to help me learn how to trust in relationships, something I had not been able to do for a long time.

Saturday following the renovation project, we had an open house. Celebrating this way, everyone involved in the endeavor could see the final result; it was a magnificent evening. Toward the end of our celebration, we all gathered together in my small living area and joined hands. We huddled in prayer asking God's blessing and protection over my new apartment. The Holy Spirit came to be there with us. I felt safety, comfort, love, and peace as God poured Himself into the room.

Two days before the open house, my sister sent me a gift in the mail. It was a funny looking, skinny, ceramic frog all decked-out ready for a fishing trip. I had no clue where I was going to put him because he did not fit my new décor at all. Nell came over the following evening, and I asked her to help find a place for Frog in the surroundings. She shared with me an acronym for "faith" she had learned years earlier. She informed me that "*F. R. O. G.*" meant that as Christians, we are to live our lives **F**ully **R**elying **O**n **G**od.

I was delighted with the meaning in this story, and I thought: *How appropriate for this occasion.* I placed Frog on the center of the coffee table so everyone could see him. Then as people commented on him, I had an opportunity to share the story of the acronym and how God was teaching me to trust Him. When the evening ended, we incorporated Frog into the prayer asking God to help us remember that we can fully rely on Him, whether in the smallest of matters or in the toughest stuff to ever come our way.

A few months after the completion of my apartment, another Jerusalem Project came to light, and I was given the opportunity to participate. This time I was a contributor, not the receiver. As we wrapped up the day, I remembered the gift of the frog. He was now gracing a spot on one of my bookshelves. I thought: *What a great opportunity to pass on a blessing.* On our last trip to gather the remaining items that belonged to the lady we were moving, I grabbed Frog and took him with me. We presented him to the woman and shared the delightful story of the meaning of his name. We prayed with her and asked God's guidance and protection over her, as she started her life in her new place.

A tradition was born. Frog has resided in several places, since his first resting place on my coffee table. He has traveled much since his early days atop my bookcase. Each time a new Jerusalem Project has been completed, he has come to rest in a new home; and, he remains there until it is time for him to hop on over to a new pad. The prophet Isaiah covers the concept of fully relying on God. He said, "Let him [man] trust in the name of the LORD and rely on his God" (Isaiah 50:10).

Another goal of mine is to seek God in all I do. I want to trust Him, even when I cannot see or understand what He is doing. I know His way is perfect, and He loves me. My prayer is that God will intervene when my faith is weak and I have the urge to lean toward something that appears to be better than what He has provided, or it seems grander than where He has placed me. I believe if we ask God to show us which "way to go" and reveal which path we are to take, then our steps will be directed by Him; thus, placing us in the center of His will. "Trust in the LORD with all your heart and do not lean on your own understanding. In all your ways acknowledge Him, and He will make your paths straight" (Proverbs 3:5–6).

CHAPTER 22

A Rich Life

God Did that for Me

In my mid–thirties, I attended a women's ministry meeting, and a dear lady told a story about losing her car keys. She was ready to come to the meeting and could not find them anywhere. She had looked everywhere and started to panic when they remained lost. When a large portion of time had passed, and she still had not found them, she stopped in her alarm and asked God to help her locate the keys. She began retracing the steps of her day. After an exhaustive search, the only place left to look was in the large black trash bag that was sitting by the back door; it was there waiting to be taken outside to the receptacle. She had spent the afternoon cleaning her house, and the trash by the door was the last remaining evidence of her efforts. She untied the top, moved a few papers aside, and there the keys lay; they were in the trash, nestled in some paper towels.

She shared this story that night at our meeting. I will never forget what she said as she wrapped up her devotional thought. "Coincidence? I don't think so. Even in the tiniest matters like finding our car keys or getting a parking space close to the entrance of our choice, God is in it; and He takes care of us. Do we take the time to thank Him for the way He intervenes in the minuscule matters in our lives, or do we only 'cry out' when massively destructive storms come through?"

She went on to tell us that from that point onward, she was determined to look for the *"God did that for me"* moments in her life. Since my deliverance and recovery, I have chosen to adopt this philosophy in my thinking. God cares about ALL of the details in my life. I do not want to miss anything He does for me. I want to be mindful of every single *"God did that for me"* moment He grants.

As I was writing the account of this event, I thought about the question: *What has God done for me*? The answer is: *"Absolutely Everything!"* From the tiniest issue to the greatest dilemma, in times of momentous joy or seasons of deep sorrow, He has been there. There are not enough words or paper and ink in existence to pen the accounts of what God has done in my life.

God placed me in an apartment complex that met all of my needs and provided many extras. He provided a congregation of believers in which I could worship, grow, and serve. He drew me out of isolation and put me back into circulation, where I could learn to trust. He landed me in the middle of mental health providers and counselors who were people of faith. He freed me from the clutches of addiction, and long-term sickness fled my body. He rescued me from the pit of loneliness and placed me in the midst of a loving family. He answered my prayers and delivered me from the abuse that kept me beaten down in life. He broke the bondage and darkness of extremely severe depression. God has transformed my life; He has brought me from a wheelchair-bound, nonspeaking, incontinent, incompetent, hopeless existence to a fully operational, fabulously blessed life. He has healed my body to a point where it functions well.

The content of this writing project holds the account of the incredible ways God has worked in my life; I pray He is not finished. The words restored and renewed are excellent descriptors, but they do not fully explain what He has accomplished. Transformation and redemption are much more expressive. Transformed meaning I was changed, I would face and react to things in an entirely different way than I use to; my thinking was reprogrammed. Redeemed meaning I have been purchased with the blood of Christ on the cross; in that redemption, I can come to Jesus for rescue when I am snared by evil and things of this world. I've been made whole (put back together) and restored to be used for a reason. I believe I am becoming the "Nora" God designed me to be, and He is unfolding my purpose before me.

God tells me in His Word: "Do not be conformed to this world, but be transformed by the renewing of your mind, that you may prove what the will of God is, that which is good and acceptable and perfect" (Romans 12:2). He *is* this powerful. How exciting to know that "where the Spirit of the LORD is, *there* is liberty. But we all are being transformed into the same image [the image of Christ]" (2 Corinthians 3:17–18).

Bloom Where You are Planted

When God landed me in Ashville, I had no idea where my life was headed. In fact, I thought I had arrived at my pinnacle, and this was as nice as it would get. My life was much better than the level at which I had been living the previous three years, and this place was perfectly fine with me. If this was as good as it would get, it was better than what I had survived.

When I moved into Hampton Hills Apartments and settled there, I came to a place of understanding and acceptance. I was dealing with the diagnosis of a serious illness, and I had to learn to live in such a way that it would remain under control. I was in a major learning season in this area as well as in many other areas of my life. I sincerely believed that I had arrived at my final home on this planet. I thought I would live out my days in this building; therefore, I set about the business of getting into habits and routines that would be beneficial to me and honoring to God.

I spent time with the Lord, and I thanked Him for my new life. I asked Him to help me adjust and do my absolute best with what He provided. I had a small income that was provided through SSI (Supplemental Security Income), and this would be my sole source of revenue. According to HUD regulations, approximately one-third of my total income was to be set aside to pay rent each month. I had to stretch the remainder of my check across the month.

Budgeting was, and still is, a vast area of learning for me. I am so much better at it now, and I hope to continue to get stronger in this subject as time goes forward. I had to discover how to live on a low-income, and I had to develop a tight budget. The most difficult part would be following it. I had to learn to save money across time for future events. One of the new friends God placed in my life through my new church was willing to help me in this area. She took me under her wing, and we started a budget journey together. Once again, I had to trust someone with a *not* so pleasant part of myself. She never judged me; she unassumingly walked beside me, guiding and helping.

We decided to organize an envelope system of money management. Rent, food, medications, and tithe were the first files created. I marked the remaining categories with the names of areas that represented expenses and the desires—like the paint. I grouped them into monthly and future needs and then prioritized them. I also had to plan for the "what if's." I even learned how to arrange for a cheeseburger and a pizza to fit into my budget; they too had an envelope. I couldn't place funds in every slot every month, so I alternated deposits. These categorical files were housed in a safe at my friend's home. For me, in the beginning, "Out of Sight, Out of Mind, and Out of Reach" was the best rule of thumb.

I have since graduated to a Microsoft Office Excel spreadsheet. I have learned to design and setup the page myself. I used to believe subjects such as technology, money, and banking were too complicated for me. The biggest lesson I've learned in all of my budgeting issues is: *No matter what my income, I can manage to save a little. I just have to decide that is what I am going to do.* God is proving to me every day the fact that we are never too old to learn. His presence and peace make me smile.

During my recovery, I have been engaging in budgeting and banking sessions with my friend. I can now balance a checkbook, and I live on less income than I have ever had. I no longer bounced checks, which had become a weekly occurrence prior to being hospitalized; and I do not spend money that is not available to me, nor money earmarked for a designated purpose. I have also learned the concepts of "putting money back" and "saving for a larger purchase." I no longer buy things regardless of the availability of funds. It does not make me happy to postpone an acquisition, but I understand the necessity of waiting in many situations. I no longer pout because I must hang tight until a purchase is feasible. Credit cards, unless they can be paid off each month and are used solely for convenience, are a major no-no. Therefore, I have none.

I will admit the temptation to buy things rears its ugly head occasionally, and I have to pray through it or seek advice from my friend. However, I now understand the principle of *just because the checkbook says I have eighty-nine dollars; it does not mean I have it to spend.* I learned this standard late in life, but I learned it. Now, I comprehend it and do my best to practice it. I wish I could tell you that I am one hundred percent accountable and accurate in every money transaction I have made since I've been in recovery, but that would be a lie. I will tell you that I am getting better at making money decisions. I know there are more things to learn in the areas of money management and finance; I am on a mission to learn them. I am much improved, but not as strong as I will be.

My Mansion at Hampton

Through the Jerusalem Project, God took care of my basic needs, provided me with many niceties, and bumped up the quality of things in my life several notches. Technically, I had been homeless, but He provided me with an apartment. It was the perfect size for one person, and the bonuses were immense. He provided heat and air conditioning, hot and cold water, elevator service, and electricity. The cost of power usage was included in the rent. I never went hungry; I always had clothes to wear, and I was safe.

I started out with few clothes and personal items. I lost almost everything in my possession along my journey; this was when God gave me a new philosophy about "things." It's all just "stuff." Is "stuff" necessary for survival? No. How many sets of clothes do we actually need? I would say two, one to wear and one to wash. How many things do we need to decorate our space? Essentially, none. How much "stuff" do we genuinely need to survive? I would say oxygen, food, water, shelter, clothing, and His Word are the most basic needs we have; everything else is an added blessing.

A phone would be nice, but it is not a must. Cable TV would help fill hours of time, but it is expensive; besides, I needed to fill my mind with healthier things. A car would come in handy, but I was within walking distance of everywhere I needed to go. God even put a burger joint (one of my favorite things) a few blocks away from my apartment. Pizza was delivered straight to my door, and tacos and sub sandwiches were right around the corner. I think I was pretty strategically placed as far as eating was concerned.

Safety is a major issue in areas of low-income housing. God could have designated any housing project that He wanted in Ashville. I think He placed me in the BEST possible place in this city because He planted me in the safest of them.

Just how strategic and perfect was it? I was four blocks from the police station, four from the local fire department, and six from my new church. If needed, I could walk to the grocery store and local pharmacy. The public library was three blocks down the street; this meant access to books, movies, and the internet at no cost. I also lived five minutes from the people who would become influential and instrumental in my life. As far as I was concerned, there was no better spot in the entire city. I settled into life in my five hundred and twenty-five square foot mansion at Hampton Hills, ready to face life and whatever was coming next.

Early in my residency, and shortly after I began meeting the tenants who already lived in Hampton, God granted me an eye-opening revelation. Every single one of the occupants residing in this building was like me; I was one of them. The occupants in this housing development all had a story; they came from all walks of life, circumstances, illnesses, and choices. They merely lived in this place; all of these things sounded descriptive of my story.

We should be aware that anyone could end up in a Hampton Hills complex, or some other living condition that seems to others as not so favorable. With this realization, I came to understand that every person in this housing facility could be facing some or all of the things I had faced and was facing. I knew, above all else, they needed a healthy relationship with God. This bond would not give them a million dollars, nor would it grant them everything they wanted in life; but it would bring peace, joy, and the ability to cope. They would be able to view life through healed spiritual eyes and a transformed, renewed heart.

God placed a burden on my heart for the people of Hampton Hills. They needed to be respected and loved, as Christ loved me; just like my new friends chose to love me. God had put me in this place to be "salt and light" (Matthew 5:13–16). A ministry was born from the thoughts God granted me with these insights.

Stepping Stones to the Savior

Seven months after God placed an incredible couple from the new Sunday school class in my life, they invited me to go on a trip with them. They were traveling to Kansas to visit their daughter and grandsons; we had a marvelous time. On our way home, I shared with them what God had laid on my heart concerning Hampton Hills. I told them about the struggles I was having concerning what I thought God wanted me to do. I shared with them the revelation I had about the people at this apartment complex and how I knew the people there were living lives of extreme need and hurt.

The greatest necessity I witnessed was the lack of opportunities to learn about Christ and grow in their relationship with God. Many claimed to know Christ, but they had no desire to spend time with Him. I witnessed many of the behaviors and emotions from which God had delivered me. I could see loneliness, defeat, and despair in almost every person I met. I knew the solution these folks needed to conquer these issues in their lives is found only in Jesus Christ. I told my friends, I had been praying and asking God to show me what part I was to play in this revelation.

First, I thought: *Pray for them*. I did, but that was not all I was to do. Then I thought: *Maybe I'm supposed to start a Bible Study*. There were already a few study groups meeting. I kept having the nagging thought: *This is not quite what God wanted; it was beyond that*. I kept praying and asking God to show me what He was trying to tell me. Before long, my new friends invited me on this trip to Kansas. We engaged in a long conversation on our jaunt home. I shared my heart with my new comrades, and they listened.

My close friend has this remarkable ability to ask fabulous questions. One of my favorites is, "*What does that look like*?" She asked me what I thought the needs were at Hampton. We got paper and pencil, and we started making a list. We brainstormed for quite a while, and then she asked another great question, "*What can we do to help meet those needs*?" Again, we brainstormed and created another list. Then she asked, "*What is the most crucial need they have*?" We all agreed it was the need of a Savior or need of His renewal in their lives.

We concluded that the most pressing issue to address was that of availability of the Gospel message. Since it was so difficult for the majority of them to get out and go to a church, we wanted to bring the church to them. For the next several hours, we put together a proposal to present to the management team at Hampton. My new friends and I proceeded to make plans on how to implement our list of "*stepping stones*" that would prayerfully lead others to a renewed, or brand new, relationship with the Savior.

We developed a list of activities and ongoing events that would place us in the middle of "what was happening at Hampton Hills" so we could build relationships with the tenants. Some of these stones were: fellowships, building a back patio, movie night, lunch bunch, domino tournaments, women's Bible study, tea and crumpets, rock and reminisce, financial advising and personal budgeting guidance, morning doughnuts, and gardening club. We decided to plant ourselves in situations where we could listen to the tenants and try to discover their interests and needs.

We met with management hoping to gain their permission and blessing on our endeavor. Instead, we encountered unexpected opposition; unexpected, because these were professing believers who claimed to have the hearts of the residents listed as a priority on their prayer list. Things did not move as quickly as I expected, and Christmas season arrived before we knew it. I asked management if we were going to have a celebration. I was shocked when she said, "No; these ungrateful people don't deserve Christmas." My immediate thought was: *No one deserves Christmas.* When I contemplated the manager's comment, I thought: *They may not deserve one, but they* ***need*** *one.*

I went back to the office and asked the manager if I could plan a party; permission was granted. She informed me there would be no funds for the event. I told her that was fine, and I reserved the dining room for the occasion. I spent the next few days scheming. Then I made a phone call. For the next several weeks, my new friends and I planned. We also recruited the help of one of the tenants who had heard about what we were doing and asked if she could help.

My friend and I went to the pastor who was in charge of our age group at church and shared our ideas. He offered to help with the Christmas Tea, and he gave assistance toward setting up the Sunday services at Hampton. He liked our whole concept. God was bringing together the people and financing for this undertaking. The WOM (*Women on Missions*) at FBC baked cookies and goodies, while my crew filled 100 goodie bags for the festivities. The church donated money for items and trinkets to go in the bags. We all had a marvelous time working on this project. All ninety-three residents received at least one Christmas gift that year, the treat bag we had prepared for them. My favorite photo of this event is the one of Brother Don serving cookies to the folks at Hampton Hills Apartments.

Our original proposal for establishing church services involved the enlistment of six different ministers from the surrounding area, all from various faith titles so we would not appear partial to any one denomination. One criterion to speak at a service was they must concentrate on the necessity of a right relationship with God which is available only through the acknowledgment and acceptance of Jesus Christ. Secondly, all teaching had to come from the Bible.

Upon our return from Kansas, I spent several months trying to enlist pastors and lay people from surrounding churches to aid in this endeavor. Before I knew it, our Christmas Celebration had come and gone, and a new year had dawned; it was almost Easter. I finally received permission from the manager to set up the Sunday services, but I could not get her to commit to a date. I was also having trouble getting the pastors in the area to show interest in the project. We kept pressing forward, regardless. We concentrated on implementing our relationship building plan, *Stepping Stones to the Savior.*

One night, in the very early hours of morning, I was awakened with the thought: *There would be no better time to start services than the season of remembrance, Easter.* I got out of bed, went to my knees, and asked God to show me how to make this happen. The next day my friend and I spoke to our pastor. He helped us organize, and we picked a date. We returned to Hampton Hills and stopped by the office. I stuck my head in the door and gave the dates for the church services to the manager.

I didn't ask her this time; I told her. She had already given me permission to plan the services, and I felt no need to ask again; I moved ahead, proactively. Our first service would be the Sunday before Easter. Don spoke, and there were nine at that first meeting. Easter Sunday there were seventeen tenants in attendance. Pastor delivered a brilliant message about the importance of finishing life well. He emphasized the fact that it does not matter what our past holds; it is about what we are doing from this moment forward. The following Sunday we were back down to seven, but that was better than zero.

Don helped with services for a while, until we were able to recruit four men from our church who were willing to bring a message on a rotating schedule. They would alternate Sundays. July rolled around; we planned a watermelon feast and "seed spitting" challenge. Sixty-five residents showed up to eat melons, and thirteen participated in the contest. Ms. Nellie won. We had a marvelous time building relationships and having fun.

God developed a ministry team with no extra effort on our part. My friends and I just put the word out in our Life Group and invited those who wanted to join us to come. Joseph and Jessa took over the music portion of the service, and Betty and Mary ended up being our permanent piano players. Of course, my awesome new friends, the couple from Sunday school, were right by my side in all of this. Clarence was instrumental in developing relationships with the men who were coming to the services.

God would grant us an unexpected blessing, something for which I had been too timid to ask. It came in the package known as James Glass. He was a lay preacher and a member of our church. We sang in the choir together. He had filled one of the rotating preaching positions a few times, and he had started coming to all of the meetings to help support the ministry; he was excited about what God had begun. God would lay it on this man's heart to become the permanent provider of His Word for the services at Hampton. What an astonishing gift. It is my understanding that as of today, the people lovingly refer to him as "Pastor James."

As I look back across the life of this ministry, the lesson I learned is this; when we offer God a willing heart, and we live a life of intentional service, He graciously unfolds His plans before us. All we have to do is recognize them and step into them. These experiences were inspirational and gratifying, as well as exciting and fun. It amazes me that the process of "blooming where I am planted" is so uncomplicated, enjoyable, and fulfilling.

God continues to bless His work at Hampton Hills. Several tenants have found salvation, many have rededicated their lives, and some have followed Christ in baptism. Some of them have reached out to a church within their chosen faith, and many have reconnected with congregations of their choice. My last contact with James quoted an attendance of thirty-two. In a facility of one hundred units that is an incredible percentage. As occupants continue to come and go, my prayer is that God will continue to touch and change lives and that His presence will remain at Hampton.

Count It All Joy

How can you consider yourself blessed when taking into account all you have been through? People have asked me this question on several occasions; many of them were hurting, facing temptations, or finding themselves in the midst of a trial or hardship. I think the answer to this question lies in scripture, where James addresses the issues of trials and temptations. The question could be asked this way, "How can you look back and 'count it all joy when you fall into various trials' (James 1:2, NKJV)?"

Finding ourselves in the midst of a trial could be God's way of correcting us, or He may be teaching us something He wants us to learn or know. We could be in the circumstance, merely because it is a natural consequence of life. It may be due to the simple fact that sin is present in this world, and the effects of sin and evil are all around us. Or it could be, we find ourselves in the center of a trying situation because of our own doing. Our choices and actions may have landed us in the middle of the trial. God, in His permissive will, could allow us to be in the midst of hardship. Whichever situation is true, there is one thing of which I am certain; trials are a fact of life, and we will find ourselves in plenty of them before our journey on earth is complete.

I think many times (not always) our personal disobedience and spiritually unwise choices land us in the toughest situations. We want to blame God for the places in which we find ourselves; but, we should be looking in the mirror of His word, checking our inner reflection because it affects our relationship with Him. Believers live in this world; but, we are to walk in His ways, not in the ways of the world (John 15:19). Instead of blaming God, we should be looking to Him for the answers to our dilemmas and confessing disobedience if it is present. This is the most difficult, yet most liberating action we can take in breaking free from the bondage of our past.

Sometime during my recovery, after studying for a life group lesson, I adopted the practice of equipping myself to face the battles that lie ahead of me. Before leaving the safety of my room each day, I would send a prayer to heaven something similar to this:

> Dear God, thank You for supplying what I need to stand strong today. I purposely take up the whole armor You have given me and claim it as my protecting force.
>
> God, gird my waist with Your truth. I place the breastplate of Your righteousness around me to protect my heart. My feet I shod with the preparation of the gospel of peace that I may walk through this day in Your calmness and comfort.
>
> Above all else, I take the shield of faith and hold it forth, for it will quench the fiery darts of Satan. God, I place the helmet of Your salvation on my head and wield the sword of the Spirit, Your Word, in my hand.

> I will continually lift prayers to You. May I walk in the presence of Your Spirit this day. Grant me boldness as I go forth that I would speak unwaveringly of who You are, what You have done, and what You will do.
>
> (Ephesians 6:10–20, The Armor of God)

Facing the trials of each day and being cloaked in the armor of God helps me handle the hardships of life. How can I say I am blessed if bad things continue to come into my life? At night when I am alone, in the dark, and there is no one around I can honestly say, "I have peace. I have joy. I am loved. I have assurance; and even though evil is present in this world, I am safe and protected." God's plan will continue to unfold from now through eternity. In other words, *GOD IS IN CONTROL*. How can I *not* call myself blessed, even when I suffer; "For I know whom I have believed and am persuaded that He is able to keep what I have committed to Him until that Day" (2 Timothy 1:12, NKJV).

The riches of this life are not measured by the amount of money we hold, and we cannot determine the quality of our lives by the quantity of stuff we acquire. The interactions and friendships we have with others are significant, but the most important relationship we possess is the one we must develop with God through Jesus Christ, His Son.

The authentic riches of an abundant life are found only in fellowship with God, through Jesus. If we come to a place where we realize that pebble-sized steps in a relationship with Him are essential, and the ability to bloom and flourish where He plants us is vital, then we will do well. Understanding that God takes care of the minor issues in our lives, even if we do not recognize it, is a crucial concept for us to learn. Acquiring these jewels of wisdom allows us to deem our dwelling a mansion, no matter the size. Procurement of these riches identifies us as blessed, and our lives are prosperous regardless of our circumstances.

CHAPTER 23

Sorting Through

Boundaries

When I awakened from my night's vigil with God in the hospital, I was foggy-headed and drained, but I was back in the realm of reality. I was aware of my surroundings, and I knew where I was. I have been in this domain ever since. I know this one thing as absolute truth, I had been in the presence of God. I had been, and continue to be, forgiven. I was starting my life completely over, but I had been face-to-face with my Holy Creator; I was, and am, radically changed. I would have to deal with things from my past, but I was not to carry them with me into my future; nor was I to allow them to take possession of my being.

God was reminding me that He is on this journey with me, and I was going to be better than okay if I walked within the boundaries He has set for me. In my therapy sessions, I learned about these margins. I discovered I did not know what healthy borders are, and I didn't know how to function within them. God revealed to me some interesting things from His Word about boundaries and their necessity. I never realized people have been operating within limits ever since the beginning of time, and they serve a purpose toward our good.

God created boundaries or a hedge in the Garden of Eden for safety and protection. When He placed Adam and Eve within the garden, God told them where the edges of the plot lay, and everything in it was for their benefit and well-being. The land that lay in the midst was the chosen area in which they were free to roam, work, rule, and tend. There was never a guarantee it would be undemanding, but it was manageable. God had only one restriction. In Genesis 2:17, He specifically told Adam he was not to eat of the Tree of the Knowledge of Good and Evil. After this command to Adam, God created Adam's helper and companion, Eve.

When the borders in our lives are weakened, or put up improperly, they cause massive amounts of damage. I would be forty-nine years old before I ever knew it is okay to establish boundaries, reinforce them when necessary, and it's perfectly fine to refuse to move them at times. Just as God designed them in the beginning, healthy boundaries help protect and preserve me; they keep me spiritually fit and healthy, and the space within them is controllable. They help foster spiritual might and fortify my character within the walls of my existence. These boundaries assist in keeping my life under His control.

The borders in my life had been placed there and established by others, and they were being moved around and changed frequently. I was like a chameleon. My operating margins were situational instead of constant, determined by whomever I was trying to please at any given time. They should have been instituted and put into place based on the words and instructions God has given me, all of which are found in His Word.

If my concentration had strictly been to please God, my boundaries would have remained steadfast. Instead, every time I tried to please others, my focus changed, and my margins moved. They grew weaker because of their feeble establishment. I learned if I would set healthy boundaries in place, every area of my existence would be fortified and manageable. Used and established properly, restrictions are perfect protectors. Jesus even tells us to "let your 'Yes' be 'Yes,' and your 'No,' 'No'" (Matthew 5:37, NKJV). Waffling is instability and leads to a fall. I discovered it is okay to say, "No."

Baggage Claim

God has delivered me to a place where I have had the privilege to do some traveling. I have discovered I love the word, "GO." A few years into my recovery, I had the opportunity to travel by air to board a ship that would take me on a delightful vacation. While waiting for my luggage at the baggage claim counter, an incredible analogy for this section of my writing project struck me. I watched as the suitcases and other bags traveled down the conveyor belt and landed in the luggage pit. As suitcases hit the turntable, people were in a position to reach out and grab the bags that belonged to them. If they missed one, they could humbly wait; eventually, the baggage would come back around.

I saw the turntable as life. The conveyor belt was the means by which Satan hurls our personal baggage (all the junk and garbage from our past) at us. If he misses, all he has to do is leave it out there; sooner or later, he'll send it our way again. There is the real possibility that we will reach out to claim it. When we take possession of it, we immediately become encumbered by the weight of the load. I found myself smiling hugely, as God was unfolding this truth in front of my eyes. I dug in my carry-on bag at my feet and pulled out my mini recorder. It felt like I couldn't document the image fast enough.

I was still in the trenches of extensive therapy at this time, and I was dealing with all of the baggage I had accumulated throughout my life. During the three years before this trip, I had reached over to the conveyor belt and pulled off many pieces of personal baggage, one piece at a time. As the bags came to me, I had to decide if I was ready to explore the contents of that particular container. Then, I had to analyze its worth and value in my life. If I was not ready, I left it lay there because, sooner or later it would come around again; and eventually, I would scrutinize every single piece of baggage ever collected.

Slowly, I went through the contents of my entire life. Some memories were worth holding onto, those I kept. The things I could not remember were not essential, and they were already lost, out there somewhere. I didn't need any of them. If they were needful, God would reveal them to me so that I could deal with them. One case at a time, case after case, I looked at the burdens that had accumulated in my life. I had to face the question: *What do I do with the tons of baggage that are of no use to me*? Its only purpose is to weigh me down, impede my travel, and make my journey arduous.

In reality, if we walk away and leave our luggage on the turntable, it gets turned into the baggage claim department. I decided to throw all of those useless pieces of dead weight back onto the conveyor, and I purposely left them there; they are now owned and controlled by the Great Baggage Claim Director in heaven. Satan no longer has the power to access them and dump them into my life, using them as weapons of destruction; they are safe with my Father. Only with His permission can Satan try to use them against me. I refuse to allow the Devil to be successful in that endeavor, ever again (The Book of Job). I also know, I will not be calling the claims department to retrieve them; they would be nothing more than a heavy burden.

Paul's writing reminds me of this principle when he says to the Philippians, "I do not count myself to have apprehended; but one thing I do, forgetting those things which are behind and reaching forward to those things which are ahead" (Philippians 3:13, NKJV). Isaiah says it this way, "Do not call to mind the former things, or ponder things of the past. Behold, I will do something new" (Isaiah 43:18–19).

My hope is to retrieve items from these cases at God's urging, for the sole purpose of offering help and comfort to others. My prayer is that this information will come to light, only when it is helpful to those who are hurting. One of the results of weeding through baggage and deciding what needs to be left behind at the claims counter is the writing you hold in your hand.

Oh, my friend, if it is time to lighten your personal load, I invite you to visit the baggage claim department; it is so worth the trip. It is a wonderful thing to travel lightly and unencumbered in life. Jesus said, "Take My yoke upon you and learn from Me, for I am gentle and humble in heart, and YOU WILL FIND REST FOR YOUR SOULS. For My yoke is easy and My burden is light" (Mathew 11:29–30).

I have learned that if I organize and keep the items in my carry cases under control as I go, I will never need to spend tons of time at the baggage claim center again; which in turn frees more time for me to enjoy my journey through life. My goal is to continue to travel lightly. Now, if I could only learn to take a real vacation with less baggage, it would be a miraculous thing.

Same Old, Same Old

As each day of my new life dawns, I find I understand a little bit more of the "why" God allowed me to experience all of the frightening events that plunged me into the depths of despair and despondency. My prayer and heart's desire to have a different life; one with happiness, enthusiasm, and filled with boundless expectations could never come about if I continued doing the *same old* things and living in the *same old* negatives. God had to deliver me from the bondage of negative influences in my life that had pushed me into the pit and were destroying me.

Groups such as AA (Alcoholics Anonymous) and DDGs (Dual Diagnosis Groups) teach a twelve-step plan for renewal. These programs give the substance abuser new tools to handle and control an addiction, and they help the individual develop a "new" plan of action when dealing with the issues of life. It is a simple fact that if we try to live out our life in the *same old* ways, around the *same old* people, with the *same old* mindset, and in the *same old* environment, we will get the *same old* results. To change the outcomes, we must make permanent changes and pour in good, positive input.

Why did I continually go back to the things that were so hurtful and damaging? In the beginning, it was my commitment to my husband and a desire to do marriage God's way. The choices to remain in my home and return to my husband in the latter portion of our relationship were based on my continued desire to do things God's way, but they also included comfort, familiarity, functionality, and fear; they entered the picture and became dominant factors in my thinking. When abuse entered the picture, remaining and increasing in severity and occurrences over time, I had every right to leave. God does not expect us to be a doormat or a human punching bag.

Deciding to stay was no longer grounded in commitment; fear of the unknown far outweighed the pain of getting over an abusive onslaught. I knew I could endure the assault. I knew I could function within the life I was living; I'd been surviving it for many years. It became painfully obvious I was being destroyed from the inside, as attacks continued on the outside.

In my humanness, I wanted familiar things around me. I feared man's judgment of me if I chose divorce. I did not want people to think negatively about me. It would be complicated to give up everything and start over. In fact, it was downright terrifying to think about it, more petrifying than staying with an abusive husband. I was also afraid for my three children. How was I going to protect and provide for them? They also needed their dad. Therefore, I made the conscious choice to stay in familiar territory, and I returned to it over and over again.

God addresses the idea of returning to that which is familiar in the book of Numbers, chapter fourteen. God delivered the children of Israel by His hand, and they witnessed miracles performed by Him as well. However, as soon as they faced adversity in their new realm of existence or faced uncertainty, they lamented for the security of what was familiar to them, the captivity of Egypt. "'Would it not be better for us to return to Egypt?' So they said to one another, 'Let us appoint a leader and return to Egypt'" (Numbers 14:3–4). Their fear of the future caused doubt, despondency, and dependency on things that "used to be." They longed for the safety of the familiarity of their past even though it included slavery, hardship, and bondage; I totally understand this thinking.

The concept of *same old, same old* heavily influenced my partnership with my husband. Why was it so difficult to make changes in our marriage? It was impossible because both of us had to desire the change for it to take place. Physical violence erupted several times in our twenty-six-and-a-half-year relationship. There should have never been one episode of this kind.

My marriage was important to me, and I wanted to be one of the seemingly fewer couples that "make it" these days. I took my vows seriously. I meant it with every ounce of my being when I said, "For better or for worse, 'till death us do part," and every vow in between. Because of my background, I thought I was the cause of the situations that led to those brutal attacks; I believed I deserved what happened. I now know this is completely wrong thinking.

The sequence of things happening over and over again and ending in a violent manner defines the "cycle of abuse." Environment, situations, events, and the people involved remain the same or similar; thus, a chain of events unfolds in a recognizable pattern with a familiar outcome every time. If some form of intervention does not take place, the cycle will continue. It must be broken to be defeated. Unfortunately, too often the victim develops behaviors of escape and survival, instead of finding solutions that bring about real change that is needed.

I couldn't change my husband. Each time I returned from my flight away from *Anger and Rage*, the *same old, same old* still existed at home. Why did I ever think things would change? My husband said the problems were mine, not his. He never took any responsibility in the troubled areas of our marriage. He never understood the issues were ours, and we needed to confront them, together. He refused to go to therapy; he didn't think he needed it, and he didn't believe in it. Counseling and therapy were just a waste of time and money as far as he was concerned. According to him, I was the one causing the issues in our relationship.

I didn't realize it at the time, but I believe the final night of my marriage was a "*God did that for me*" moment. Even though it was brutal and painful, I was at the point where I could not, and would not, let go of a situation harmful for everyone involved. I believe God removed me from that environment because I couldn't find the strength to do it myself. God took the decision to leave and escape to safety out of my hands. I believe God removed me from the *same old, same old*, so I could finally get different results.

My dear, new friend and I were having lunch one day. I love how she put it: "Always doing what you've always done, will always get you what you've always gotten."

Breaking the Cycle

Our Christian walk calls us to take action and be purposefully involved in life; when we do, we experience the blessings of abundant life that Christ has for us. If we fail to bring ourselves to be actively engaged in strengthening our walk with Jesus, it will be lacking and unfulfilling; we will be spiritually malnourished. The same holds true when we are trying to rebuild our fractured thinking. Unfortunately, some of the misguided notions, philosophies, and teachings I received during my years growing up would follow me into adulthood. I discovered it is most difficult to break the cycles of negative thinking, claiming baggage, doing the *same old* things, and abuse; but it is doable.

Change is hard. If we desire things to be different, our resolve to alter our life must be stronger than the hold of our past. It takes a lot of hard work and consistent, constant effort. I wish these alterations were instantaneous, but most of the time things do not change overnight. It takes a lot of strength and endurance; both of which we find in dependency on Jesus. One day, somewhere down this transforming road, we discover we have crossed over into a whole new way of facing life.

I hope all I have been through and experienced culminates with the empowerment of all who find themselves caught in these cycles. I pray you will be granted the strength and tenacity to refuse the use of learned patterns and behaviors that are abusive or destructive in nature. It is not easy, but it is possible in Christ Jesus.

CHAPTER 24

Stinkin' Thinkin'

Such as a Man Thinks

One of the compartments of my brain that had to be wholly vacated, disinfected, and aired was the area that held descriptions of things I knew I loved, but my view of them had become polluted and twisted. This holding cell also housed my opinions of myself. The recesses of my heart became marred by falsehood. Over the years, I had listened to negativity and destructive criticism. The positives were choked out by the vigorous manifestations of disapproval, disparagement, and condemnation; eventually, they took over and permeated my life.

"One bad apple spoils the whole bunch." This adage is an interesting saying and accurate. Placing a damaged apple among healthy ones eventually corrupts the accepted, causing them to become bruised and bitter. The unflawed apples have zero effect on the sick. If only one ruined apple possesses the power to destroy the whole batch, I found myself wondering what a multitude of tainted apples would do to a barrel containing wholesome fruit. Over time, I imagine the stench would be quite rancorous. We must always be on guard, looking for the development of a corrupted or defective influence, and continually cull these negative factors from our lives.

I think the breaking point at which I found myself in life is a pretty graphic picture of what happens when this analogy plays out in reality. The end results are toxic. We would do well to separate the spoiled fruit and remove it from our contaminated barrel as soon as possible.

<u>ONE BAD APPLE</u>

Nora J. Alexander

To the barrel of life, dissatisfaction found its way.
Dissatisfaction led to resentment.
Resentment triggered selfishness.
Selfishness morphed into envy.
Envy produced discontent.
Discontent generated antagonism.
Antagonism bred disdain.
Disdain manufactured malice.
Malice created hate.
Hate fed bitterness.
Bitterness chilled the soul.
The chilled soul reaped heartlessness.
Heartlessness quenched the Spirit.
A quenched Spirit fostered impure thoughts.
Impure thoughts drove uncontrolled behaviors.
Uncontrolled behaviors brewed restlessness.
Restlessness fueled anxiety.
Anxiety nurtured intimidation.
Intimidation sowed loathing.
Loathing gave birth to worthlessness.
Worthlessness transported depression.
Depression begot hopelessness.
Hopelessness ended at Death.
The barrel became toxic.

I had spent a lifetime listening to garbage about myself, my abilities, and the things that were important to me. It felt like I was being held solely responsible for everything wrong in my life. It was all my fault; I had made a mess of everything. I couldn't do anything right. I spent a portion of my life hearing statements that proclaimed: *My parents and siblings did not care about me*; when in reality, they did. I grew to believe the lie that *I hated my students and teaching school*; in actuality, I cared for my students deeply and always felt led to be a teacher. I loved being an educator. Before illness devastated me, I was a decent mom; but I was led to believe *everything wrong in my home hinged on my moods and behaviors alone.* This maxim is partially true because mom's do heavily influence the atmosphere at home, but they are not entirely responsible for it; it is a shared responsibility of the father and mother.

Through the years of our marriage, my spouse managed to twist the truth of these things, and I came to believe these falsehoods as factual certainties. My thinking was in need of an overhaul, or transformation, and my heart needed an infusion of truth. God's word tells us this about humanity: "For as he thinks within himself, so is he" (Proverbs 23:7). The revamped compartments of my damaged mind now function in newness, completely restructured. Paul says, "Do not be conformed to this world, but be transformed by the renewing of your mind" (Romans 12:2). Through Jesus Christ we find the power to rid ourselves of stinkin' thinkin'; we come to live victoriously in a new mindset.

More Tests

When being released from the hospital, doctors told me I would never be able to work again, let alone teach. In the beginning, I never questioned that. Over time I grabbed onto the belief that if I could reacquire the skills and knowledge of an educator, I could build myself back to the level of being a competent teacher. There was the real possibility that I could reclaim my career if I so desired. I knew if I mastered this achievement, I would experience a rare form of victory, and it would be empowering.

God placed a special friend in my life who would be instrumental in this portion of my healing. Through her positive influence, I saw this dream come to fruition. God planted her in my life; and for whatever reasons, she believed in my abilities. She was always mindful of recognizing areas of improvement or increased strength in my life on a continual basis.

I could study on my own to regain information from all of the targeted subject areas for which I would be responsible, and I could study to update my professional conduct and pedagogy data. I prepared to do this, but math was another story. I could barely remember how to add, subtract, multiply, and divide. I was about to discover something incredible about my new-found friend.

My new comrade offered to help me. I found out her professional credentials are impressive. She has a master's degree in mathematics, and she taught upper-level math courses for twenty-plus years. She is a retired high school teacher and an excellent one at that. She is still sharp as a tack in her field. She continually reminded me that I could do this. She told me I was smart, and I was doing a great job. She never made me feel stupid or dumb. With her help and support, at the age of forty-nine, I entered into a season of study to regain and improve my math skills.

I began to dream and hope that I might teach again. I studied hard. I did homework every night. A few months after my fiftieth birthday, I took the professional pedagogy portion of the State Teacher's Exam, and I achieved a phenomenal score. It was better than any score I had ever made in my entire career. Having been out of the classroom for fifteen years, I felt this was quite an accomplishment.

While preparing for future possibilities, God afforded me an opportunity to see if I could handle the stresses of working every single day. I had passed the first portion of my professional certification, and I bought the materials to prepare for the General Knowledge and Content Areas of the test. I continued my tutoring sessions for math and studied the rest of the information on my own.

At this time, the low-income housing project in which I lived was under new ownership; after their first year in control, the owners opted to release the manager of the property from her duties.

There was now a job opening where I lived. Someone jokingly said I should apply for the position. "Yeah, right," was my only reply. For two seconds, I entertained the thought and then laughed it off.

There was a resident in the facility that was having trouble with her rent payments. I befriended her, and she asked me for advice and help. With the resident's permission, I introduced her to my new friend from church; the one who was helping me learn about budgeting, spending, money, and how it all works. The three of us were sitting in the lobby waiting to see the owners. We had a three o'clock appointment to meet with them concerning the eviction notice they had issued to the resident. This notification was one of the last acts of the departing manager. She was following HUD guidelines and had every right to issue this expulsion decree. The resident was there to beg for mercy, ask for time, and plead for one more opportunity. My friend and I were there for emotional support.

The supervisor of the ownership company came out and headed toward us. She pointed at us and curled her index finger to motion "come here." The three of us rose and moved toward her. I can still hear her accent to this day saying, "No; no, just Nora." My two friends sat down, and I continued to follow her to the office. I figured they were going to ask me about the core issues of this meeting and why we were all there. I walked into the office ready to help my fellow resident if I could. Before I realized what was happening, the owners were asking me about my work history. They asked me if I might be interested in helping them run the property.

I asked them, "Why me?"

They said that one of their husbands had been watching people for the last several days, while they were there for a federal inspection. He had focused his professional attention on me. He didn't realize I was a resident. He thought I was an outside citizen who came to Hampton Hills Apartments every day to visit and support the residents. He said I had a great rapport with the people.

I told them that I had never thought about managing rental property; and I was preparing, trying to get to the point where I could teach again. We talked for the next hour or so; but in the end, I agreed to help the owners until they could find someone, and I said I would consider the idea of making it a permanent position. At four, forty-seven—I looked at the clock—that July afternoon, they handed me the keys. I became the new manager at Hampton Hills.

For the next year and a half, I learned the processes involved with being a HUD property manager. I gave it my best effort. My bosses were patient, and they knew from the start I had no background from which to draw any knowledge. I was starting at ground zero. I am thankful for the opportunity they gave me.

I enjoyed my job as manager. As with any position, some things can become distasteful, and we become disgruntled, but they come with the territory. Being cursed and yelled at were not my favorite things. God showed me His presence could keep my spirit fortified and peaceful, even in the midst of someone else's uncontrolled frenzy; this was something I needed to know I could do.

In October of the following year, I was ready to see how I could do on the state teacher's exam. I went in with the mindset: *If I did not pass, the results would contain indicators of the areas in which I needed to concentrate more effort. If the opposite happened, then I would pass; and, there was nothing wrong with that outcome*. I was also praying about which career path to follow. I sincerely loved what I was doing at Hampton Apartments, but everything in me was telling me: "*You are a teacher.*"

I arrived at the testing center, and before I clicked the computer to start the assessment, I paused to pray. I became disturbed at the beginning of the test period because I had not received a calculator to do the math portion of the exam. It was my understanding that the proctor would issue one to me before testing began, and we were not allowed to bring one to the center. Only participants who were taking the mathematics specialty area were issued calculators that day. I lifted another quick prayer and worked my way through the test. I did all of the computations the good old fashion way, with my brain and hopefully with some reasoning and common sense.

I was the second to last person to leave the testing center. It took me over six hours to complete the exam. I was exhausted. I left thinking: *I'll be coming back.* Several weeks after the evaluation, I found out that I passed. My score was super good. I cried tears of joy. I passed every section, even the math portion. Once again, my Father had blessed me beyond measure.

She's Back

I immediately felt the draw in my life to step back into the classroom and give it a try. I called the owner of the apartments and asked her if we could talk. She came to town for a visit. We had a long conversation, and I shared my heart with her. I told her some of what God was doing in my life, and I thanked her for giving me a chance. Her decision to believe in me meant more to me than she will ever know. She graciously agreed to let me try my hand at substitute teaching a few days a week, while I continued to work for her.

By Thanksgiving, they offered me a permanent substitute position that would put me in the classroom, as the lead teacher, full-time for the second semester of the school year. God had delivered me back to the world of teaching. I turned in my notice to corporate and told them that as of the last day of December, I would no longer be in their employment. I would be teaching sixth grade World History for the city school district.

It was like I had never left. The thrill of being in the classroom and challenging my kids filled me with instant gratification. I went home at night reeling with ideas and possibilities. I was in a great place in my life. I fell in love with my students. One day as I stood in my classroom doing my thing and loving it, this thought ran through my head: *At one time in my life I was really sick, but not anymore; I'm not sick anymore*!

In February, the principal of the school interviewed several other candidates and me for a job opening that had come into existence for the next school year. I went before the panel for my interview, and then I waited to hear from them. A few weeks later, I was offered a permanent position at Jamison Middle School. I was beyond excited. I accepted and went back to work with a gigantic smile on my face. Joy oozed from within me and spread all over me.

Show Me

By the time mid–April rolled around, I realized I was becoming fatigued and stressed. I also noticed that to keep up with the workload, I was letting many of the administrative tasks of teaching fall to the wayside; they should have been finalized, but I let them slide. I felt bad about this; but above all else, I had to protect my relationship with God and my newly restored health. Everything else had to take a backseat to these two priorities in my life. As a full-time substitute, teaching the kids was the central focus of my job. That decision was satisfactory, but it was not an acceptable game plan for a full-time teacher under contract. I was beginning to wonder if I had the stamina to make it through an entire school year. I made this a matter of much prayer, and I asked God to show me what the right decisions were concerning full-time work.

Over the next several weeks, God would orchestrate events in my life that showed me exactly what to do. Because of district-wide budget cuts, the job offer left the table. The position I was hired to fill no longer existed; therefore, I no longer had a job for the upcoming year. Believe it or not, I cried tears of relief and joy because this was an answer to my prayers. When the principal called me into a conference to tell me about the developments in my job offer, he was upset, not with me but for me. He said he had been to the school board and asked if there was any way he could hire me in any position so that he could have me on staff. Then later, he would place me where he needed me; it was flattering.

He thought I was crying because of the job reversal. I was crying for two reasons: one, I cared about my students; second, I loved what I was doing. I would miss being a part of the kids' lives. Greater than this was the fact that God had given me the answer to my prayers, part of which was whether I should be working or not. My thought at that instant was: *Oh God, when you put the writing on the wall you make it so big, there is no way to misinterpret it.* (Daniel 5:13–30, Interpreting the Handwriting on the Wall)

Through work, the job season in my recovery, God helped me come to grips with some realities. When we have been involved in a crippling battle and have looked death in the face, we will have scars; they are reminders of where we've been and what we have been through. God revealed to me the reality that I have been through a major war, and some of the battles were harrowing. Though the bruises, bumps, and cut lip have long ago healed, I still have war wounds and scars that remind me of where I've been; and they alert me to be cautious, for I never want to return to the heat of emotional battle, turmoil, and severe depression again. The marks on my wrists remind me of the truth of restoration; the scars from my journey help me remember His divine deliverance.

I have come to realize I do not have to prove anything to anyone, and I don't have to live up to the expectations anyone else in this world has for me. My responsibility is to live up to God's expectations, and I am to fulfill His calling on my life. As long as I seek to be in His will and ask for His guidance, I know He will hear me and provide the answers I need; being in this fantastic place is exactly where I need to be.

CHAPTER 25

Forgiveness

Accept It

God delivered me into a brand-new life, yet I still had to handle many issues as I traveled along my path of healing. Forgiveness was one of them. I had to deal with this portion of my journey in therapy, and I had to deal with it spiritually. I knew God had forgiven me, but I had to accept it and walk in it. I had no doubt that He had granted me forgiveness. However, I had to ask Him to help me with the other phases of forgiveness.

Part of accepting this gift is being able to exonerate one's self. I had to find a way to forgive myself. Satan would love nothing more than for me to sit around and bemoan the things that had happened to me in the past; things I cannot change. I also needed to absolve myself of the things that were my fault. I had to admit them, and let them go. I cannot tell you how nor why my Father who loves me has freed me from the guilt I could so generously heap upon myself, but He has. I unquestionably know I asked for the strength to forgive myself, and God granted me the capability to do it. I trust Him.

Seek It

Not only did I need to receive and accept forgiveness when offered, but I also needed to seek it from others. I had to identify all those I had wronged, and then I had to offer my apologies and request forgiveness. I was not responsible for their responses, but I had to do my part in making things right.

The initial list started with my children and ex-husband. I was responsible for the presence of some issues and emotional pain in their lives. I had caused some of the hurts in our family's relationships, and there were times my behaviors were abusive in nature, even though I never intended them to be. First, I had to identify what these issues were and make sure I was the actual responsible party in some or all of it. It is effortless to pick up more than what is ours to carry, so I looked carefully at the things for which I thought I was accountable.

I felt the need to apologize to my kids for leaving them. The day I exited my home to escape my abusive spouse, I didn't realize I would not see my children for two years. The first time I saw my daughters, I didn't know if I could survive the meeting. I was terrified and thought they probably hated me; I wouldn't blame them if they did. I had to continually lift my voice and repeat God's promise that He "has not given us a spirit of fear, but of power and of love and of a sound mind" (2 Timothy 1:7, NKJV).

I had to spend a season in prayer to prevent Satan from having victory over this one. I had sought my daughters' forgiveness, and they said they were granting it. I knew they had a lot of heartache and issues to work through concerning all that had happened, especially my youngest. I also knew it may be a very long time, if ever, before they could actually forgive me. My baby girl went through childhood without her mom; I could only hope that one day she would recognize me as her mom. For now, I had to accept and believe that they wanted to move forward.

My son's forgiveness was instantaneous, and I felt it the first time I saw him. I had not seen Nathan in over two years. The number one lesson my special needs child has taught me in all of this is the meaning and power of unconditional love; he showed me what it looks like. He poured his acceptance out to me like soothing oil. It was as if we never skipped a beat in our relationship. The first thing out of his sixteen-year-old mouth was, "Mommy!" He said this, as he ran to me with open arms and wrapped me in an enormous bear hug. He topped it off with his special giggle. God did that for me.

Next, I had to take responsibility for the things I had thrown into my marriage that caused major issues; this was emotionally painful but necessary. Not every case has two perpetrators; some marriages end because of only one of the individuals involved. In our case, I was not entirely innocent. I wrote a letter seeking my ex-husband's forgiveness for as many things as I could identify, like the money issues; and toward the end, it was the horribly hurtful words that spewed forth from my mouth. I also let him know I was offering forgiveness for his part in everything that happened, including the physical abuse. When finished, I put this letter in the mail.

I have never received a response. I know this: I did what I was supposed to do, and I am not responsible for my ex's reactions or lack of a reply. My personal obedience is what is required, and that is what I did.

Bestow It

Granting forgiveness to those who have wronged us, whether they think they need it or not, is the only way to release the captive hold blame uses to keep us in bondage. The inability to forgive will keep us in oppression, and it will starve our relationships of the blessings in life. We must find the courage to deal with our hurt and bestow forgiveness. This act is not for the benefit of the perpetrator; it is so the victim can enter the recovery stage and experience true freedom.

Forgive the men who took advantage of me? Forgive the insulting crushing remarks that damaged my emotions? Forgive the physical pain wrongfully inflicted on me? Forgive grown-ups who unrightfully blamed and accused me? Forgive the emotional mind games? Forgive my ex-husband for not loving me unconditionally?

Forgive him for abusing me? I kept asking God, "HOW?" He finally revealed the answer. I would do it the same way He has forgiven me.

In the parable of the *Unforgiving Servant*, Jesus tells us we must forgive the trespasses of our fellow servants. The master represents God, and we are the servant in the story.

> His master said to him, "You, wicked servant! I forgave you all that debt because you begged me. Should you not also have had compassion on your fellow servant, just as I had pity on you? So My Heavenly Father also will do to you if each of you, from his heart, does not forgive his brother his trespasses" (Matthew 18:32–33 and 35, NKJV, selected sections).

How much must I forgive?

> Peter asked Jesus, "Lord, how often shall my brother sin against me and I forgive him? Up to seven times" (Matthew 18:21)?
>
> Jesus answered Peter saying, "I do not say to you, up to seven times, but up to seventy times seven" (verse 22).

I began praying, asking God to help me work through the emotional pain of all that had been inflicted upon me by others. I asked Him to help me find the courage and strength to forgive. The number of offenses was trivial; the ability to grant my enemies true forgiveness was paramount.

We do not always have to confront our enemy, sometimes we can merely come to grips with an issue in our heart, and it resolves. However, there are times we must have some form of confrontation. In this act, there is healing for us and hopefully for the other party. Whatever we do, we must deal with each situation and ask for guidance as to how to implement the forgiveness.

I made a list of all who had wronged or hurt me in some way. There were individuals I could not go to and offer this forgiveness face to face because they had already passed from this life. I could tell my Lord of my desire to do so, and He would grant me release. Over the course of many months, I worked my way through the remainder of my list. I chose one of four avenues to deal with them: leave it with God, make a phone call, write a letter and mail it, or call for a face-to-face meeting. I prayed over each circumstance and asked God to show me which course of action was appropriate in each case. Some incidences were tougher to handle than others; but eventually, I worked my way through each and every one of them.

Forgiving my ex-husband was grueling. I had to come to grips with the fact that he has shown no remorse about what happened, and he has never admitted any responsibility in the ending of our marriage; he has made no attempt to apologize for anything. I just had to release the idea that he might express regret one day, and realize I have no control over his actions. No amount of stewing or worry will change that fact. I had to let go of the pain and bitterness his abandonment and abuse caused for me. The only way for me to do that was to forgive him; this was going to be exceedingly hard and more challenging than I imagined.

In the beginning, my first reaction was to pull away and isolate myself from the problem. I was so hurt I couldn't even think about forgiving this man; I cried every time I thought about it. Then, I became angry. I had to focus all of my energy on not allowing the anger to drive my actions, specifically those concerning my children and their well-being. I wanted them with me more than anything, but I knew I had to look beyond my wants. I could not act at the expense of their emotional health. Then I became indifferent; I convinced myself that it did not matter if I forgave him or not. Because of this, I fell into the role of the victim. It would take over a year to move past this phase, but God showed me how to move on.

I finally reached the point where I was no longer mad. I stopped regretting and mourning my lost marriage. I accepted reality, and

I was ready for the emotional pain to be gone. I reached the point of acceptance. I am God's child, and I am called to forgive as He has forgiven me (Ephesians 4:32). I would never get well if I didn't do this. Dealing with this issue caused me many tears. I knew what the scripture said; now, I had to ask God for the strength to carry it out; it was time to apply it. There are still times I deal with memories, but that's the point; I deal with them. They do not cause me anger at every turn, and they do not consume my thoughts or drive my actions.

Relationships with Our Fathers

In my early twenties, God taught me a valuable lesson concerning unconditional love and forgiveness. After becoming a Christian, I began to pray for my entire family. When I reached twenty-two, I had been praying for my dad's salvation for many years. I became convicted about my relationship with him. Through a series of events God would unfold in my life, I became withdrawn and non-responsive to my dad. I thought for several years that I could no longer tolerate him; I had given him enough chances. I was ready to write him off and kick him out of my life. He had hurt my mom, me, and my family way too much.

God's Word tells me I cannot have the right kind of love within me if I hate someone. "Beloved, let us love one another, for love is from God. The one who does not love does not know God, for God is love. Beloved, if God so loved us, we also ought to love one another" (1 John 4:7–8; 11, selected sections). I needed to find a way to love my dad.

One day, as I pondered the situation between my dad and me, it hit me. I had been praying for his salvation for years, and I wanted him to experience the love of my heavenly Father so his life would become transformed. I suddenly realized I had never heard anyone, not even my mom or his parents, tell my dad they loved him. I had never personally told my dad that I loved him. I expected and wanted him to discover the love of a Savior, yet he had not experienced or heard love from those who should have shown it the most, particularly his Christian daughter.

I began praying, anew. I asked God to forgive me for not being the witness I should have been. I requested the strength to forgive my dad and the empowerment to love him the way my Father-God loves me. Through that time, God revealed to me that I had to apologize to my dad and ask him to forgive me for treating him so disrespectfully. Does this sound anything like what God requires of us, His children?

I also had to tell my dad I forgave him for the abuse and harsh words he had inflicted on me during my childhood. I could not express this to him if the declarations were false, and I did not mean it. After a few months of hashing things out with my Heavenly Father and getting my heart right, I was ready to visit my dad.

I would like to share the account of my relationship with my dad in the form of a story. I had occasion to share this format when I was asked to teach a life group lesson on the healing power of forgiveness.

<u>The Power of Forgiveness</u>

Nora J. Alexander

> She came from an abusive home. Spankings were in ample supply; some qualified as beatings. The lashes grew in intensity as the years passed, and the person administering the discipline would strike over and over until they were tired of hitting. It was always with a belt, a switch, or some object. Later years involved the inclusion of slaps, shoves, and fists.
>
> God found this little girl when she was fourteen. He brought her salvation through Jesus Christ. As a Christian, she began to change quickly. Before long, she became convicted about the fact that she was to

honor her father and mother. She made every effort to be respectful of them.

Shortly after her twentieth birthday, she was severely beaten by her father, again. This time it was because she didn't do something her father had told her to do, but her mother had told her *not* to do it. After the thrashing, she left and went to a friend's house with the intent of never returning home.

A few days later, she received a call from her mom telling her she could come home. Her mom had packed her dad's things and told him to leave. After twenty-nine years of marriage, it looked like the end.

Six weeks later, this young lady's dad wanted to return home. The mom had agreed, but only if the daughter was okay with the arrangements. The grown child received a phone call at work; it was her dad. He told his daughter that the mom had agreed to let him come home, but *only* if it was okay with her.

Was she supposed to decide the future of her parent's relationship?

"Fine, give me about thirty minutes before you normally come home, and I'll be gone." the daughter said.

"No. Mom said you have to agree to live at home, too."

There was silence on the phone.

"Fine," she said coldly, as she hung up.

When she got home, her dad was waiting on the porch. She didn't look at him. She stopped for a moment and looking passed him she said, "Just because we both live here, it doesn't mean I have to talk to you."

She went straight to her room. She stayed pretty much to herself and didn't speak to her dad. Though they were under the same roof, things remained strained between them for many months.

Fast-forward, she is now twenty-two and married. She has been listening to a series of sermons on forgiveness. From the first words, conviction about her relationship with her father materialized. The third message finally pierced her soul.

Her thought: *How could her dad understand the love of a Savior he could not see if no one in his life showed him their love*? He had nothing in his life to which he could compare the message of God's love. *How could he ever comprehend love if it was never demonstrated to him*?

She knew she loved her dad, and she had to forgive him. She came to the realization that she wanted to forgive him. After much prayer and seeking, she called her father and asked if she could come over; she had something important to say. She drove the twenty-five miles to her dad's house, praying the entire way. He was waiting for her on the front porch.

As she mounted the steps, she informed him that she would not be staying. She needed him to listen and not say a word; she had something to tell him. In a broken voice and fighting tears, she asked him to forgive her for specific things she had thrown into their relationship. There were no blanket statements; she read from a list.

Then, she forgave him. Being precise in identifying matters of pardon, these were read from the list too. She did this without asking or knowing if he thought he needed the mercy and grace being granted to him.

Next, she told her dad that she knew God had placed her in this family; and because of that fact, she was proud to be his daughter. She stated, "The past is the past. 'It is like water under the bridge,' gone forever. I will not hold any of this against you ever again. I forgive you."

She put her arms around his neck and with tears streaming down her face, she kissed him on the check and told him that she loved him. She turned, ran down the steps, climbed into her car, and drove home.

She left that day, vowing she would tell him she loves him at every opportunity. Maybe in time, he would come to understand the love of the unseen Savior. For now, the demonstration would come into his life through his daughter.

After that, every time the daughter spoke with her dad, she always finished with, "Remember dad, I love you." From that point on, when she came home to visit, it was "roll out the red carpet, blow the trumpets, and kill the fatted calf; my daughter is coming home!" (Luke 15:11–32, Parable of the Lost Son)

Three years later, her first child died. The evening of the baby's death, her dad hugged her and whispered in her ear, "Don't let this take whatever it is you have away." She looked him in the eye, and with tears in her eyes and a trembling smile she softly said, "Oh, dad, it's only because of what I have in Christ that I can even fathom getting through this."

Over the next several years, this daughter enjoyed her new relationship with her father. It was unlike anything they had ever experienced together.

After the loss of her child, her dad began the habit of checking on "his girl" relatively often.

At the end of one such check-up call, she finally heard the words she had waited her entire life to hear. She closed with the traditional goodbye and ended with her pronouncement, "I love you, Dad." She cried tears of joy when, "I love you too," rang out from the other end of the line. She was twenty-five.

Fast forward seven years into the future of their new journey, her father had a massive heart attack. Doctors were going to attempt surgery, but things did not look hopeful. Her dad said to her mom, "Call my daughter and see if she'll come."

Of course, she came. Because he did not want to ride in an ambulance, she transported her dad from one medical center to another. The second hospital was where the surgery would transpire. The night before the operation, she went into her dad's hospital room and shared the loving forgiveness of Jesus Christ, one more time.

He went into surgery early the next morning. He made it to the recovery room, but he never woke up. The Gospel Message was the last words she ever spoke to her father.

Later, this young woman came to the realization that it was at the point of her obedience to forgive her father where she found peace and joy in the relationship. She no longer feared him, and she was freed to love him.

One day, I will know the outcome of our last meeting. I have complete peace in knowing that the last two things my dad heard from me were: the unconditional love of a Savior does exist, and "I love you, Dad."

I did not have to seek a restored relationship with my dad, but I did have to grant the forgiveness. The future relationship that developed was purely an added blessing given to me by God, yet another "*God did that for me*" moment in my life.

I have been able to forgive my ex-husband in the same manner that I forgave my dad. Only this time, healing took the form of leaving him and *Anger and Rage* behind. After fleeing the abuse, I struggled for five years with my commitment to my marriage and my feelings for this man. I came to realize I did not have to seek a restored relationship with him. I no longer desire this, nor do I think it is required.

Some people have questioned my ex's salvation and call to the ministry with great skepticism. I was there when God dealt with him. I witnessed firsthand as God grew this man in knowledge and prepared him for that work. I sat and marveled week after week as he rose to stand in the pulpit and began to preach, with no trace of the stammer he desperately fought when he had to speak publicly. Some individuals have asked me outright how God could call a man with severe anger issues to the ministry and use him.

I cannot answer that inquiry; I look to God's word to help me cope and find answers. Who am I to question how God works in a person's life? Moses was a murderer, and Paul was an enemy of believers; yet, God used them in compelling ways. The calling God had placed on my life at age sixteen had come into existence through this man. How could I second guess that? I also know what scripture says about how husbands are to treat their wives (Ephesians 5:28–30; 1 Peter 3:7). I know what it states about how to identify true believers and those who are not; it also declares how believers are to love (1 John).

The evidence in one direction is compelling, but so is the other; however, one is weightier than the other. There are only a few absolute truths I know for sure. One, I will not judge my ex-husband, that is under God's authority. Two, my place is to pray for him, hoping he does know the Savior and if not, requesting that he will. Third, I am responsible for my own personal relationship with God, no one else's. I think I will do what God has commanded of me as His child and let Him handle the rest.

Being able to forgive the hurts and wrongs inflicted upon us, especially those that are painfully grievous, is terribly challenging. I agree with those who say it is unrealistic and humanly impossible to do so. In our power, we cannot. However, in the model prayer of Jesus, he says, "Forgive us our debts, as we forgive our debtors" (Matthew 6:12, NKJV). Outside of the power of Christ, we have no hope of being able to forgive; but, "I can do all things through Him who strengthens me" (Philippians 4:13).

Seeking, accepting, and granting forgiveness, and working my way through the process of implementing all of these elements released me from the bondage of a bitterly-entangled, unforgiving heart.

CHAPTER 26

The Ultimate Blessing

Friends

I have been privileged to have some great friends in my lifetime, though the number of them is small. My earliest recollection of a "Best Friend" is from elementary school. We moved from the city to the suburbs when I was in second grade. The government bought our house so that they could demolish it. The new interstate was going to run straight through our neighborhood. We transferred to our new residence, and the youngest Alexander children attended Walton Elementary School; this is where I met my first ever "BF" (*Best Friend*), Christy.

I remember the day shortly after we met when she fell off of the monkey bars and broke her arm. She was the only friend I had with whom my parents would allow me to spend much time. She was also the only one permitted to spend the night at my house; I, in turn, had my parent's approval to stay at hers. Her mom worked at a *Dunkin' Doughnuts,* and I loved staying at her house because we always had fresh doughnuts for breakfast. That is not the only reason, but I must admit it was a "biggie."

Christy was the person God would use first to introduce me to the idea of church, though it would be six years in the future before that seed would be watered and take root in my life. She was also the person around whom I would experience my first memorable bout of envy and jealousy involving someone outside of my immediate family. My dad always bragged on her, and he would make statements about what a good daughter she would be. On occasion, he would say, "Why can't you be more like Christy?" It cut me to the core every time.

I don't know if she ever knew why I became so angry with her, but I stopped talking to her or being around her for a long time. I knew it wasn't her fault, but she was getting the recognition from my father that I craved. I was young and immature, and I didn't know who else to blame. It took me two years to deal with my jealousy and anger. Christy and I became friends again, and we remained so until seventh grade. Her mom remarried, and the family relocated to a different area of the state. We lost contact, and our friendship dwindled.

When God placed me among believers, I developed new friendships; they were more fulfilling than any I had ever come across. It would be a few years before I would experience the gift of strong friendships outside of the church. In fact, it would not be until our move south. God moved me a long distance and across cultural lines, and that is when I made some remarkable new acquaintances. They made my move tolerable. They were patient with this Yankee; we celebrated the first time I ever said, "Y'all," instead of my northern, "You Guys."

I treasure my high school memories. These friends introduced me to high school basketball games; peanuts poured into Dr. Pepper; and my favorite pizza, Canadian bacon with onions and mushrooms. My senior year best friend and I never missed an opportunity to enjoy one of these pizzas as often as possible. I cannot omit my favorite remembrance, my new southern discovery—*blue jeans.*

I didn't have a college best friend. I was too busy worrying about my mom, adjusting to school, and working to spend time developing relationships. I was painfully shy in those days as well. As I look back, I find I had only one prolonged friendship on campus; I married him. Throughout my adult life, I would be in a variety of situations where I would gain friends; most of these developed at church and work. Some of these relationships were stronger and more distinctive than others, but only one of them became life-long.

A New Best Friend

God brought me through some pretty terrifying experiences over the span of a few decades. Then He landed me on the threshold of a brand-new life, and He introduced me to someone who would become my BFE (*Best Friend Ever*). Typing that last line brings tears of amazement and joy to my eyes. She is such an incredibly awesome person. Because of the wellspring of emotion that rises within me when I think of what God did for me by placing this extraordinary woman in my life, I have purposefully saved this chapter for the last to compose. I am so unworthy of the gift God bestowed upon me when He allowed our paths to cross, but I am so glad He did. I am so very thankful that He did.

I had just started my new life in Ashville when I walked into First Baptist Church; it was a beautiful Sunday morning in February. I selected a Sunday school class and headed that way. I picked a chair and sat in it, not knowing what to expect next. I was a thin, pale, frail-looking, scared piece of humanity. People began arriving for the morning activities, and I sat there almost hiding behind a pillar. None of the people gathering in this room knew how terrified I was at that moment; my anxiety level was very high; the emotional strain was so great, I returned to my apartment and threw up, cried, then slept the entire afternoon.

The first time I ever saw the woman who would become my best friend was two weeks later when she and her husband arrived to class. They had been out of state visiting their daughter, so they had not been in attendance during my first two visits. She stopped and spoke with the teacher; they were both looking my way. Suddenly, I realized she was heading my direction with what seemed to be a purpose. She continued coming toward me, stopped, put her things down on the table next to me, put out her hand, and introduced herself. That morning I heard the words that would change my life, "Hello, I'm Kathryn Todd."

She and I like to tell people that when she walked into the room that morning, she looked toward her regular chair with the intention of going there; but someone was sitting in it—*ME.* A friendly warning from us to you: *Beware of strangers sitting in your seat in Sunday school*!

The person God planted in my life to be instrumental in my healing had just introduced herself. That was the instant God blessed me with the ultimate gift of a true best friend; I just did not know it at the time. I do not recall the exact moment when I realized this new relationship formed into something special, but I do know it was soon after we first met. She treated me like I mattered; I couldn't figure out why she seemed to care so much. After some time had passed, I realized I meant something to her because she believed I mattered to God.

I cannot tell you what she was thinking over the first few months of our acquaintance. Whatever it was, I'm glad she was contemplating it. There were plenty of thoughts racing around in my mind. The biggest one, *fear.* I knew that scripture says: "A man *who has* friends must himself be friendly" (Proverbs 18:24, NKJV). Knowing this meant if I wanted a new friend, I had to be friendly, and that meant I had to trust and put myself out there. It meant I would be vulnerable. I did not know if I had the courage to be in a situation that might lead to rejection. I was not sure if I could endure that again.

Love One Another

Jesus said, "Love one another, just as I have loved you" (John 15:12). Later in the same scripture, Jesus is talking to his disciples and speaking of His relationship with those who believe in Him. Jesus said, "You are My friends if you do whatever I command you" (verse 14). Therefore, as a believer, Jesus is my friend. Then Jesus calls them friends again, and He says, "You did not choose Me, but I chose you" (verse 16).

I understand that theologically this means God chooses us, His creation; this is evident from *Genesis* through *Revelation*. However, I would like to look at this phrase through the eyes of Jesus calling us a friend and combine it with His command for us to love each other the way He loves us. In this sense, this incredible stranger "chose me" that day. She initiated the hello and the introduction. Afterward, she was intentional in reaching out to me. I do not know when she consciously made that decision or why she chose me, but she did. My life has never been the same.

Shortly before finishing this chapter, we were studying the uniqueness of Jesus in Sunday school. The leader of the class asked me, "What is the rarest thing Jesus has ever done in your life?" I did not answer then because it would have taken too much time to explain; but I knew without question, one of the most distinctive things Jesus had ever done for me was granting this incredible friendship.

If we love others the way Jesus loves us, then our love should be unconditional. This woman did that. One of my deep-seated fears was that she would reach a point where she would learn too much about me and my past, and then decide she didn't want to be around me anymore. What person of means wants to be friends with someone who lives in HUD housing? Who would tolerate a woman that seems to have walked away from her children? Who intentionally befriends a recovering drug addict only a few months out of rehab? I was afraid that sooner or later something from my past would surface, and that would cause her to pull away.

She never did. I decided to trust her with the worst parts of me and my past which meant telling her the absolute truth. Some of which was pretty ugly. She chose to love me regardless of what she heard or discovered about me, just like Jesus does.

Am I in tears right now? Oh, yes!

God's Word tells us to be kind to one another (Ephesians 4:32). Her kindness has been phenomenal. We are commanded to treat others as we would treat ourselves (Romans 13:9). She does. God's word clearly tells us we are to look to the needs of others and fill them if we are able (1 John 3:17). She chose to meet numerable needs in my life; she even added extras along the way. She never counted the cost of helping me. To this day, she continues to pour herself into my life.

My Jonathan

Everywhere in the pages of this book where you have read of "the friend" God sent into my life to accomplish something, or bring an event to fruition after my hospitalization and arrival in a new city and state, it is this one incredible woman. She is the one who believed in me. She is the one who fed me, countless times. She is the one who bought me a winter coat because I didn't have one. She is the one who allowed me to do laundry at her house every week at no cost so that I could save the twenty-dollar expense. Many times, she did my laundry for me.

She put me on her phone plan so she could stay in contact with me. She is the person who made sure I got to doctor and therapy appointments. I no longer had to spend an entire day in a medical transport van because of her willingness to drive me to these places. When I was sick, she brought me food and medicine. She always called and came by to see if I was ok. She spent the night with me in the hospital so I would not be alone. She made sure I had shoes and warm clothes for winter. She helped me learn math. She was the driving force that encouraged me to get my teaching certification. She has been my loudest cheerleader and number one fan.

She determined that I would *not* spend Christmas or any other prominent day alone. She has guaranteed every birthday is incredible, for she celebrates me every year. She has helped me learn about finances and budgeting. She has enriched my life. She has adopted me into her family and provided me with a home; she even includes me in family vacations. She speaks spiritual truth into my life. She has made it possible for me to have time to work on this manuscript, and she is the force behind its publication. She holds me accountable. She comforts me when I am sad. She counsels me when I need wisdom. She always listens. She encourages me. She accepts me. She trusts me—which is enormous.

This list contains only a fraction of the blessings I have, simply because I am privileged to call her my friend. Since I have known her, she has shown me more love, care, concern, compassion, and acceptance than I have known my entire life. In the words of my therapist, "She has chosen to love me well."

I know her well enough at this point to say that she is not excited that I am singing her praises and doting on her at this moment. She would prefer I not include this portion of my story in the book. Because of my respect for her, if I could do it any other way, I would; but I do not know how. This section is her part in my story. I am not doing this to toot her horn or to raise her above any other. I am sharing this to let others know that my life is drastically different because this servant of God intentionally chose to reach out and touch my life. I wonder what our world would be like if all of God's children would elect to love this radically.

She is like a sister to me, and she is a remarkable friend. Not only because she loves me, but because she is brave enough to call me on things when necessary. She questions me, to make sure I do not have "stinkin' thinkin'" creeping around in my head. She was dear enough to challenge some things I was doing that were causing me to trip up in some of the new habits I was trying to implement in my life. She did not leave me there to struggle. She stepped in and helped me create a plan for something better, and then she helped me carry it out. She never stopped to count the costs monetarily, emotionally, or physically; nor has she calculated the amount of time she has invested in me. Day after day, she pours herself into my life always with a smile and encouragement.

I can never thank her appropriately. I can never pay her back for all she has done. The only thing I can do is try to find the words that tell her what she means to me. The beauty of our relationship is, I do not have to pay her back. I desire to, but it is not a requirement. Because of her heart, my friendship with her mirrors my relationship with Christ. I pour as much as I can back into these relationships knowing my contributions will never be equivalent, though I wish them to be.

God ordained a special friendship for David in the person of King Saul's son, Jonathan. God's word says: "The soul of Jonathan was knit to the soul of David, and Jonathan loved him as himself" (1 Samuel 18:1). I know God has established a heavenly friendship between me and this amazing person, my sister-in-the-Lord. He has joined my life to that of my dear friend in a special bond. I believe God ordained our relationship; it is not a coincidence; it is by divine plan. Our friendship is priceless, and I treasure it. He has knit my soul to that of my friend, and I love her. She is my Jonathan.

<u>My Jonathan</u>

Nora J. Alexander

Father in Heaven, thank you for creating this incredible person.
Thank you for the appointed time in my
journey that placed her in my path.
Thank you that she listened to You, and she did not pass me by.
Thank you that she heard You, and she chose to be obedient.
Thank you that she lives out Your Word in her life.
Thank you for blessing my life with the treasure of her friendship.
Dear God, Thank you for this:

K— kind-hearted,
A— awesome,
T— talented,
H— helpful,
R— intelligent,
Y— yearning,
N— nice,

B— beautiful,

T— tremendous,
O— obedient,
D— devoted,
D— dazzling,

M— marvelously magnificent,
Y— youthful,

B— bold,
E— energetic,
S— sensational,
T— terrific,

F— fabulously fantastic,
R— radical, reliable,
I— incredible,
E— extraordinary,
N— notable,
D— dedicated

Woman named Kathryn B. Todd.
Father, Thank you for my Jonathan;
I Love Her.

There is not a word in existence that describes what this precious friend means to me. There is, however, one in God's vocabulary that is descriptive of her, ***disciple***. I know beyond the shadow of a doubt that my beloved friend will hear: "Well done, good and faithful servant" (Matthew 25:23, NKJV).

Adopted

I have suffered many significant losses in my journey through life. The one that left me reeling the most was the demise of my family. It was as if I had lost them all to an instant death with no warning. I felt abandoned and alone in this world. In those moments, it felt as if something was ripping my heart and soul from being. In one fatal night, I lost my husband and all three of my living children; though not in actual death, I lost them just the same. This event knocked me off the roller-coaster of life and sent me into a tailspin, culminating in near death. In the beginning, I didn't think I could endure it, and I didn't want to survive without them.

In His marvelous provision for me, God placed me in the midst of an entire family who would come to love me and treat me as if I was born into their lineage. They have chosen to bestow their acceptance and love on me. At a time when I had given up on many of my ideas as false, this clan arrived in my life to prove that families do care about one another, and they celebrate life together. They do not allow distance or time to be their enemies. They treasure the challenge of each of these factors and seek every opportunity to be as involved in each other's lives, as much as they can. Spouses love and adore each other, and they show their love and support of one another. They strive to communicate, and I have yet to hear hateful, hurtful words between any of them.

I have the grand privilege of being right in the middle of it all because I am adopted. I always knew deep in my heart a family like this could exist, and God has a design for families. The Benton family is this model. They are none other than my Jonathan's (Kathryn B. Todd's) extended family. Once again, His Word rang true in my life: "God sets the solitary in families; He brings out those who are bound into prosperity" (Psalm 68:6, NKJV). God uses the analogy of adoption to describe our relationship with Him when we become a member of the Family of God. The Apostle Paul says, "When the fullness of the time came, God sent forth His Son, born of a woman, born under the Law, so that He might redeem those who were under the Law, that we might receive the adoption as sons [children]" (Galatians 4:4–5).

When we recognize Jesus as God's Son and acknowledge why He came, we have the opportunity to enter into a relationship with Him. Establishing this relationship through faith by believing that God's word is true and trusting in what Jesus has done on the cross means we are adopted. We become a legitimate part of His family: "if a son [daughter, or child], then an heir of God through Christ" (Galatians 4:7, NKJV). When we are adopted into the family of God through belief and acceptance of Jesus Christ and understand that we are not naturally born of God, we become equal to Jesus in God's eyes. Because we are in His family and equal, we will inherit everything along with God's one true Son, Jesus.

I spent decades serving among the ashes, being abused and mistreated by those who were supposed to love me. The family I had spent my entire adult life nurturing disappeared at the stroke of midnight. My ballroom life as a wife and mother turned into pumpkin waste on the roadside. My earthly prince had abused and abandoned me. However, The Prince of Peace (Jesus) heard my cries and rescued me from the cinders. I want everyone to know, there *is* such a thing as a "fairytale life," and we can all live it. I will settle for nothing less than my Prince Charming and happily ever after. I love my abundant life. Just call me, *Norella.*

CHAPTER 27

With A Cherry on Top

Spoiled Rotten

When I moved to establish residency in my new life, I had few possessions from my former existence. One item that managed to survive the drama was a purse filled with a handful of photos, and I had my Bible. I managed to hang on to two suitcases of clothing (none of which were originally mine) and a few boxes of trinkets. My sister kept these for me until I was ready for them. I am thankful for these few reminders that tell me my old life did not consist of only trauma and bad experiences; there was much good in it. These leftovers from the past are some of the memories I nurture and claim.

At this moment, I must admit to you I am utterly spoiled. "Rotten" would be an understatement. From the beginning of my restoration, since my hospitalization until now, God has blessed me with extras and bonuses; things I do not deserve, but He lavishly showers them on me anyway. I recently told someone, "God allows me to live a lifestyle like the rich and famous."

I thought Ashville was my stopping place in life's journey. Whatever God was going to do with my new life, I figured He was going to do it in my new hometown. I settled there with the mindset that I would never move again; this was it. I got established and started to build my life in this new area. In time, God would reveal to me I was only at the jumping-off place of my renewal.

Today, I reside in a great neighborhood that lies within a gorgeous portion of our nation. My home is a two-story brick with hardwood floors and some carpeted areas, two and one-half baths, a deck, and a beautiful yard. Within this home, I have a large room with a study space, a full bath, and a big closet. For the last several years, I have had access to a vehicle whenever I needed one. I have not gone hungry. In fact, God allows me to eat out fairly often. (This is my absolute favorite thing to do.) Occasionally, He allows me to enjoy new clothes and travel opportunities along my journey.

God has been performing a miraculous work in my life. The years of my recovery journey have been complicated and demanding, but they have been worth every effort and second. I am now free to live life with whipped cream, nuts, and a cherry on top. As I close this endeavor and move toward the next phase in my life, I ask all who have shared this project with me to pray. I do not know what God holds for my future, but I know He has a plan for me. I desire nothing more than to be in His will, and I want to share God with a lost, dying, and hurting world. Though I do not know names, I will continue to pray for all who travel through these pages.

Power in Prose

I love writing poetry, and have done so ever since I can remember; even as far back as elementary school, my first introduction to it. I would like to close this undertaking with a few pieces of prose I have penned during my journal therapy sessions and restoration.

<u>Found in Christ Alone</u>

Nora J. Alexander

Of things most important in life,
I wish to discourse at this time.
We make mistakes along our way;
Yet, we need not faint or die.
The bondage of our past,
We must simply come to face.

There is a key that sets us free;
It allows us to live and once again breathe.
The source that breaks this mighty lock
Is found in Christ alone, the solid Rock.

At some point in this writing endeavor, I asked God to help me convey the simplicity of Himself and salvation to the readers. I received the thought: *He is as easy to comprehend as 1, 2, 3 and A, B, C.*

The A. B. C's of God
Nora J. Alexander

Who is the one true God I serve?
He is **AWESOME** and **ALMIGHTY**,
BEAUTY for the unlovely, and
COMFORT to the troubled.

Who is the one true God I serve?
He is the **DELIVERER** from bondage,
EFFICIENT in all things, and
He is **FAITHFUL** to the obedient.

Who is the one true God I serve?
He is **GRACIOUS** to the needy,
HOPE for the hopeless, and
He is **INVINCIBLE**.

Who is the one true God I serve?
He is **JOY** to the miserable,
KIND to those who seek Him, and
He **LOVES** the unlovely.

Who is the one true God I serve?
He is **MERCIFUL** to those who are repentant,
NEAR to those far off, and
He is **OMNIPOTENT**.

Who is the one true God I serve?
He brings **PEACE** to the conflicted,
QUICKENS the spiritually dead, and
He is **RIGHTEOUSNESS** to the sinful.

Who is the one true God I serve?
He is **STRENGTH** to the weak,
The only **TRUTH** among lies, and
He brings **UNITY** to the divided.

Who is the one true God I serve?
He gives **VALUE** to the worthless,
WEALTH to the poor, and
He is **eXALTED** on High.

Who is the one true God I serve?
He is **YAHWEH of Israel,**
And **ZEALOUS** toward those whom He loves.
It is Jehovah God whom I serve.

Being showered with all of the material goods and monetary wealth we desire does not indicate we are enjoying and living an abundant life. When God takes a life of every possible situation and scenario that we can imagine and fills it to overflowing because of the relationship between Himself and the person involved, then we see abundance portrayed. When the created seeks the Creator and finds Him, their new life begins.

What happens when God divinely intervenes in someone's life? What does it look like when the Holy Spirit overshadows and fills a life? How did God ultimately transform my existence?

<u>TRANSFORMED</u>

Nora J. Alexander

That was then, this is now;
Before the Maker I did bow.

I called to Him; He heard my cry,
"Oh, God no strength have I to try."
Forgive me Lord in Your Holy name;
I wish no more to be the same.
Change my heart, Oh God, this I pray:
Please transform my life today.
You have taken me:
From homeless to a house made of bricks,
From two outfits to a closet overflowing,
From two pair of shoes to more than enough and boots too,
From church food boxes to multiple grocery choices,
From always dining at home to meals in restaurants,
From aimless wandering to life with direction,
From sick and tired to health and zeal,
From no transportation to a brand-new car,
From stricken to the ability to function,
From untrustworthy to trusted,
From devastation to joy,
From chaos to peace,
From voiceless to singing,
From sadness to happiness,
From darkness to Light,
From beaten down to lifted up,
From defeat to victory,
From condemnation to forgiveness,
From captivity to freedom,
From storms to calmness,
From wounded to health,
From hatred to love,
From worthlessness to treasured,
From insanity to a sound mind,
From spiritual poverty to a heart filled with riches,
From evil influences to Holy protection,
From paralyzing fear to sweet tranquility,

From danger to safety,
From the desire of death to the joys of life,
And from bitter and broken to utterly blessed.
I asked the Master my life to save;
My messed-up life to Him I gave.
He reshaped me and created something new;
I pray my future mistakes will be few.
To the cross I nailed my sin repugnant;
I rose to walk in Life more abundant.
(This poem resulted from contemplation on what God
has done in my life since coming to me in the hospital
and rescuing me from the ravages of mental illness.)

To be blessed in the areas of the essence of life is an incredible gift, worthy of thankfulness and a grateful heart; it should be treasured. We, like all the saints and patriarchs of the faith who've gone before us, face adversities and trials, even demonic attack at times. The only difference between us and those without the power of God in their lives is spoken of by the Psalmist. It is God who will "give us help from trouble, for the help of man is useless. Through God we will do valiantly, for it is He who shall tread down our enemies." (Psalm 108:12–13, NKJV) He will fight for us (Exodus 14:14).

God will call me home one day, according to His timetable. He has proven to me quite sufficiently, I have no power to change the number of my days. I am excited to know that the remainder of my life has been delivered from the years I spent in painful darkness. He has banished the evil that stormed through my existence. God has brought me through and redeemed my life.

I knew I had to share my journey. My prayer is that every life touched by these pages will uncover their story. Understanding that it begins at physical birth but gains meaning and purpose in the discovery of Jesus Christ; this is our *second birth*. Jesus said to Nicodemus, "Truly, truly, I say to you, unless one is born again he cannot see the kingdom of God" (John 3:3). This man asked Jesus,

"How can a man be born when he is old" (verse 4)? Jesus answered Nicodemus and said, "For God so loved the world, that He gave His only begotten Son, that whoever believes in Him [the Son] shall not perish, but [he] will have eternal life" (verse 16).

Nothing can, or ever will, match the awesomeness of my God and His Son, Jesus. Absolutely nothing can change Him. He is "the same yesterday and today and forever" (Hebrews 13:8). Always remember God's truth: Cry Out, He **WILL** hear you (Psalm 145:19, bold caps are mine); Knock, and He **WILL** answer (Matthew 7:7, bold caps are mine); Seek Him with your whole heart, and you **WILL** find Him (Jeremiah 29:13, bold caps are mine); He **WILL** listen to the honestly repentant (Psalm 34:4, bold caps are mine).

The writer of a Psalm declares the following truth about God: "Your faithfulness *continues* throughout all generations" (119:90). He still listens today.

<u>LORD God, I Love You</u>

I Love the LORD,
because He hears my voice
and my supplications.
Because He has inclined
His ear to me,
Therefore I will call *upon Him*
As long as I live.
The cords of death
encompassed me
And the terrors of Sheol
came upon me;
I found distress and sorrow.
Then I called upon the name of the LORD:
"O LORD, I beseech You,
save my life!"
Gracious is the LORD,
And righteous;

Yes, our God is compassionate.
The LORD preserves the simple;
I was brought low, and
He saved me.
Return to your rest,
O my soul,
For the LORD has dealt
bountifully with you.
For You have rescued
my soul from death,
my eyes from tears,
my feet from stumbling.
I shall walk before the LORD
In the land of the living.
(Psalm 116:1–9)

"I have come that they may have life and that
they may have it more abundantly,"
(John 10:10b, NKJV)

Thank You, Jesus, for my abundant life.

Epilogue

God continues to add new chapters to my life. Each day a new page is written. My journey is not complete, but He knows the ending. I have the distinct privilege of discovering the rest of my story over the course of my remaining days.

"The LORD is the strength of my life."
(Psalm 27:1, NKJV, italics are mine)

Nora

I am available for speaking engagements,
workshops, retreats, and other events.
If interested, please contact me at:
noraalexander1210@gmail.com
or
bonniekdavis@gmail.com